A perfect gift to uplift your loved ones

A perfect gift for someone who needs enlightenment and uplifting

101 MOTIVATIONS FOR THE AMBITIOUS & TALENTED

Santosh Kumar

BlueRose ONE
Stories Matter
NewDelhi • London

BLUEROSE PUBLISHERS
India | U.K.

Copyright © Santosh Kumar 2025

All rights reserved by author. No part of this publication may be reproduced, stored in a retrieval system or transmitted in any form or by any means, electronic, mechanical, photocopying, recording or otherwise, without the prior permission of the author. Although every precaution has been taken to verify the accuracy of the information contained herein, the publisher assumes no responsibility for any errors or omissions. No liability is assumed for damages that may result from the use of information contained within.

BlueRose Publishers takes no responsibility for any damages, losses, or liabilities that may arise from the use or misuse of the information, products, or services provided in this publication.

For permissions requests or inquiries regarding this publication,
please contact:

BLUEROSE PUBLISHERS
www.BlueRoseONE.com
info@bluerosepublishers.com
+91 8882 898 898
+4407342408967

ISBN: 978-93-6783-468-8

Cover design: Shubham Verma
Typesetting: Sagar

First Edition: February 2025

The Success Mantra to All

Nothing is predestined if you have strong will
Nothing is lost until you lose your patience
Know no hate when love is your habit
No disappointment when passion is aspired
Adapt these principles to lead a noble, fulfilled and desirable life

SANTOSH KUMAR

My Inspiration

The thoughts, teachings and quotes of our great spiritual guide Swami Vivekananda, alongside his work to uplift the underprivileged, his pursuit of wisdom and his quest for inner peace and in leading the world to enlightenment and harmony have inspired me immensely. His words made me think deeply, and opened my eyes as to what the purpose of my life is.

"It is a privilege to serve mankind, for this is the worship of God"

Preface

The world is going through a period of a steep decline in moral and ethical human values. Ultimately, our thoughts are filled with regrets, resentments, sorrows, and anger. There is no place for traditional values like love, genuineness, empathy or honesty in today's world. Today's youth are swaying away from these values and it's high time that we as a society should emphasise these values of integrity and humanity in our lives.

With this noble intention in mind, Mr. Santosh Kumar, the author of "101 MOTIVATIONS FOR AMBITIOUS & TALENTED", through this book thinks of serving today's miserable youth, uplifting their hopes for a better future. This book is not only for the youths but also for students and normal working class people, enabling them to recognise their true worth as well as reflecting on their ideological immaturity that led them to their unhappiness.

Mr. Santosh simply believes that if any problem has no solution, then, it is not a problem at all and recommends that whatever the past might have been, it's over now, but don't let this hold you back for any reason. Don't completely ignore it but let the learnings from those problems guide you in taking your next steps wisely.

- SANTHAVE KALIYANKARA

Acknowledgement

I am grateful to the universe for blessing me with the wisdom, resilience, life experiences and determination to compile these life lessons. My heartfelt thanks to everyone who has inspired, supported, and encouraged me on this journey. To my loved ones, mentors, and fellow dreamers, thank you for being the spark that ignited the fire within me. May these lessons inspire and empower to unlock your full potential that shines through.

For years, I've dreamt of writing a self-help book to empower individuals struggling with goal-setting and motivation. Through my experiences as a volunteer and member of a school management, I've witnessed countless people and students grappling with discipline and concentration issues. This sparked a crucial realisation: life is inherently uncertain, yet every phase offers invaluable lessons on growth, healing, and resilience. This insight fuelled my passion to compile '101 Motivations for Ambitious and Talented'- a guiding light for those seeking direction and purpose in their lives.

I am deeply grateful to the incredible individuals who supported me on this journey. My heartfelt thanks to my loving sibling, and my wonderful nephew, whose unwavering encouragement and patience have meant the world to me. Your unshakeable trust in me has been a constant source of strength and inspiration. I also extend my sincere gratitude to Mr. Santhiave Kaliyankara for his valuable wisdom and guidance. My beloved mother & father, an inspiration since my childhood, deserves special thanks for nurturing my dreams. Additionally, I appreciate the efforts of the entire team of

Bluerose Publishers, who ensured the publication of this book. Your collective support has made this dream a reality, and I am forever thankful to each one of you!

As I close this chapter of gratitude, I perceive that the true essence of this book lies not in its words, but in the positive impact it may have on the lives of its readers. I hope that the lessons shared within these pages will inspire, motivate, and empower you to unlock your fullest potential. Thank you once again to everyone who has been a part of this journey. May the light of knowledge and wisdom continue to guide us all.

Dedication

"In every heartbeat, in every moment shared, Maa Sarawati's love blooms like a flower, pure and eternal."

Introduction

In this fast-paced modern world, having self-harming beliefs that limit ourselves can hinder us from achieving our greatest potential. Whether it is due to our circumstances or lack of right guidance at the right time, our minds get conditioned overtime into believing that achieving something great is almost impossible!

Surprisingly, with the right mindset, self-guidance and effort, we can definitely overcome these negative thoughts, our fears and we might find ourselves to be more accomplished and capable, contrary to our prior beliefs. So breaking free from these self-limiting thoughts and by bravely facing the difficulties, we can definitely achieve greater heights.

Welcome to the journey of a lifetime! Are you ready to unlock your full potential, break free from your limiting beliefs, and unleash your inner strength? Then look nowhere else! This book will rightly guide you towards making you feel more empowered and motivated than ever before! It will be your roadmap to achieving your dreams and aspirations, and will catalyse that real change within! Within these pages, you'll discover the collective wisdom of 101 secrets to help you set and achieve your goals through:

- Inspiring stories of resilience and triumph
- Building unshakeable confidence and self-belief
- Tips and practical strategies for overcoming fear and doubts
- Cultivating a growth mindset and teaching how to embrace challenges

- Generating the power for moulding life as per your desire
- Making a meaningful impact and thereby leaving a lasting legacy
- Turning your dreams into reality by learning to pursue your passions
- Unlocking and finding your true potential and thus transforming your life forever!

You have the power to create the life you desire, to pursue your passions, and to make a meaningful impact in this world. It's time to believe in yourself, to take the first baby steps, and to embrace the incredible journey that awaits you towards your goal. With each step forward, you'll unlock new opportunities, build resilience, and discover the strength and courage that lies hidden within you.

In the pages that follow, you'll discover the '101 Motivations For Ambitious and Talented', a comprehensive guide to help unlock your full potential and to manifest your dreams. You'll learn how to clarify your vision, break free from self-limiting beliefs, and to cultivate a growth mindset. You'll discover the power of intention, the importance of accountability, and the art of creating a supportive environment that fosters success.

You'll gain insights into the habits and routines of high achievers, and learn how to stay motivated in the journey to success. Most importantly, you'll develop a deeper understanding of yourself and your unique strengths, passions, and values, and learn how to align them with your goals, leading to a life of purpose, fulfilment, and greatest joy. So, take a deep breath, let go of your doubts and worries, and set yourself to unleash that inner strength.

As you turn the pages of this book, remember that you have already started achieving greatness, by thinking of beginning the journey to achieve your dreams. You are strong, resilient, and deserve to be living an extraordinary life. Let's embark on this journey together and discover the incredible things that will happen when we start believing in ourselves, by taking actions that's needed, and by never giving up on our dreams!

Contents

PART 1: Laying the Foundations 1
   1.1. "DEFINE SUCCESS ON YOUR TERMS" 2
   1.2. "THE POWER OF GOAL SETTING" 5
   1.3. "HAVE CLARITY IN YOUR VISION" 8
   1.4. "SET SMART GOALS IN LIFE" 11
   1.5. "MANAGE YOUR TIME WELL" 13
   1.6. "PRACTICE SELF-DISCIPLINE" 17
   1.7. "DEVELOP YOUR INNER TALENTS" 20
   1.8. "TRAIN YOUR BRAIN" 22
   1.9. "BE INSPIRED BY GREAT MINDS" 26
   1.10. "ALL THAT BEGINS WELL ENDS WELL" 29

PART 2: Self-Improvement 33
   2.1. "FOCUS ON SELF-IMPROVEMENT" 34
   2.2. "BECOME THE BEST VERSION OF YOURSELF" 38
   2.3. "BE CONFIDENT IN YOUR APPROACH" 41
   2.4. "PUT FORTH YOUR MAXIMUM EFFORT" 43
   2.5. "COMPETE WITH YOURSELF" 45
   2.6. "CULTIVATE MATURE THOUGHTS" 48
   2.7. "HAVE MEANINGFUL DISCUSSIONS" 53
   2.8. "BEFRIEND GOOD BOOKS FOR KNOWLEDGE" 58
   2.9. "SEIZE OPPORTUNITIES" 62
   2.10. "STAY CONSISTENT" 66

PART 3: Personal Growth and Development 69
   3.1. "REALISE YOUR STRENGTHS AND WEAKNESSES" 70
   3.2. "NURTURE A PEACEFUL MIND" 74
   3.3. "STABILISE YOUR FINANCES" 79

3.4. "BE MATURE, YET ADAPTIVE" 81
3.5. "BE DECISIVE" 85
3.6. "PROCURE WISDOM AND KNOWLEDGE" 90
3.7. "BOOST YOUR ENERGY LEVELS" 94
3.8. "DISCOVER YOURSELF THROUGH NOVEL EXPERIENCES" 98
3.9. "EMANATE CONFIDENCE AND CHEERFULNESS"..... 101
3.10. "ELEVATE YOUR PASSION WITH A PURPOSE" 105

PART 4: Relationships and Communication 109
4.1. "BE GRATEFUL" 110
4.2. "CHOOSE YOUR CIRCLE WISELY" 114
4.3. "BE A GOOD LISTENER" 119
4.4. "PRACTICE TOLERANCE" 122
4.5. "COMMUNICATE EFFECTIVELY" 126
4.6. "RECIPROCATE RESPECT" 130
4.7. "TAKE ROLES & RESPONSIBILITIES SERIOUSLY"...... 134
4.8. "GRASP THE POWER OF LOVE" 138
4.9. "PRACTICE LOYALTY AND FAITHFULNESS".............. 142
4.10. "JOY VS. PLEASURE: KNOW THE DIFFERENCE" 145

PART 5: Positive Mindset and Habits 149
5.1. "THINK AND ACT WISELY" 150
5.2. "MINDSET MATTERS" 153
5.3. "NURTURE A POSITIVE ATTITUDE" 157
5.4. "KEEP POWERFUL, POSITIVE THOUGHTS" 161
5.5. "BE OPEN TO NEW IDEAS & PRINCIPLES" 165
5.6. "SELF-EFFICACIES ARE IMPORTANT" 170
5.7. "GROW YOUR EAGERNESS AND ENTHUSIASM"....... 176
5.8. "CHOOSE A HEALTHY LIFESTYLE" 179
5.9. "YOUR TIME IS PRECIOUS - VALUE IT"....................... 183
5.10. "CULTIVATE UNIQUENESS IN YOUR THOUGHTS"186

PART 6: Overcoming Obstacles 191
6.1. "PREVENT HAZARDS AND OBSTACLES" 192
6.2. "AVOID TEMPTATIONS" 197
6.3. "DISTRACTIONS ARE DESTRUCTIVE" 201
6.4. "RECOVER FROM PAST TRAUMAS" 204
6.5. "ELIMINATE YOUR TIREDNESS" 206
6.6. "AVOID SHORTCUTS LIKE THE PLAGUE" 208
6.7. "RULE OVER UNCERTAINTIES" 211
6.8. "BREAK AWAY FROM LONELINESS" 213
6.9. "AVOID COMPARISON" 217
6.10. "DEFEATS - STEPPING STONES TO SUCCESS" 220

PART 7: Character Development 223
7.1. "BUILD YOUR MORAL CONSCIENCE" 224
7.2. "SELF RELIANCE LEADS TO SUCCESS!" 227
7.3. "BACK UP YOUR WORDS WITH ACTIONS" 230
7.4. "TURN MISTAKES INTO LESSONS" 232
7.5. "TRUST IN THE PROVIDENCE OF GOD" 235
7.6. "PERSEVERANCE ALWAYS PAYS OFF" 239
7.7. "ATTAIN PERFECTION THROUGH PRACTICE" 242
7.8. "BE A GOOD ORGANISER" 245
7.9. "TRUTH ALWAYS TRIUMPHS" 248
7.10. "COMMITMENT FACILITATES SUCCESS" 251

PART 8: Self-Awareness, Resilience and Courage 255
8.1. "FACE CHALLENGES HEAD-ON" 256
8.2. "DEFEAT *FEAR* - YOUR WORST ENEMY" 259
8.3. "ELIMINATE SELF-DOUBT" 262
8.4. "SHAPE YOUR FORTUNE" 265
8.5. "HAVE COURAGE TO TAKE ACTION" 268
8.6. "DESTROY YOUR INFLATED EGO" 271
8.7. "ELIMINATE NEGATIVE COMPLEXES" 273

8.8. "BE PASSIONATE WITHOUT GREED" 276
8.9. "VALUE GENUINE ADVICE" 280
8.10. "MASTER THE ART OF SELF-REFLECTION" 283

PART 9: Leadership, Teamwork and Empowerment 287
9.1. "BE PRUDENT BUT DIPLOMATIC" 288
9.2. "JOURNEY TOWARDS PERFECTION" 291
9.3. "TAKE A HELL-BENT RESOLUTION" 293
9.4. "MAKE HARD WORK YOUR MOTTO" 295
9.5. "STICK TO YOUR WORK ETHIC" 297
9.6. "MOVE TOWARDS EMPOWERMENT" 299
9.7. "BE A PLAYER, NOT A SPECTATOR!" 302
9.8. "PRACTICE WORKING IN TEAMS" 305
9.9. "BE AUTHENTIC" 308
9.10. "HOLD YOURSELF ACCOUNTABLE" 311

PART 10: Legacy and Impact 315
10.1. "REALISE YOUR UNIQUENESS AND POWER" 316
10.2. "TRANSFORM THOUGHTS INTO ACTIONS" 319
10.3. "CELEBRATE YOUR TRUE FREEDOM" 322
10.4. "LEAD A PRACTICAL YET MEANINGFUL LIFE" 325
10.5. "TURN YOUR VISIONS INTO REALITY" 328
10.6. "SET YOUR SOUL ABLAZE" 331
10.7. "BE A BEACON OF LIGHT AND WISDOM" 334
10.8. "LEGACY IS BUILT THROUGH NOBLE ACTIONS" ... 337
10.9. "BE A GAME CHANGER" 340
10.10. "EXECUTE LIKE A TRUE VISIONARY" 344
CHAPTER 101: "UNLOCK YOUR FULL POTENTIAL, MANIFEST YOUR DREAMS" 346

PART 1:

Laying the Foundations

1.1. "DEFINE SUCCESS ON YOUR TERMS"

This chapter will help you recognise your needs and purpose in life, along with the importance of setting goals to guide your perception of a successful life.

So what exactly is success?

Success is the sweet spot where hard work, determination, and passion converge. It's the culmination of efforts, the fulfilment of dreams, and the realisation of one's own potential. Success is not just about achieving goals; it's about growing as a person, learning from failures, and making a meaningful impact on the world around us. We can say that happiness is a key to success, and vice-versa.

"Success is the key to happiness"

Is success the same for everyone?

The meaning of success differs from person to person, according to their needs. For some, it's the mere attainment of peace of mind. For others, it might be to stay fit and healthy. For some of us, success is about getting skilled, recognised and having a healthier life. But for the majority of people, success means being wealthy and financially strong. Success is never accidental, but rather the result of consistent effort and a zeal to deliver the best. Thus the perspective of success may vary from individual to individual, while the factors contributing to success are largely similar. Once you recognise what success personally means to you, you'll be able to set your goals with the right mindset, confidence and commitment. By setting yourself to goals that ignite your passion, you can also push the boundaries of knowledge in your chosen endeavours.

Pursue your passion for success

Have you ever wondered why very few people achieve success in life? There are several examples of successful people from different walks of life and success matters a lot for them. Success is something very subjective as for a sportsperson - it's something that brings them fame by delivering their best in a match, breaking records, and achieving personal goals; for an artist, it may be providing their best performance to get a place in the hearts of millions; for a politician, it's all about winning positions and power so as to get respect from fellow citizens.

For a professional, it's equivalent to delivering exceptional performance, exceeding expectations, and continuously striving for excellence, thereby leading to a great career. Similarly, for a student, success is about achieving academic excellence, gaining knowledge, developing skills, and building confidence, all of which can help them achieve a bright and promising future. So the best qualification a person can possibly possess is success. You just have to boost your inner passion to achieve greatness in life. So start your journey to success now.

Key takeaways for success:
- Work with purpose - It's Objective.
- Add value to your life - It's Integrity.
- Wise action & thinking - It's Wisdom.
- The greatest of all virtues - It's Gratitude.
- You can transform your life - It's Consistency.
- Accept the reality of what you are - It's Resilience.
- It's your ultimate choice to work with - It's Work Ethic.
- The key factor to achieving success is a positive attitude.
- Be grateful for existence and belief - It's the Providence of God.

Conclusion

So, success is all about the inner contentment and sense of accomplishments of an individual in their current life. Here we will explore the many facets of success, and provide inspiration, guidance, and practical tips to help you achieve your goals and live a life that you truly deserve. By embracing a holistic approach to success, one shall encompass personal growth, meaningful relationships, and a sense of purpose in life. You'll thus be empowered not only to create a life with accomplished dreams, but will also bring joy, fulfilment, and an everlasting impact.

"Success is all about fulfilling one's purpose with joy"

1.2. "THE POWER OF GOAL SETTING"

This chapter will reiterate the power of goal setting. It will explain how this powerful tool has proven to have a profound impact on one's life and has been used by successful individuals throughout history.

The Importance of Goal Setting:

From Olympic athletes to businessmen, goal-setting has been the secret weapon to turn their dreams into reality. By setting clear and specific goals, you can:

- Create a roadmap to your success: "Set, Work, Achieve, Success, Repeat"
- Have clarity in your vision and purpose: "Define Your way and Direction"
- Stay motivated and focused: "Fuel Your Passion and Drive"
- Boost confidence and self-belief: "Empower Yourself with Positive Thoughts"
- Enhance creativity and innovation: "Unleash Your Imaginative Inner Genius"
- Build accountability and responsibility: "Encourage to Take Responsibility"
- Control and overcome procrastination: "Own Your Actions and Outcomes"
- Encourage resilience and perseverance: "Embrace Challenges, Persist, and Rise"
- Improve time management and productivity: "Focus, Prioritise, Review, Repeat"
- Achieve more than you ever thought possible: "Dream Big, Work Big, Succeed"

- Enhance overall well-being and life satisfaction: "Revitalise Body, Mind, Heart, Soul, Spirit"

Without Goals, You May Feel:
- Lost or Aimless: Drifting Without Purpose or Direction
- Stuck in a rut or stagnant: Tapped in a Life Standstill
- Overwhelmed or uncertain: Lost in a Sea of Doubt
- Lacking purpose or meaning: Feeling Empty of Life's True Purpose
- Directionless without purpose: Adrift Without a Clear Purpose

Goal Setting Matters Because It Helps Individuals:
- Stay focused and motivated: Keep Your Eyes on the Prize
- Make progress towards their aspirations: Move Closer to Big Dreams
- Creates a sense of purpose and direction: Define Path to Life's Meaning
- Channel their energy and efforts effectively: Focus Your Energy on Clear Goals
- Fosters a sense of accomplishment and fulfilment: Yields a Sense of Pride
- Develop a growth mindset and learn from setbacks: Embrace Challenges as Learning Opportunities

Conclusion

By setting your goals right, you can harness the power to transform your life and unlock your full potential. So, set your goals, work towards them, and watch your life transform in amazing ways. Setting goals help you navigate life's challenges with purpose and resilience. As you continue to push beyond your limits, you'll discover that the true power of goal setting lies not in the achievement itself, but in the person you become in the process- a stronger, more capable and wiser you! As you reach new heights, you'll realise that the journey itself is a treasure trove of important teachings, memorable moments, and a sense of purpose that will stay with you for a lifetime.

"Goals give life meaningful direction"

1.3. "HAVE CLARITY IN YOUR VISION"

This chapter emphasises on the importance of setting your mind clearly on the right path to success. A clear vision provides direction and purpose and helps in setting relevant and meaningful goals. Having a clear idea and vision of how to achieve your goals is essential for achieving the desired results. It can help a person to get motivated, to boost their overall self-confidence and prepare him to tackle various challenges in their life.

It also promotes personal responsibility and accountability for progress. It helps enhance a growth mindset that accepts learning and improvement. Having a clear picture of what you want to achieve will be enormously helpful in the planning stage. It can help us to break larger goals into smaller achievable targets in different phases. Precise objectives and setting time limits will help individuals to stay focused and avoid putting off the responsibilities that come with it.

Why Is Setting Clear Goals Important?

High achievers have clarity in their aspirations which enables them to develop a roadmap for success, and cultivate a motivated mindset to achieve their desires. They create a work schedule, review it regularly and stick to it by delegating tasks properly and with priority. If needed, one can also sublet their tasks to the person who is equally responsible while working in a team setting. The delegated person has to be provided with the authority and resources needed to accomplish them.

Setting clear goals also helps prioritise tasks through proper time allocation, enabling individuals to increase productivity, minimise distractions, and maximise the output. One can enjoy better work-life balance by reducing stress levels. Life can be unpredictable, so be prepared to adjust your goals as circumstances change and have a backup plan if things get worse. Assess your current situation and set an action plan in place in case things don't go as planned.

These plans should be well monitored and should be adjusted as needed in frequent time intervals. It's advisable to share your thoughts with your well-wishers and family who'll provide you with much needed feedback and words of encouragement. This will help you gauge the pros and cons of the idea and ambitions you have. After getting success, it should be acknowledged and celebrated along the way. Reflecting on goals and checking your clarity of vision should be an ongoing process. It can be considered as a continuous journey and not a destination. It is a process that helps you grow, learn, and evolve over time.

Conclusion

Life becomes truly magical when you have a clear ambition and set goals accordingly. Once you've worked hard in achieving these goals, you will experience a sense of satisfaction and pride knowing how you have grown and evolved in life. You will feel a surge in confidence that will empower you to take on and tackle new challenges. You will have the right set of attitudes to develop new skills and knowledge in multiple disciplines and different domains. Achieving goals can create a sense of accomplishment and momentum, motivating you to set new and even more ambitious goals.

This momentum builds confidence and propels you towards a lifelong journey of growth, self-improvement, and fulfillment. You are unstoppable now! As you continue to push yourself beyond the limits, your potential expands, and your impact as an individual grows, leaving people around you inspired and motivated by your success. And as you reflect on your journey, you'll realize the true measure of success lies in what you've made in the lives of others.

This profound understanding will empower you to continue striving for excellence, inspiring others to do the same, and creating a ripple effect of positive change that will resonate for generations to come. Thus, the clarity in setting goals and achieving it becomes a never ending path of growth, transformation, and impact, leading you a life of purpose, fulfillment, and everlasting legacy.

"Always believe in your inner strength"

1.4. "SET SMART GOALS IN LIFE"

In this chapter, we'll see what SMART goals are and why setting them will help you reach your desired results much faster. It's often said that a person without a goal is like a body without a soul. Goals are an integral part of a successful life. Everyone should set a clear goal to live their dream life. Most of the time, people confuse goals with dreams. Dreams are mere fascinations without direction, aspiration, or purpose. On the other hand, goals are dreams with plans, set timeframes, directions and destinations. Goals can vary, including personal, professional, artistic, educational, and social goals..

How to Set SMART Goals

Before setting goals, take some time to think about the results you want to see in the future. Make a list of the various goals you want to achieve in different areas of your life. Then think of setting your goal smartly by drafting an efficient plan for it. Make your goal specific by asking yourself about your passions and what exactly you need to accomplish from your life.

To create a milestone, first quantify your goals to make them easier to track. You should set your tasks, concentrate on your daily work routines and rate your daily progress. Although you can"t measure progress quantitatively, regularly tracking it and ensuring you're hitting your target will definitely help.

Setting clear goals is the most effective way to feel motivated and achieve your desired outcomes. Constantly guide yourself and check that you're on the right track. .The next step is to balance your short-term, mid-term, and long-term goals.

Regularly define and re-define each goal by articulating it periodically. The goal that you want to achieve in less than 2 years is a short-term goal; medium term shall be for 2-5 years and a long-term goal is something that you are planning to achieve after 5 years.

Most people are not bothered about goal setting in their life as they don't know how to do it. Remember the 'S-M-A-R-T' way of setting goals. Every alphabet of a SMART goal stands for: S-specific, M-measurable, A-achievable, R-realistic, and T-time bound.

The way individuals set goals depends on their approach to accepting challenges. If someone says they want to lead a healthy life, that's not a specific goal. On the contrary, if they add the statement that they want to reduce their weight each month, then we can classify their goal as a specific one. The next step is that we need to make their goal measurable. Let's say Ashok wants to reduce their body weight by 5kgs in a period of six months - this is a quantifiable goal he can work towards, which is also achievable and realistic.

Conclusion

The most observed mistake that some people make while setting goals is to raise the bar so high for themselves that there is no practical way of achieving them. There should be a reasonable milestone in goal setting. These are the specific checkpoints that help you measure your progress and ensure that you are still on to reach your goals. A goal oriented roadmap is necessary, which emphasises what you want to achieve and then listing it. Remember, your world will only change by setting the goals right, not by mere speculations.

"Setting goals turns the invisible into the visible"

1.5. "MANAGE YOUR TIME WELL"

This chapter emphasises the importance of cultivating effective time management skills. Effective time-management is an essential skill that one needs to cultivate to maximise their productivity. Good time management leads to improved efficiency, reduced stress and increased productivity in life. A better utilised day will give you immense satisfaction and confidence to finish your tasks on time.

How do we enhance the effectiveness of our time?

From morning till evening, your time needs to be properly planned and managed. Start your day with a nutritious breakfast to energise yourself. Draft a list of tasks you need to accomplish for the day before you set your hands on those. Prepare an effective, realistic and achievable plan depending on your needs.

Assess your previous day's performance and identify your most productive time. But before making plans to manage your time, you need to know what tasks you need to prioritise.

A list of tasks, ranging from common to critical priorities, will help you get an understanding on what needs to be prioritised to get your tasks done in a way that alleviates the most stress quickly.

Assign realistic priorities to each task:
- **Priority 1**: Due today by 6 pm.
- **Priority 2**: Due tomorrow by 6 pm.
- **Priority 3**: Due by the end of the week.
- **Priority 4**: Due during next week, weekend.

You can further prioritise tasks within these groups by adding subgroups. For example, a Priority 1.0 task needs to be done immediately, whereas a Priority 1.5 task simply needs to be done by the end of the set period.

- **Balance your effort:** Work on small portions of tasks each day, focussing on those due by the end of the week.
- **Finish the daily tasks:** Complete your daily tasks by focusing on what needs to be done and maintaining your concentration. Try finishing the tasks that's set for the day, and don't allow yourself frequent free-times before finishing them off. Once the tasks set for the day are over, mark them as finished, after reflecting on the quality of your work.
- **Arrange tasks day by day:** Set small, manageable tasks and avoid the carryover of unfinished tasks. Setting small portions of tasks everyday is better than one huge, laborious task that might stress you out and make you feel exhausted. By setting smaller tasks everyday will help you keep up the pace towards finishing the tasks on time with greatest quality.
- **Keep track of your work:** Reflect on your work at the end of the day and make plans for the next day accordingly. This will help you plan the tasks for the next day and the things that need to be improved. Each day should end reflecting on the work that you did that day and with a proper plan for the next day to keep you going.
- **Identify your most productive time of the day:** Identify your most productive time of day, whether it's morning or evening. Choose what's yours, to optimise your schedule!
- **Manage time in increments:** Manage your time in increments by practicing task segmentation and allocating specific time slots. This will train you to manage your time efficiently.
- **Take regular intervals:** Take regular breaks, such as 15-minute, 30-minute, or 1-hour intervals, between tasks. Breaks provide incentive by giving something to look forward to having. It's scientifically proven that doing 45

minutes of work followed by a 10 minute break is beneficial for an average manager.

- **Set a time-goal**: Set time-based goals by estimating a time frame to finish a particular task. Then set yourself a time goal to finish that particular portion of a task or an entire task.
- **Take breaks if necessary**: Take breaks when necessary to avoid burnout and maintain productivity. Try clearing your mind and refresh yourself to refocus and carry on with your activities.
- **Observe frequently**: Monitor your progress precisely on frequent intervals of time, which will help you be on track for the day.
- **Update your tasks regularly**: Cross things off the list as soon as they are accomplished. This will help you add and manage more tasks if necessary.
- **Get motivated by completion**: Completing daily tasks will leave you feeling more relieved and relaxed. Not only will you be getting things done, finishing tasks will give you a sense of satisfaction and will spur motivation to do well further.
- **Reassess your list**: Regularly review and prioritise your task-list. Add new tasks as needed, based on your priorities. This should be done on a daily basis, especially when you're just getting started with a time management regimen. Eliminate or adjust tasks that are completed, or fall in priority.
- **Assign tasks**: Delegate tasks to others when possible. Contrary to our beliefs, you don't need to do it all. You can be much more effective if you can delegate tasks as necessary.
- **Streamline task management**: Utilise technology to complete tasks efficiently or accurately. Today's mobile technology features hundreds and thousands of apps

that will help you manage and even accomplish your tasks much efficiently.

- **Leave time for fun:** Although it's necessary to focus on large projects, make time to relax and recharge.. Not only will it refresh your mind and body, but will also help you work efficiently. It doesn't necessarily need to be a large amount of time, but make sure that you do!
- **Give your body its desired rest:** Adequate sleep after a long workday helps maintain focus and energy. It will help you to think clearly, and your brain and body to function at its highest level.

Conclusion

Effective time management offers numerous benefits. Creating and following a task schedule reduces work-related anxiety and stress. When checking off the daily schedule and 'to-do' list, you can see some tangible progress which will give you immense satisfaction. It will provide you with extra time which you can spend on family and other personal pursuits.

Effective time management leads to increased opportunities and reduced time waste on non-essential activities. Good time management skills are one of the key qualities that these days employers look for. The ability to prioritise and schedule work is extremely desirable for every organisation. If you practice good time management, you will be able to achieve goals and objectives in a much shorter time.

"If you manage your time, you can manage your life"

1.6. "PRACTICE SELF-DISCIPLINE"

In this chapter, we will look into the importance of following discipline in our lives and why it is necessary for us while working towards achieving our goals. Studies show that learning to discipline oneself adds many benefits to one's life. It reduces anxiety thus helping you in effective decision-making. It increases your confidence and ability to achieve short-term and long-term goals. When you cultivate discipline, you increase your agility towards progress. Researchers have found that learning to be more disciplined, positively impacts your attitude, assertiveness, and conscientiousness. It helps improve your mood and outlook on things you have to accomplish, irrespective of which phase in life you are in.

What is Discipline And Why Is It So Important?

The word 'discipline' originates from the word 'disciple', meaning 'follower'. Discipline refers to following certain rules. Without it, the world would be plunged into complete chaos and disorder. Discipline plays a vital role in our day-to-day life and in our society. A family will be disoriented if its members do not follow certain rules of conduct in it. A teacher cannot teach in the class if the students are not well behaved and disciplined. Similarly, no fair game is possible if the players reject the rules of the game.

Discipline enables employees to follow guidelines that facilitate effective performance and for an employer to implement and take disciplinary action in an organisation if the rules are violated. One can only succeed in their goals by developing the ability to work with utmost discipline. A person who lacks this essential quality can never be organised in their life. An army will lose a battle if the soldiers are disorientated and do not follow and obey their commander.

There are numerous examples of individuals and nations that have achieved greatness through disciplined work and leadership. Japan was destroyed in World War II, yet through the hard work and determination of its disciplined people, it has become one of the most financially strong and largest economies in the world!

Here is an interesting story of two men who got drunk on an island. Late at night, they got into their little boat and began to row to the mainland. As morning approached, they were still nowhere near the mainland. They had forgotten to untie the rope that held it to that island, thinking that it was already untied.

Many of you are like these two men, working tirelessly but failing to achieve your goals. Observe your situation and cast away your tiredness. Work in a well-organised and systematic manner with self-discipline until you discover the land of success.

Conclusion

Through self-discipline, you'll discover the power to shape your destiny and create the life you've always desired. With every small victory, your confidence will grow, and your resolve will strengthen. You will feel the master of your thoughts and emotions.

Your inner strength will radiate outward, earning respect, and inspiring others to follow. And when the journey gets tough, as it sometimes will, your self-discipline will be the beacon that guides you throughout the darkness, leading you to a brighter, more triumphant tomorrow.

With each step you'll become more attuned to your wisdom, more grounded to your values, and more confident in your ability to shape your destiny. When the journey comes full circle, you'll look back on the person you once were, and marvel at the transformation that has taken place, knowing the fact of your power to create the life of your choice was within you all along, just waiting to be unleashed.

"Self-control is the cornerstone of strong character"

1.7. "DEVELOP YOUR INNER TALENTS"

In this chapter, we'll explore how nurturing and developing inner talents over the time, leads to a world full of opportunities and possibilities. Talent if nurtured properly is that potential which can aid any individual to achieve wonderful results.

The creator has gifted each of us, regardless of our abilities, with inherent talents and abilities. One of the most important tasks for a man is to recognise and discover these innate hidden treasures and bring them up to perfection for the world to witness.

What Are Hidden Talents, and How Do We Recognise Them?

Talents can be categorised into intellectual, cultural, physical, and humane types. We all are well aware of the different aspects of the first three divisions. Many of us consider someone talented only when they possess certain physical, cultural, or intellectual abilities. For instance, if he can sing well, give inspiring speeches, draw beautiful pictures, or excel in their studies, carrying a high rank or position, everybody calls him 'well talented.'

On the contrary, those who lack these qualities cannot be classified as 'less talented.' The only mindset that is carried by one who doesn't work hard is that he might highly believe in fortune and luck or else he might be just not driven. Remember that destiny lies in your persistent hard work, and someone will merely not hand it over to you.

You must find your way and recognise what you excel at. Even those who do not have limbs also work on their talents for existence and show the world their presence. Now take some time to reflect on your successes and failures in the past and what your career aspirations are for the future. Through self-analysis, you'll identify areas where your talents haven't been utilised.

With this talent, you could have made your critical career decisions wisely and that would have made you more successful and feel much valued. I'd like to emphasise the importance of human talents based on love, sharing, and empathy. Those who cultivate healthy relationships and friendships are equally talented as those who excel academically.

The one who is willing to extend a helping hand to the needy is not less valued or talented than the one who sings melodiously. Individuals who perform their tasks with dedication and responsibility are equally gifted as those who create beautiful art. We all have observed on various television channels that many talented youngsters in reality shows are given opportunities with many music directors and choreographers.

There are various platforms for the present young generation to show their talents to the world. Many talented children and youngsters dig in for opportunities to showcase their talents and emerge as idols at a very tender age. Most of these excellent talented children achieve these accolades along with their academic excellence.

Conclusion

By nurturing your inner talents, you'll unlock a sense of purpose and fulfilment that resonates deeply within your soul. Accept your unique gifts as talents, cultivate them with dedication and don't be afraid to share them with the world. As you do, you'll discover that your talents are not just a source of personal joy, but also a powerful tool for making a meaningful impact on others. And at this moment, you'll realise that the true beauty of your inner talents lies not in what it can do for you, but in what it can help you do for the world.

"Harness your inner strength: multiply your talents and gifts"

1.8. "TRAIN YOUR BRAIN"

This chapter will help you understand the importance of developing and maximising your brain's potential through training and understanding the habits that might unknowingly damage your brain's ability to perform effectively. We will also look into different techniques that can help improve our memory and understanding. Training your brain by doing activities that involve testing your memory periodically will help in maximising your brain potential. During student life, our memory power is constantly tested through various examinations and competitive tests. In later phases, as we age, it might be tested through various stages of interviews and aptitude tests for jobs or placements.

How Can We Increase Our Memory And Brain Potential?

Having a sharp memory is always a bonus for humans to emerge as successful. Unlock your brain's full potential and improve your memory power using these proven techniques!

- Pay attention to and focus on the information or subject you want to remember.
- Rehearse the piece of information you want to remember and read it aloud.
- Using your memory, try writing down the piece of info you want to remember.
- Practice using the information daily during other activities.
- Practice reading informational books and try learning something new.
- Organise and structure information into categories or lists.
- Use visualisation techniques to associate images or videos with memories.

- Use mnemonics and acronyms to support in memory recall.
- Stay mentally sharp with challenging puzzles and learning new skills.
- Most importantly, get enough sleep and rest for your brain every day.

By incorporating these simple techniques in your daily routine, you'll be amazed at how quickly your memory improves! As we all are aware, we humans are visual beings, and the things that we hear and see are very hard to erase from our memory. I recommend that you watch movies such as "peaceful warrior." If you just care about the final scores the character made or how many flaps he took at the end, trust me, you didn't learn anything! "*As in combat as in life expect nothing, but be prepared for anything*" were the great words from Socrates to Dan Millman. Brain performance depends on how well we can manage concentration and emotions.

What Are the Common Brain-damaging Factors, and How Can We Avoid them?

There are some brain-damaging habits most of us possess, that at all costs should be avoided. Not getting enough sleep is the most damaging factor. Our brain requires rest to function at its best. For a normal adult, a minimum of six hours are needed for a productive rest of the day. Personally, this has proved to be beneficial, and I have found myself to be very productive after practising sound sleep. Rudolf Steiner suggested a technique for Waldorf pedagogy teachers. He suggested that at night, before falling asleep, to make a retroactive recount of all the daily activities. Go back to the beginning of the day when you woke up early in the morning, count whatever activities you did throughout the day and write it down if possible. These are good signs for a person who wants to enhance the skills of self-assessment and memory. Remember this old saying:

*"Early to bed and early to rise makes
a man healthy, wealthy and wise"*

    Train your brain to focus on a specific task when feeling distracted. It could be watching an inspirational video, or a quote, a page in a book, or maybe talking to a friend on a particular topic. When feeling low at times, these techniques will lift up your mood and inspire you to work. Avoid thinking about issues that don't concern you. Stop giving unwanted opinions on matters that don't cause any harm to you or anyone, or are of the least importance in this world. Do not get into unnecessary arguments that can drain you out and disturb your mental peace. Abstaining from these will help reduce your mental burdens. This will definitely help you get back to work with much concentration and with double vigour than before. Remove distracting sources like phones and consoles from your line of sight while working. Put your phone on work-setting and turn off your notifications while at work if possible.

    While doing important tasks with tight deadlines, let your friends and family know that you have turned off the notifications, so if in urgency let them know of an alternative way of contacting you. If you still feel compelled, check your phone in a regular fixed interval, so as not to compromise your work. Always remember, you are the one who should control your gadgets, not the other way round. The next brain-damaging habit is not eating healthy and nutritious food. Relying on the diet patterns that are unhealthy like processed foods, refined carbs, high in sugar and rich in unhealthy fats for a long term can lead to memory-impairment and other learning difficulties.

    It's not banal, but let me emphasise that the intake of nutritious and healthy unprocessed food has a relatively significant benefit and practicing this habit can be a huge determinant for your memory and concentration. Eat until you're satisfied, but not full, for a productive day. Try not to fill up your stomach with your entire favourite as it will make you feel lazy for hours!!! Drink water in regular intervals to replenish your electrolytes and body fluids.

Stress is another significant obstacle to memory and concentration. You might have heard some mental health researchers emphasising on practicing yoga and other forms of meditation in-order to relieve one from their stressful life. If you have tried it before, then you'll know that it is not untrue! The immediate effect is calmness from within and it further leads to mitigating stress, anxiety and depression. It gradually helps you to develop your outlook and perspective in a way that won't disturb your mental stability. Engage in brain exercises, such as memory games or sudoku, solving crossword puzzles, and jigsaw puzzles, just as you would with physical exercise.

Conclusion

Finally, let's explore additional tools that can enhance memory which are the interconnection of ideas and the cultivation of verbal fluency. Let me elaborate it by giving you an example. The majority of people may have difficulty in differentiating the meaning of two similar sounding words. Here, for example, bored and bored. The former one (in verb form) is *'to get on to something'*. The latter is *'to feel annoyed being unoccupied or due to the lack of interest'*. You can be able to see the difference after inter-connecting in a single sentence - After getting 'bored' without friends, I 'board' a bus to leave the place. Practicing the use of rhyming words and verbal fluency tasks help us to build our cognitive abilities. Verbal fluency tasks are now commonly used as a tool in neuropsychological testing when it comes to test a person's cognitive abilities.

"Exercise your brain, boost your power"

1.9. "BE INSPIRED BY GREAT MINDS"

This chapter will provide insight into how following inspirational personalities and reading their personal experiences can positively impact our thinking and worldview. Most of the time, reading motivational books and success stories of great people helps us stay inspired and keeps us focused on attaining our goals with perfection.

People often wait for the new year to come and make resolutions and promises for significant change.. They forget the fact that every day brings an opportunity and hope for you to change yourself or to bring a change in something that you need to. Even a small positive thought in the morning or reading an inspirational quote by someone can bring a big change in your day. This will contribute to bringing the change you want to see in yourself over a month. Then one day looking back, you will realize how far you've come and how different and matured a person you've become. Life is based on several principles, including using things, not people, and loving people, not things. There were great personalities in the past, and people still get inspired by their valuable teachings and thoughts.

Swami Vivekananda is a great personality who continues to inspire millions of students and adults. Swami. He was altogether a different personality who never condemns any one or any individual practices. He preached only about the un-manifested infinite strength and divinity in every living soul. With a boundless love and respect for others, their wisdom was versatile and profound; their emotions were exuberant which is very rare to find in this selfish world. Their words never fail to infuse fresh energy and enthusiasm whenever I have gone through their teachings.

Inspired by his life and teachings, I sought to explore our ancient scriptures and Upanishads further. As he is a quintessential representative of Indian Culture, today's youth, irrespective of their religious beliefs, have immense love and respect for this great man's teachings and ideas. The best thing I have seen in Swami Vivekananda is that he seemed to be an awakened, pragmatic and enlightened persona. He never followed beliefs blindly without experiencing them first.. For instance, he checked their Guru Sri Rama Krishna Paramahamsa whether he is in a meditative state by touching his eyes.

He spiritually awakened many disillusioned souls and worked towards building a stronger nation. He was a modern thinker who taught people to think beyond caste and superstition. He supported women empowerment in India. He preached the gospel of truth in every nook and corner of the world. He felt sorrow about struggling and unawareness of the youths and masses that were in despair, and helped spread the message of courage and strength to gain their uniqueness.

His remarkable qualities made me a devoted admirer of this great social reformer. To get inspired by great minds, start by finding a personality whose teaching and life resonate with you. It doesn't necessarily need to be a social reformer, or a philosopher. It can be anyone who you see often, who has overcome the challenges, and like whom you aspire to become one day. But to get inspired you have to study their journey and their shortcomings alike.

Here are some ways to get inspired by their thoughts:

- **Learn about their lives**: Discover their struggles and experiences that shaped their thinking. Also, know about their achievements.
- **Read their work**: Go to a deep study about their biography, and quotes to get the ideas and perspectives.
- **Reflect on their ideas**: Apply their principles and concepts to your own life and challenges.
- **Surround yourself with their true wisdom**: Display quotes, images, or books by great thinkers or idols in your space.

- **Identify with their values:** Replicate the qualities and values that made them great thinkers. Simply follow their footsteps.
- **Find ways to master yourself:** Intelligent people always try to know themselves very well and find ways to improve, master what they really know and will do their best to be better than before.
- **Integrate their wisdom into your daily life:** Apply their insights to your goals, relationships, and personal growth.
- **Inflow of their thoughts to remake you:** Integrate their insights into your daily life and decision-making.
- **Share their wisdom:** share their wisdom with others to reinforce your knowledge and understanding.\

Conclusion

Continue to inspire yourself with the principles of great individuals who have contributed to humanity's betterment. You look at their life with the resilience they had, the hope they held on and the success that they achieved in spite of the odds they experienced. There's always something to learn from the people or things that withstood all odds and still keep going. You can even learn something from nature and its other habitats. Just look around you. Our mother earth is full of hope and possibilities.

"Inspire yourself, so that one day others will get inspired by you."

1.10. "ALL THAT BEGINS WELL ENDS WELL"

As I sit here, sipping my morning tea, I remember the wise words my loving uncle told me once:

"A good beginning is like a strong foundation; it sets the stage for successful completion."

The phrase:

"All that begins well, ends well"

has guided me to approach each new endeavour with focus, determination, and a clear plan as I grew older.

The Importance of a Perfect Start

A perfect start is crucial in our daily routines. It signifies that a good beginning is always the base of great ventures. To make a good start, we should fill our hearts with smiles, happiness, and all the good things in life. As I reflect on my own life, I realize that my daughter's journey is a perfect example of this. Since she was born later in life, we took extra care of her, limiting her interactions with the outer world, which affected her social skills with other children. So to give her some exposure to other children of similar ages, we decided to send her to a play school at the age of two.

Although she struggled initially, hesitating to integrate with other children, she gradually started enjoying playing with them. Her social skills since then have helped her to become a very sociable, kind and loving child. My adorable daughter, whom I'm incredibly proud of, has found her footing and excels academically and socially..This personal experience has made me realise that a strong start might not always guarantee success, but it certainly sets the tone for a brighter future.

Overcoming Invisible Hurdles

We've all been stuck in a rut, unable to take the first step toward our goals. Fear of failure, fear of the unknown, and fear of confronting challenges can be significant obstacles. But, as I've learned from my own experiences, the key to overcoming these invisible hurdles is to kick-start our journey with a positive attitude, a clear plan, and a willingness to take calculated risks.

The Dangers of Complacency

While a strong start is essential, it's equally important to avoid complacency. Early success can breed complacency, leading to stagnation. Early achievements boost our confidence but they also inflate our egos and foster unwanted tendencies. As I look back on my journey, I realize that this was a trap I had fallen into before. But, since then I've learned that the key to continued growth and success is to stay focused, keep pushing ourselves, and strive for continuous improvement.

The Story of the Hare and the Turtle

The classic fable of the hare and the turtle teaches a valuable lesson about perseverance and consistent effort. While the hare started strong, they became complacent and lost the race. On the other hand, the turtle began slowly but kept pushing himself, ultimately winning the race. This story reminds us that a strong start is just the beginning; sustained progress and perseverance are essential to experience continuous growth in our lives.

Starting Early vs. Starting Well

While starting well is important, it's not always the most critical factor. Starting early can be just as important, if not more so. By getting a head start, we can gain a competitive advantage and set ourselves up for success. Starting early doesn't necessarily mean that you need to focus only on starting your career early. Starting early can also mean to start your day early. As I reflect on my own life, I realize that starting early has helped me immensely to utilise my day in a more organised and structured way. Whether it's meditating, exercising, or enjoying a quiet cup of tea, starting the day on a positive note sets the tone for a productive and fulfilling day.

Conclusion

In conclusion, a strong start is essential for achieving success in any endeavor. By beginning things on the right foot, overcoming invisible hurdles, and avoiding complacency, we can set ourselves up for a successful outcome. However, a perfect start is just the beginning; continuous dedication, sustained progress and perseverance ultimately lead us to success. So, let's make a conscious effort to start each new day, each new project, and each new endeavor with focus and determination.

"Do Your Good Deeds with Great Start,
It Is Almost Completed"

PART 2:

Self-Improvement

2.1. "FOCUS ON SELF-IMPROVEMENT"

This chapter will guide you through the process of developing the right mindset and the basic behavioural skills needed for leading a successful life. Having a mindset to improve oneself offers numerous benefits.

What is self-development, and how do we develop good thoughts and habits?

Self-development is the process of developing yourself through your thought process and deliberate learning from your past experiences. Once you start working on self-improvement, make a weekly note of your progress. The door to development will always be locked in your mind if you don't give it a key of thought.

You should have the right mind-set and resources to work towards it. Most importantly, you must be your own friend and saviour first. You must spend time finding and organising the right resources for yourself before developing others. Always remember that no one other than you, is responsible for your progress.

Self-development offers numerous advantages in life, including a significant boost in confidence. It enhances decision-making, goal-setting, and career progression through resilience and advanced skill sets. It grows your sense of purpose, and can change your life's boring situations into a learning opportunity, thus improving your overall mental stability and relations. It's up to you to take the initiative and exchange your despair with the willingness to learn new skills that can change your life.

People attract failure only due to their negligence and unwillingness to devote their time and effort to improve themselves. Those are the people who always blame their circumstances, and complain about the lack of resources and time, but wouldn't do anything to change it. The moment they start believing in themselves and start taking initiative to self-improvisation, the change occurs!

They'll find themselves more skilled and confident in their approach to life challenges. Some of these skills are acquired through practice and some by constant learning process. Putting the right effort and having the right mindset are important in order to achieve these goals.

Like personal development, social development is also an essential part of your life. Here you must learn how to communicate empathetically with others and express your emotions and feelings to others. Meeting people and cooperating with them are also a part of these developments. Empathy is the ability to deeply understand others' feelings and perceive situations from their perspective, fostering strong bonds. It is that feeling that is reflected in you at a time when you see someone suffering in despair while losing their beloved. At that moment you might envision yourself facing a similar experience and feeling their distress. While people can be well attuned to their feelings and emotions, getting that into someone's head can be a difficult task.

The feeling of empathy allows you to walk a mile in others shoes without experiencing it personally. If you are like me, you might feel drained or overwhelmed in such conditions and sometimes you'll find it difficult to set boundaries with your emotions. You might feel like you are absorbing the emotions and experiences of others in such a way that sometimes it interferes with your own mental well-being! At times I have noticed that I'm easily distracted by loud noises or certain smells others might not evidently notice. During those moments, I tend to unnecessarily get hyper-aware of such small things and have been told off several times for being too sensitive. Being in crowded or emotionally charged spaces too sometimes overwhelmed me. I worked on myself regularly to decompress these thoughts and to restore my mental energy levels. With much dedication, so can you too!

Children should be taught social skills like cooperation, compromise, negotiation, sympathy, empathy, respect for others, care, and attachment at a young age. They should also be kept away from anti-social behaviours such as selfishness, bullying, dishonesty, aggression, egocentrism, destructiveness, prejudice, etc.

Every child's self-esteem grows with each experience of successful and positive interactions with adults and their peers. It's important to build a child's belief and confidence that they can handle their life well. Their emotional health depends on their self-esteem and the positive thoughts you cultivate in them. Liking ourselves and feeling capable are the foundations on which emotional health rests. You have to provide them the freedom, encouragement and respect which will feed and grow their self-esteem.

Here are seven simple yet important steps parents and teachers can take to build self-esteem in children:

- Listen to and acknowledge the child's thoughts and feelings.
- Create situations that will help your child experience success, or learn from his failure.
- Set clear and appropriate expectations, offer a reasonable amount of help, provide adequate incentives and remove obstacles.
- Give the child a feeling of reasonable control over his own life.
- Reinforce that the child is lovable, capable and worthy of your respect.
- Show your child that you have a positive view of yourself and him too.
- Give them their share of responsibility and expect cooperation.

Conclusion

Personal development or self-improvement stimulates your mind to learn continuously and upgrade your skill-set. It puts you in the right mindset to expand your understanding, acquire new skills, and maximise your capabilities. New experiences and opportunities will come your way if you are ready to step out of your comfort-zone and make up your mind to continuously challenge yourself.

Thus, it is really important to identify and work on the weaknesses that might potentially drag you down and might hinder your success first. Another important element to consider just like personal development is the 'social-development'. It is the process by which you learn and internalise the values, skills, and behaviours necessary to interact efficiently and effectively with others.

An empathetic person can understand the emotions that others are feeling. Being a part of society, you have to be kind towards others feelings too and will have to play your role to meet the social responsibilities that are expected from you as a human. People often say that the pain you feel today will be the strength you feel tomorrow. So sometimes being empathetic helps in strengthening your own mind for any adverse situations later on.

*"Your growth is the greatest contribution
you can gift to others"*

2.2. "BECOME THE BEST VERSION OF YOURSELF"

In this chapter, we will learn how important it is to build ourselves first and show a willingness to improve our weaknesses before focusing on transforming the world. We will focus on how to be a better version of ourselves.

Why is change necessary for personal growth, and how can it positively impact society?

As you stand at life's crossroads, gazing out at the vast expanse of opportunities and possibilities, remember that the most profound revolution begins within. The journey to transform the world around you starts with a single, courageous step: transforming yourself. It's a path that requires unwavering commitment, unrelenting curiosity, and an unshakeable belief in your own potential. As you embark on this transformative journey, you'll unlock a life of intention, ignite a fire of purpose, and unleash a boundless potential that will forever change the trajectory of your path.

A famous Sanskrit saying, ततिविरतन भाव (tat parivartan bhava), translates to:

"Be the change you wish to see in the world"

Being your best self means living a genuine and contented life. It brings a sense of happiness when you know that your life and mind are in your own control. You should understand the purpose of your life and be willing to unlock your potential. You might have to sacrifice a lot of unwanted things in order to bring harmony into your life. Life's circumstances differ for each individual. Unexpected events will undoubtedly arise as you go through life. There may be a situation that might puzzle and confuse you for what is right and wrong. There is no one right path towards success and to live a meaningful life!

At times, you must embrace failure to understand what went wrong. Regretting past mistakes and missed opportunities serves no purpose. Be willing to change the way your life is at present, if you are not happy with it. Put some effort into thinking of ideas that can help bring a positive change in your life. Remember that where there's a will, there's a way! If you want to see positive changes in the world, the best place to start is with you! As Abraham Lincoln once said:

"The way to change the world is not to work upon the world, but to start working and introducing changes in you"

By setting your goals correctly, you can catalyse positive change in your own life. True transformation begins with self-reflection, marking the start of personal growth journey. You need to bring changes in yourself so as to feel better in every field you perform. Before pointing fingers at others, you should take a look at yourself. By self-reflecting, you'll become more aware of your own thoughts, words, and actions, and make a conscious effort to avoid negative words for others. This self-awareness is the first step towards positive change, leading to a more fulfilling life and improved relationships with those around you.

"Everyone thinks of changing the world, but no one thinks of changing himself."

Leo Tolstoy.

Another way to bring change is by prioritising the things that you love and that matter most. By prioritising and taking time to practice those things every day, you'll find yourself excelling in that particular skill after a few months. This will boost your confidence to do the tasks better, and who knows that someday it might become your career and main source of income! For the positive changes, you need to recognise the good qualities you possess, which will help you to cultivate those qualities within. You sometimes need to listen to others about their perspectives as well to get some ideas that you can apply in your life too. Be appreciative to people and their views and return the favour by being good to them when needed.

Conclusion

Try exploring your talents and improving them. Don't be afraid to do new things and acquire new skills. Recognise the goals you want to achieve and set them. Live honestly, practice self-control and forgiveness, listen to people carefully without interrupting, never be jealous of other people's success and never hold grudges. Be a role model to your family and society. By accepting this journey of growth and self-improvement, you will unlock your full potential and become a shining example of what it means to live a life of purpose, compassion, and service to others. By investing in yourself, you'll reap a harvest of happiness, fulfilment, and success that will bless your life and the lives around you.

"Don't try and be perfect, just be a better version of yourself"

2.3. "BE CONFIDENT IN YOUR APPROACH"

In this chapter, we will focus on building confidence when facing life's challenges. It will also teach you how to stay positive and optimistic about the challenges you've set for yourself. To achieve a certain level of confidence does take time and skill.

Why is confidence crucial for a successful life?

As you enter life's vibrant tapestry, remember that your attitude weaves, crafting a narrative of either tribulation or contentment. Confidence and cheerfulness are the golden threads that can transform the fabric of your existence, illuminating even the darkest corners with alluring and resilient radiance. By cultivating these illuminated attributes, one can unlock the doors to a brighter life, where challenges become opportunities, fears transform into courage, and every day begins with a purpose and a promise!

At times, simply being confident isn't enough! When you feel less confident, you might consider faking it until you make it. But it's never a long term solution; rather it will hinder our ability to work towards attaining our set goals. To feel confident, one must continually improve their skill set. It might be time-consuming and equally frustrating at times while learning new skills, but believe me; there will definitely be light at the end of the tunnel.

Confidence in your abilities will make you feel more accomplished and motivated. With this trait vested inside, you can develop the strength to face any challenges that come your way. The skills developed will give you the confidence to push yourself through the difficulties and to lead a successful life. A famous quote by Henry Ford says:

> *"Obstacles are frightful things you see when you take your eyes off your goal"*

Confidence stems from consistent self-care, learning from mistakes, taking accountability, reflecting on achievements, embracing challenges, maintaining a positive outlook, practicing simplicity and living a disciplined, purposeful life. Building confidence requires consistent self-care. Keep track of both your progress and failures while taking challenges. Reflect on your mistakes and achievements alike.

Don't fear taking challenges or setting personal and professional goals. Let no one's negativity influence your optimistic approach. Stay away from anything that drains your positive attitude. Believe in yourself and your ability to achieve your goals and never lose sight of your final destination. Be humble, knowledgeable, disciplined yet cheerful at all times. These right attitudes will help you sail through almost all the difficulties life might throw at you. Always remember, that challenges are inevitable, but succumbing to them is a choice.

Conclusion

Feeling satisfied and cheerful brings positivity and reduces stress and other ailments. Practice gratitude and self-care. Focus on the sunshine, not the shadows. Dissatisfaction leads to unhappiness and negative consequences.

Avoid it at all costs! Lead a healthy lifestyle, allocate time wisely, nurture relationships, cultivate hobbies, motivate yourself and others, set ambitious goals, and work towards achieving them.

A great mathematician, and a known public intellect, Bertrand Russell, revealed a wise secret to avoid stress:

> *"The secret of happiness is this: let your interests be as wide as possible, and let your reactions to the things and persons that interest you be as far as possible friendly rather than hostile."*

2.4. "PUT FORTH YOUR MAXIMUM EFFORT"

From childhood, we were encouraged to put in extra effort to achieve greater results.

As adults, we work long hours and give our all to meet certain deadlines, to chase promotions or higher returns from business. Cultivating a habit of putting forth maximum effort is necessary in every aspect of life. Virtue is a commendable quality that significantly influences an individual's character and personality. Individuals with virtuous attributes are considered fair in their relationships. They own the quality of being honest with their partner and always possess compassion in their hearts.

This quality will transform them to cultivate a society and generation that's upright and with great moral values. Remember that growth is directly proportional to you achieving your small and big goals. Education is the primary method for teaching individuals how to cultivate virtue, emphasising consistent dedication and hard work. Education is considered the most powerful tool that can be used to promote moral values and instill virtuous qualities in a person. An educational institution teaches how to focus on ethics, morals, values, honesty, etc.

The one who understands the importance of being virtuous and how to develop and practice these qualities throughout his life will rise like a champion. Individuals with these characteristics can become role models, positively influencing others in society. As a mentor, they can have a significant impact on shaping people's behaviour. My mother, knowing my passion for writing, often used to say 'Either write books so that people can remember you, or live your life in a positive way, so that people can write about you!' The world has both virtues and vices, and our perspective can change its meaning. One only sees what he thinks and believes in. To see a better world, change your sight, not the site. To maximize your efforts in tasks, you should avoid multitasking. Multi-tasking can lead to loss of focus on individual tasks, affecting work quality.

It has been proved that multi-tasking can reduce the productivity of a person by 40%. Planning and prioritising tasks, setting small achievable targets and milestones, without getting distracted also helps maximise our efforts. Effective time management skills and communication skills will also help you to delegate some tasks to the people whom you can trust.

Positive reinforcement of efforts can encourage frequent virtuous behaviour. Recognising and rewarding individuals who exhibit qualities like honesty, kindness, and sympathy can encourage others to emulate those behaviours. In the same way, effective criticism can be used to rectify negative behaviour and encourage them to learn from their past mistakes. Efforts put on activities such as volunteering and charity works, community services, and other social gathering programs can enable individuals to practice virtues by helping the needy. Being part of such programs can help people develop qualities such as empathy, compassion, and kindness.

The virtue of effort is a rich source of strength, resilience, and growth. Celebrating the rewards of hard work, industriousness, and perseverance can transform obstacles into opportunities, and struggles into stepping stones for success. So, celebrate the sweat, the tears, and the triumphs that come with effort, for it is the virtue of your endeavours that you will discover your true potential, and forge a legacy for others to do the same.

> *"The only way to reach greatness is through the path of effort and hard work"*

2.5. "COMPETE WITH YOURSELF"

This chapter emphasises the importance of competing with oneself as the healthiest form of competition. Although competition can be stressful, it's an important motivating factor to an individual's successful life. You can find competitions that are encouraged in different fields like chess, athletics, games, racing, sports and even during a public election.

But there are individuals who taste success without them engaging in any unhealthy competition. They don't believe in competing with any other person, other than themselves. Unhealthy competition can harm performance and productivity, while self-competition and comparing oneself to past achievements can boost productivity and progress. Comparing oneself to others has limited benefits.. While competing with others can bring success, it may not be lasting or fulfilling in the long-term. Competing with your past self can lead to improved performance and better results. If you really have to look into other people's successes, look for the methods through which they attained success. Competing with yourself can be a powerful way to challenge yourself, grow, and improve in various aspects of your life. You are born to live up to your maximum potential. Try to be the best version of yourself.

The education system often fosters unhealthy competition from the outset. Often their academics involve different kinds of competitions in exams and in various other tasks. Some schools place progress trackers to track the progress of individual students and then set the work accordingly. Some schools give equal importance to academics and other activities like sports and arts too, understanding the needs of differently able students.

They understand that each child is unique and hence have unique strengths and weaknesses. It's unfair to compare athletes and artists, as each excels in their own field. Without understanding this basic concept, most often students are asked to be best at everything. This gives them a sense of failure and disappointment that they are good for nothing. Expecting an athlete to be that good in the field of art and culture is pointless.

Likewise, an artist might not be a good performer at sports. So it's better to find what your forte is and revel in that particular field. Remember, life is a competition, but it's definitely not a race against someone else!

How to compete with yourself effectively

- **Set specific SMART goals:** Define clear, measurable, and attainable objectives to work toward.
- **Track your progress towards your goals:** This can help you to see how far you've come and where you need to focus your efforts next.
- **Reflect on your performance:** Regularly reflect on your performance and identify the areas where you need to improve. Be honest with yourself.
- **Create a plan:** Develop and set a daily routine to help you attain your goals. Break down your goals into smaller, manageable tasks to make them achievable.
- **Stay motivated:** Find tricks and ways to stay motivated and focused on your goals. Celebrate even small successes. Use setbacks as learning opportunities.
- **Challenge yourself:** Continuously challenge yourself to do better. Raise the bar for existing goals to keep yourself engaged. If you accomplish one goal, aim for the next. The moment you stop trying is when you leave the battle of life.
- **Stay disciplined:** Develop good habits and routines that support your goal. Commit to your plan even when you face hurdles and setbacks.
- **Practice self-compassion:** Be kind to yourself throughout the process. Acknowledge your efforts and

pat your back, even when you haven't reached your final destination. The fruit of your hard work will be healthy and glorious.

- **Practice self analysis:** Start analysing yourself and your actions. Think about the actions you might take in a particular situation and think about your previous actions retrospectively. Spend at least 15 minutes daily practicing self analysis.
- **Practice to win yourself:** Practice meditation to help you to increase your ability to concentrate and enhance your memory. Understand that the hardest battle in life is to win yourself, which can be time consuming.
- **Don't lose patience and focus:** Be faithful and true to yourself. It's observed that 99% of people are busy winning over other people, whilst the other 1% make efforts to win themselves. Those 1% are the ones who make history.

Conclusion

Draw inspiration from others' abilities without doubting your own! You can admire good qualities like someone's talent, their character, personality and so on. When you compete with yourself, you will spend your energy on progress rather than on envying someone else who is in a better position than you are!

You might feel good temporarily by being a jack-of-all-trades. It's like fluttering in all and flying in none. However, mastering one skill will help you soar to new heights! Competing in a healthy and constructive way, will make you grow, improve and help you achieve your fullest potential.

> *"What others see in you doesn't matter;*
> *what you see in yourself is important"*

2.6. "CULTIVATE MATURE THOUGHTS"

This chapter sheds light on mature thinking and the unique characteristics of mature individuals. Mature individuals are thoughtful about their choices and opinions. They tend to be reliable beings, and will often be grateful, humble and respectful. They will be responsible for their own actions and committed to their values and morals. They will be independent and know their responsibilities well.

They will also be considerate and understanding of other people's needs and wouldn't hesitate to help. In contrast, immature individuals avoid responsibilities and disregard others' needs and feelings. They will be erratic, reckless and self-absorbed most of the time. Mostly they will show impulsiveness, arrogance and rudeness in their behaviour. They will never show gratitude and will never be thankful to people's efforts for them. Once their need is fulfilled, they will turn their back and will never acknowledge any favours they had. They will be heavily dependent on other people and will throw tantrums and be dramatic when things won't go their way.

How does one think maturely?

Mature individuals can control their emotions and respond positively to situations. They will behave like how an adult should be while responding or dealing with others. There are some positive traits that a mature person or a person needing to be mature should possess.

- **Honour your commitments:** Avoid being erratic and keep your promises.
- **Practice self-control:** Practice controlling your actions and words and never let your emotions control you in any way. Never allow yourself to do anything that might hurt others and never compromise your values and morals for anything.

- **Try being self-sufficient**: Try being self-sufficient by taking care of your own needs financially. This might need you to live independently, on your own, and find an honest way to make a living for yourself.
- **Make thoughtful and informed decisions**: Before you make any decisions, take time and think carefully about the pros and cons of taking that decision. If in doubt, seek others opinions and advice to have another perspective of the situation.
- **Stay humble and grounded**: Be humble and accept that you don't know everything. Accepting that you have limited knowledge and resources will help you to stay motivated to gain more knowledge and experience.
- **Set your goals**: Be aware of what you need to achieve. Once you fixate your goals, try breaking them down to smaller tasks and achieve them one at a time.
- **Stay dedicated and focused**: Delaying gratification helps you prioritise long-term goals over temporary impulses. A mature individual will show restraint with resilience when faced with events that offer instant gratification.
- **Work persistently**: Work regularly and persistently to attain your goals. Never stop trying when unexpected hindrances occur and when things get tougher.
- **Never stop putting in effort**: When the goal seems impossible and making progress is a challenge, taking small steps and being persistent will help you reach your destination even if it takes time.
- **Balance your work and life**: Maintaining a balance between your needs and others' is crucial. Your agenda shouldn't solely revolve around you, but it also shouldn't cater exclusively to the needs of the individual around you either, to the extent that you neglect yourself.
- **Learn to set boundaries**: Care for others, but by all means, take care of yourself.

- **Be respectful to others**: Appreciate others viewpoints and understand that people's perspectives can vary. So treat individuals and their opinions respectfully, even if you don't agree with them.
- **Have a routine and maintain it**: Maintain and build a healthy yet stable routine. Fix times to wake up, sleep and other activities in the day. Find time for exercise and other hobbies that will help you deal with the day to day stresses of life.
- **Accept setbacks and mistakes**: Take ownership of your mistakes, just as you would your achievements. Never blame others for your failures, as this will feed unnecessary hatred and suppress your ability to recover from your circumstances. Owning up your mistakes will help you find ways to rectify it.
- **Eliminate harmful thoughts and habits**: Remove the harmful habits, activities, ideas or even relationships that weigh you down in your progress or no longer benefit you.
- **Express gratitude**: Be thankful and grateful to the people and things that add value to your life. Never hesitate to express how grateful you feel for their existence in your life.

Many young people believe that they cannot fulfill tasks, roles, and responsibilities assigned by teachers or parents. Students who fall behind in their class or exams often try escaping from these responsibilities as they find watching TV, playing games and browsing through their social networks more effortless and entertaining. They don't understand that these set tasks and responsibilities groom them not only to be successful but to become a man/woman of abilities and responsibilities. There is no particular age to start your journey of fulfilling your dreams.

Some people, in their adulthood too, lose their hearts by thinking that all opportunities for success in their lives have come to an end as they have reached a particular age in their lives. This kind of person takes a negative approach towards their life which is dangerous and takes away from the beauty in their life. Such people will not feel enthusiasm towards their work and gradually lose their drive and energy to attain success.

Always remember, there is no age limit for success as it can come early or later depending on a person's mature attitude and willingness to work. You have heard the story of the founder of Kentucky Fried Chicken (KFC), Colonel Harland Sanders Pete Harman who founded it at the age of sixty-five. Initially, this man experienced a series of failures, one after another. His recipe was rejected 1009 times, before it became a hit. This recipe of his was also termed as a 'secret recipe' of KFC, and has since become so popular that it's still considered as its unique selling point. Now as you know, KFC has become one of our favourites, and it has branches all over the world! It has 29000 plus outlets spreading over more than 147 countries on this planet.

Lata Mangeshkar, the 'Nightingale of India' and 'Queen of Melody' started her singing career at the age of 13, and her career spanned over eight decades.

Likewise, Michelangelo, a famous Italian sculptor and painter of all time, continued his painting and creative works until he turned 90.

Former Prime Minister of India, Morarji Desai was elected as PM when he was 81 years old.

Age is never a factor and old age is never an obstacle to anyone's journey to success.

In some cases, old age brings a few disadvantages such as bad health conditions. There are some advantages of mental health such as high self-esteem, moral integrity, patience, and wisdom in a person as he grows older. This stems from the need for a peaceful life during the last stage of his life.

He might often reminisce and talk about the journey of his life and share his personal struggles and experiences with the youngsters for them to learn from. Age is just a number and never a state of mind for a good start-up. So stop worrying about the wrinkles on your face, and do whatever you wish to do in your lifetime. Just try doing it persistently and without any regrets of your wasted years.

Conclusion

Maturity helps build stronger relationships, reduces conflicts, and brings stability to your personal and professional life. Immature people often miss out the bigger significant picture and get caught up with unnecessary arguments and conflicts which eventually drains them out. They often act on impulses and leave behind the most important task that needs to be prioritised. The immature people also tend to depend on others for a longer period than they should be.

Maturity is not something that can solely be measured by your age, but your ability to handle certain situations, responsibilities and in maintaining your emotional stability. Your personality should reflect in such a way that you radiate positivity that it gets reflected onto anyone who comes in contact with you. You can determine your maturity level by looking at how well you react to others' criticisms, adapt to your life changes and challenges, and accept responsibilities, show love, affection and respect towards youngsters and elders alike.

"Rise above your years, embody maturity and wisdom"

2.7. "HAVE MEANINGFUL DISCUSSIONS"

Effective yet meaningful communication is the foundation of any successful relationship, be it personal or professional. In today's digital age, where communication is often reduced to brief texts or social media updates, the messages can often be taken in different contexts which might result in many relationships to fall apart. Many youngsters of this generation lack emotional intelligence and empathy due to the lack of having proper meaningful conversations in their day-to-day lives.

Lack of communication and not putting through your ideas and thoughts straight can cause drifts and misunderstandings both in your life, and in your work. Moreover, you cannot dream, plan, or collaborate at work without gaining the art of communication skills. Communication has that important part to play when it comes to teamwork. While working as a team player in a team, you need to establish an effective communication system first, and have a mutual agreement among the team members on the schedule of meetings, its purposes and the outcome that needs to be achieved at the end.

Finally, it's always good to check and verify with your teammates, if you have been understood properly and the tasks have been mutually agreed on. Discussing your issues and matters shall help others to get on board and join a good argument with you. The person listening can put forward any concerns, disagreements or confusions he has in a positive tone.

Practicing the art of meaningful conversations can help you build deeper connections, foster empathy, and is even good for your mental well-being. It will help you understand if the person whom you are conversing with has comprehended your thoughts exactly in the same way you intended to put across or not.

For effective communication, you need to be an active and good listener too. If in doubt, you need to ask questions to get a deeper understanding on the matter. Avoid assumptions at all costs. If you want to know about other's perspectives, don't hesitate to ask open-ended questions, which will require the other person to express their thoughts deeply and elaborately.

Try speaking clearly and specifically according to the person you are communicating with. The tone and words that you select to communicate with an adult won't be the same while communicating with a child. When it comes to communicating with a much younger generation, you would use a stern yet compassionate tone and the words used might be easily comprehensible to them. While listening to a child you might need to listen to him without being distracted by your work or chores. Set aside some time to communicate with your child if he persistently craves for your attention.

Keep a good eye contact with him and if needed kneel down to his level, so that you can look straight into his eyes while listening to his concerns or stories. Engage in small talks with him quite often. Listen to him empathetically and ask questions in multiple ways so that you could understand what he is trying to put across to you. While answering back to them or explaining a matter to them try reinforcing your intent with your body language if needed. Use non-verbal communications if needed to make them understand your point in the right sense. Using eye-contacts, objects like pencil or a pen, or a compassionate touch might be very effective to put the message across.

Find ways to master the art of communication and unlock the power of effective communication. In this chapter we will briefly discuss the importance of effective communication, and how to practice it. Wisdom always plays a vital role when it comes to understanding others' viewpoints and the way it should be perceived. People who are poor listeners, tend to be more argumentative and might make fuss out of matters because of their poor understanding of the topic. Effective communication should be a balanced act where everyone's points are valued and listened to without any interruption.

Every person in the conversation should get a fair chance of speaking their minds up, and every view should be valued respectfully. Always remember that a message sent is not always the message received and it applies to both written and verbal communications alike. The communication can be interpreted rightly or presumably wrongly depending on one's past experiences, the person's own thinking and perspectives, and the words used to put the message across. It's advised not to judge others by one's limited knowledge, their way of thinking or the way they chose to communicate the message to you. If in doubt, ask them questions until you get the context and message properly.

Small actions when practiced everyday can create a significant change in one's life. You will see your communication skills getting better by practicing it in day-to-day life. Ask yourself some questions and try to give suitable, specific and thoughtful answers.

Try to be part of a charitable organization, or institutions where you can apply your communication skills publicly to a larger group whenever you get a chance to. In some events or programs, try to take advantage of opportunities to present.

Remember, practice makes everything perfect! With practice and applying it to real life, be assured that the skill of effective public speaking will come easily to you. Being equally good at written communication is necessary to grow yourself as an overall effective communicator. Each mode of communication (Email, WhatsApp, Messenger etc.) plays a significant role in flexing your written communication skills.

Communication is involved in nearly every field. Your words, body posture, and emotional intelligence to understand and listen to other's viewpoints carefully and empathetically will contribute to your success in effective communication. Building up on these strategies means you are confident and mature enough to handle things carefully.

What are meaningful conversations? Why are they so important?

Meaningful conversations are exchanges that go beyond small talk and superficial discussions. They involve active listening, empathy, and a genuine interest in understanding the other person's thoughts, feelings, and experiences.

Meaningful conversations can:
- Deepen relationships and build trust
- Foster empathy and understanding
- Encourage personal growth and self-awareness
- Improve communication skills and conflict resolution
- Enhance mental health and well-being

Habits to practice to have meaningful conversations
- **Active listening**: Give the speaker your undivided attention, and focus on understanding their perspective.
- **Ask open-ended questions**: Encourage the speaker to share their thoughts and feelings by asking open-ended questions.
- **Show empathy and understanding**: Reflect on the speaker's emotions and show that you understand their perspective.
- **Be present**: Put away distractions like your phone or other tasks, and be fully present in the conversation.
- **Be vulnerable**: Share your own thoughts, feelings, and experiences to create a safe and supportive space for meaningful conversation.

Tips for starting meaningful and mindful conversations
- **Start with a thoughtful question**: Ask a question that encourages the other person to share their thoughts or feelings.

- **Share a personal experience:** Share a personal story or experience to create a connection and encourage the other person to do the same.
- **Find common ground:** Look for something you both have in common and use it as a conversation starter.

Conclusion

By incorporating meaningful conversations into your life, you can build stronger relationships both personal and professional, improve your communication skills, and even enhance your mental health. Remember, meaningful conversations are a practice that takes time and effort to develop, but the rewards are innumerable.

"Cultivate meaningful conversations that inspire, educate and uplift each other"

2.8. "BEFRIEND GOOD BOOKS FOR KNOWLEDGE"

Progressive and goal-oriented people are always on the hunt for ways to become the best version of themselves. While personal growth and success is important, it's equally challenging and demands a lot of sacrifice, dedication and commitment. Most successful people take inspiration from others' work and experiences. They usually are very good at motivating themselves and taking actions based on other people's experiences. They read books that help them to understand other people's journey towards success.

In the vast expanse of human connection, there exists a unique and enduring bond- the relationship between a reader and a book. Like a trusted confidant, a book secretly offers a listening ear, a supportive hold, and an enormous wealth of wisdom. Its pages whisper secrets, share experiences, and kindle imagination, developing a deep and abiding connection that can last a lifetime. Within those books or articles, we often find reflection of our own thoughts, a validation of our emotions, and a solace that soothes our souls, reassuring us of a better tomorrow.

We all know that just like how the ancient Vedas and Upanishads have guided us through ages, the books continue to be our gurus, imparting knowledge, wisdom, and spiritual growth in us and our children. Like the sacred rivers of India, books nourish our minds and souls, quenching our thirsts for understanding, healing and feeling connection. As we turn each page of knowledge and information, we undertake a path of personal growth, navigating the complexities of life, feeling motivated and gaining strength from the words of influential writers, storytellers, and poets.

Through the stories and insights shared by writers and thinkers, we gain a deeper and better understanding of ourselves and the world around us. We begin to see the interconnected threads of human experiences, which make our own journey richer, more meaningful, and purpose-driven. In the embrace of a good book, we find the comfort of a familiar home, the warmth and caring of a loving family, and the wisdom of a revered guru.

As we delve into the pages of great books, we unlock the secrets of the past, present, and future. We discover how the likes of Gandhi, Tagore, and Vivekananda found a purpose in their struggles and transformed their lives into testaments of courage, enlightenment and wisdom.

We learn how to distill life's lessons from the success stories of pioneers like Albert Einstein, Martin Luther King Jr., and Marie Curie. We realise that the journeys of these visionaries hold the keys to our own growth, possessing an enormous capability to empower us, to help us set goals that ignite our passions, values, and dreams. By harnessing this timeless wisdom that we gain from the experiences of these great people, we can draft and prepare our own course, aligning our actions with our purposes, thus becoming authors of our own extraordinary stories.

The basic purpose of reading is to gain knowledge about a particular topic or subject. Knowledge is something that we can gain through our own experience or through someone else's experiences. You can gain knowledge through reading about other's experiences on that subject matter. Secondly, the purpose of reading is to acquire wisdom through knowledge. This wisdom helps us to make decisions based on those knowledge and to distinguish right from wrong and good from bad. It enhances our decision making capabilities and helps us avoid unnecessary risks at various stages of life. We can take wise advice and learn from the principles of great authors or deep-thinkers whose ideas we are most likely to get influenced by.

We can also grasp information from various other learning platforms such as the internet, media, newspapers and television. Based on the information and knowledge gained through reading, we can construct a life based on those values and principles. I advise against reading something just for the sake of reading only, but to grasp the concept and context of the content in the book or article that you read. If you choose to read a motivational book or article, choose a quiet place and concentrate fully while reading and understanding the ideologies expressed there and if applicable, try to implement them in your life. Different authors have different perspectives about the subject they choose to write about. When a scientist sees a rainbow, he might visualise it as a phenomenon of refraction of sun rays as it passes through the water droplets on a rainy day. While a poet might envision it as a garland of vibrant flowers adorning a sky nymph's cloud-like dark tresses.

I vividly recall a moment that sparked a sense of wonder and awe in my young nephew's eyes. Before starting my journey to meet him at our parental home, I asked him what he desired for a birthday gift, and his response left me beaming with pride. He eagerly requested books about space and astronauts, showing his passion to explore more about the subject.

He has since then explored topics related to space, robotics and even programmed a space game at a very young age, which then got featured on Scratch. This achievement ignited a passion in him for coding, propelling him towards a future filled with promise. Fast forward to today, and that curious and enthusiastic child has blossomed into a brilliant young adult, pursuing his passion at the prestigious Imperial College London.

As an influencer on social platforms, he also provides guidance on various topics related to his subjects, his experiences and the projects that he undertakes during his free time. It's a great testament to the power of nurturing curiosity and the boundless potential that lies within every child.

Conclusion

Beyond the surface level of our everyday life experiences, lies a profound realm of emotions and subconscious feelings waiting to be discovered. While many of us claim to be great readers, book lovers or writers, only few truly accept the transformative power that words can carry. To read with curiosity, to absorb the thoughts with passion, and to integrate the wisdom gained into our lives- this is the rare pursuit a genuine reader, and a seeker of knowledge should possess.

For it is through this depth of engagement that we gain the insight and the purpose of our lives. A person can enhance his empathetic mind, conversational skill, knowledge and intelligence through reading. A person, who has a habit of reading often, will possess a curious mind. He will have in-depth knowledge on various topics, and can most likely engage in conversations that will help others to gain valuable insights on those topics.

"Wisdom, guidance and companionship at every turn"

2.9. "SEIZE OPPORTUNITIES"

Every day brings new hopes and opportunities in everyone's life. Grab what today can offer you, so that you can build a better future. Take every opportunity that comes your way, believe in yourself, mold yourself with the new knowledge, and watch yourself transform into a better person. The transformed you will be a happier person in every aspect, whether it is with your family, your social circle, or your professional life. Focus on staying with good people that keep up your positivity and want to see you succeed.

Make sure you have good thoughts to stay positive. Never take anything, anyone or any day for granted. Grasp every opportunity and route that will help you grow, even if it's a challenging one. Every person thinks differently and so will have different perspectives of dealing with opportunities that come with risks. Some approach it with much enthusiasm, whereas others might turn their heads away in much fear and anxiety.

Remember that great opportunities never knock on your door twice. You have to identify those and give yourself a chance to make use of it to achieve something great. Never turn it down with fear and self-doubt. In this competitive world, the secret to failure is to not take any risk at all. There are at times when you doubt yourself and your abilities thinking about the failures you had to face in your business. You should know that your past experiences have the power to change your present. You now know what you need to change and what you need to do to achieve success. You shouldn't waste your time looking back and reminiscing about the bad experiences of your past as this will obstruct you from moving forward and grabbing some good opportunities.

You all know that the human lifespan is comparatively shorter than most of the other mammals. We have achieved a greater lifespan than before with the help of medical advances and research. But still we all feel that it's not enough! With this limited time frame, we still can achieve a lot and live a happy and contented life if we set our mindset right. If you look through the history of great men, the common thing you can observe is that the basic mantras of accomplishments were nothing but the proper utilisation of opportunities and time that was available to them. The privilege of success will only come to those people who can identify the prospects and possibilities at the right time and utilise them for the betterment of the world.

Some people experience stagnancy as they abstain from trying something new and rather prefer to wait endlessly for better opportunities to come through. Also, while waiting for something great, they fail to notice the various opportunities knocking on their doors that might help them get out of their present situation. If you want to be successful, you have to live in the present, recognise the chances and avail it on time, rather than waiting for other opportunities that are yet to show up.

You can funnily say that opportunities are like a biscuit dipped in tea; a little delay and it disappears. It's not only applicable to individuals but can be applied in national interests too. A diplomat has to identify and grab every opportunity to strengthen socio-economic ties with other countries.

Similarly, if you look at multinational companies, you can find that these companies have to tie-up and work in collaboration with several other internationally renowned foreign companies as part of their foreign investment policies.

Here, local companies wait and watch with much resilience and patience for a perfect investing partner. When it comes to individuals looking for work, trying local Government jobs at the right time is important. Most of the government jobs have age caps, so try grabbing these opportunities within that age limit. Most of the people try looking for jobs in the private sector, as there is a better flow of money in various projects they find in major cities than in rural areas.

Most of us at a certain age will try to look out for ways to create active and passive incomes. Sometimes, you might find difficulties even after several attempts to succeed and waiting patiently for an insanely long duration. Yes, it is vital for all of us to learn and know how to make a better living and how to manage money. But what most of us don't realise or never try to learn is the importance of setting clear paths to generate income.

Money being the most important factor for many, it has nowadays become the biggest reason for unlawful and deceitful activities. People nowadays are desperate to 'anyhow' make money, no matter what means they take. They don't hesitate to lie, cheat and use cunning tactics to somehow accumulate wealth. There is a lack of integrity and empathy in people when it comes to making money these days.

Always remember, being honest and trustworthy is more important and valuable assets in the eyes of the civilised world. It's better to die poor than to live as a dishonest human. No matter what, try living a contented and happy life. Pursue your passion and work with utmost dedication. Just stick to your core values, without compromising your integrity and honesty, pursuing your passions, grabbing opportunities at the right time, taking responsibilities one at a time, exuding confidence, delivering excellence, constantly evolving and working in coalition where-ever and whenever is needed.

This is the perfect recipe for a great and successful life. For most of the adults later in life, they regret spending too much time at work and all unimportant things, without spending enough time with their children as they grow up. Up till the middle age, most of us focus mainly on providing a better future for ourselves, possibly trying every way to excel in life, often forgetting that our families will not be with us forever. Put trust in yourself and believe that what was lost in your past can be repaired and regained just by clicking the cursor of life with various opportunities that can bring both endless happiness and guaranteed results.

Conclusion

During the final days of your life, you shouldn't regret what you have lost in your past. So if time and age doesn't suit you to try various paths, recognise your strengths, pursue your dreams and stick to your passion. There might certainly be things that can make us hesitant to grab opportunities. Some of them are fears and confusion from our past experiences that might have traumatised us from trying something new.

But if we constantly think of our past experiences, we will never overcome our fears which might hinder our ability to pursue the things that can be beneficial and might change our lives drastically. Take chances at the right time to avoid regretting later after it's gone. So come out of your comfort zones and your fears, try grabbing the opportunities before it disappears, and explore the possibilities of your future.

"Seize opportunities at the right time, before they're gone!"

2.10. "STAY CONSISTENT"

This chapter throws light on the importance of working consistently and persistently without losing passion to lead a progressive life. With so many distractions in this world nowadays, it can be hard to stay focused and consistent in maintaining good habits and day-to-day routines. Without consistency and persistence towards your work, your professional life, academics and even personal life will swiftly start breaking down. Even the most successful people must produce consistent further efforts in order to maintain their positions.

Consistency is the one common quality that every successful person possesses. No matter how challenging it may seem, staying consistent in your efforts and making even just a little progress everyday will inevitably lead you to the successful life that you have always dreamt of. The first major step is for you to make a list of objectives of your life, and set a short-term plan towards attaining those goals, and consistently work every day so as to reach that short-term goal in the set time period. Start off by making a list of your old habits that were proven to be effective, and then add new habits you would like to adapt in your daily life. The final step is the simplest to think about, but the hardest to execute: work relentlessly to finish off your daily set tasks. In other words, consistency is the commitment that you must take and put into action daily, so as to achieve your aspirations. Remember that dreams without action will always stay as dreams.

"I've learned from experience that if you work harder at it, and apply more energy and time to it, and more consistency, you get a better result. It comes from work."

Louis C.K

Goals can only be achieved if we envision our dreams and take necessary actions to achieve them. One such action is 'staying consistent', which makes our path easier by each step towards achieving the set targets. It's an art of staying focused and dedicated, doing tasks persistently without any fail, no matter how less motivated you might feel or whatever obstacles come your way. Consistency is that driving force along with motivation which can lead a person towards the destination in a much lesser time. It's a slow, but constant progress that one makes towards achieving their goals.

Success can't be measured as a result of one's intelligence or mere fortune, but rather it's the result of persistent commitment, perseverance and effort. If you are a businessman, or a professional, your consistency in finishing off your assignments and tasks on time, without failing your promises will help you build credibility and trust among your clients or customers. The only way a person can maintain his success after achieving it is through consistent efforts to do better, or else he might become stuck and stagnant without any progress and might even lead to failures.

> *"Small disciplines repeated with consistency every day lead to great achievements gained slowly over time"*
>
> **John Maxwell**

For most of us, the word success sounds more enticing than the word consistent, as most of us start off our work with much motivation, but after a certain period it wanes away, leaving our tasks often incomplete and unfinished. We often feel less driven and get distracted by unwanted thoughts and activities that the main task slips off from our routine, thus leaving our work without any further progress. It's natural to feel skeptical about the decisions and changes that you make in your day to day life, in order to achieve your goals. Most of us, before going to bed, think of waking up early in the morning, maybe at 5 O'clock, completely disregarding the time that we hit the bed. You can't expect to wake up that early after having a late night party or after watching movies or soaps till late night.

Your body needs to revive and will only function or regulate properly the next day, if you get at least 7 hours of sound sleep at night. Researchers claim that an adult who sleeps less than 7 hours a night will have many health issues compared to adults who sleep more than 7 hours! Maintaining a regular sleep schedule with set timings for going to bed and for waking up will help regulate our body's internal clock.

Only consistency can provide you with better sleep quality and enhance your body's natural sleep-wake cycle. Try to wake up every morning at the same time, even during weekends and holidays. A fixed wake up time plays a surprisingly important role in improving your overall health and day to day habits. So, in the olden days, people used to say that it takes 21 days for a person to form a habit, while if they continue the same habit for 90 days, it will become their lifestyle.

Conclusion

Consistency and perseverance are things that any person with purpose should always practice. Being consistent in your efforts will give you the results you desire and keep you ahead of your competitors, whether in business or in your academic lives. It's a subject that many feel easy to talk about, but usually fail to implement in their own lives. Many forget the fact that consistency just means taking a few simple steps daily without fail.

Consistency needs continuous dedication and efforts everyday so as to reach your set goals. It involves continuously taking small gradual steps, building the momentum and regular habits that help utilise your time effectively, thereby contributing to a successful life and career.

With a little consistency, you can achieve greater tasks through simpler steps without getting overly exhausted. Habits are behaviours that are operated by our system on auto-pilot, remarkably without disturbing other activities. So in your day to day life, always cultivate good habits with steadiness, and be consistent with your efforts to attain your goals.

"Stay focused, remember consistency leads to excellence."

PART 3:

Personal Growth and Development

3.1. "REALISE YOUR STRENGTHS AND WEAKNESSES"

We all have our own weaknesses and strengths, but not all of us try to recognise those and work on them. A person who is self-aware will always have the ability to identify their weaknesses and strengths. Many employers look for this desirable trait in their potential employees. An employee who is aware of his own strength will try using his fullest potential and will never hesitate to work on his weaknesses when needed. He will always find ways to improve his skills and performances.

Identifying and working on it is the crucial part which will help you grow and succeed in your career and personal development. Identifying these strengths and weaknesses will allow you to improve yourself and enable you to make positive changes in both your career and your personal life too. Periodically checking these strengths and weaknesses can help leaders and superiors to make proper decisions on their professional and personal development. They can guide the subordinate team to discover themselves, help them select their roles and make them understand their responsibilities wisely.

Nobody in this world can boast of their perfection, either in professional life or in character. So knowing your strengths and weaknesses will give you a better understanding of yourself and how you will function. Knowing your weaknesses gives you a clear understanding of things that may be holding you back. Once you recognise these, you can work around finding different ways and methods not to let it pull you from behind. You should never be extremely proud and overconfident of your strengths.

You should always be open to improvement even on your strengths and try to develop them further. On the other hand, you should also not run away from your weaknesses and shortcomings. You can do everything possible to get rid of them as it can create hurdles on your journey to success. You can turn your weaknesses into strengths only if you recognise and accept your weaknesses. You shouldn't deny yourself the way you are.

Moving on to working on your weaknesses, the first thing you need to do is to identify what you are lacking in to achieve your goals or professional attainments. You'll just need to learn a particular skill to keep up with your growing job requirements and demands.

Understanding your power and strengths will make your goals attainable and lead you to success, whereas, recognising your weaknesses will enable you to work on the areas that need improvement. It's better to focus on your own strengths instead of comparing what others can do.

Different people have different strengths depending on their life choices, experiences, exposure and circumstances. A person who is trained to be an athlete since their childhood cannot be compared with a professional singer who is trained in that specific field. Focus on what you are good at rather than getting upset about what others are excellent in.

Sometimes, you think that it's very difficult to realise your weaknesses. But it is a myth. You have to recall and reflect on your past experiences and your school, your college, past hobbies, and other co-curricular activities you were previously engaged in. Make a note of your accomplishments as well as your major setbacks. Ask yourself how you succeeded in those moments and what weaknesses obstructed you.

While I was a high-school student, I used to love playing hockey. I had a competitor named Manoj whom I grew really jealous of. He was an excellent runner, but I wasn't. When compared to many, I was very fast, but when compared to Manoj, I wasn't. My fast running was my strength when compared to the majority of my peers, but when compared to Manoj, my performance was always poor. From this I learnt - Strength makes us feel proud which results in ego which is a bad sign; whereas weakness makes us feel bad which gives birth to jealousy, which is again a negative trait to possess. This made me realise that I can turn powers into weaknesses depending on the way I perceive them.

In your life, you may have to encounter a difficult interview for a particular course or a job. First and foremost thing to remember is not to panic; listen to the question carefully, pause for a moment to think about the possible answers while handling it tactfully with confidence. Many interviewers want to see whether you stick to your thoughts or not. They may interrogate you differently. When it comes to your strengths, "Experience counts". Mostly the student who sits for competitive examinations doesn't clear it in their very first attempt.

You should maintain a positive mindset, dedication and personality while facing such an examination. How can you understand and improve your personality? For that, you should keep challenging yourself by experiencing new things considering the risk factors. In many cases, only a few seconds of insane courage will magically do something you normally wouldn't, which may result in an enhanced ability and personal growth. You will be able to grow new skills and thereby enhance your strengths and improve on your weaknesses.

Conclusion

We are deemed naturally good when it comes to our strengths and the things that need improvement so as to become better are our weaknesses. Some of the examples for strengths can be strong determination, listening skills, leadership skills, adaptability, honesty, time management, versatility, confidence, communication skills etc. Examples of weaknesses can include negativity, anxiety, poor judgement, poor communication skills, laziness, less motivation, poor listening skills etc.

You might find yourself related to some of these positive and negative traits. You can be powerful enough to protect yourself from failures through concentrating on your talents. Never let your weaknesses like insecurities and fears hold you back.

Instead let your strengths lead you to focus on what you can do to turn these weaknesses into strength by constantly working on it. Once you are successful in turning your weaknesses to strengths, find ways to assist people with similar problems. Always try ways to use your talents in the right place and the right direction, and this will make you never feel sad and defeated again.

"Power is 'I can do it'; weakness is 'I can't do it' "

3.2. "NURTURE A PEACEFUL MIND"

This chapter emphasises the importance of nurturing a calm mind for a healthy body and a successful life. A relaxed stress-free life and a refreshed mind-set is what a person needs when he gets into a conflict or trouble. Anyone can fall into a depressive state if he feels abominated by both his family and society. This state of mind can occur to anyone in any phase of their lives, be it professional or personal.

In this situation, a person might feel overwhelmed and exhausted. First of all, keep calm and remind yourself that you are not just your thoughts! You have the ability to turn over any adverse situations by controlling your negative thoughts and mind. This may seem difficult, but don't you think a calm mind is more content and efficient than the stressed one? So why add more?

How can one nurture a peaceful mind?

Start your day with positive thoughts and wake up in anticipation that something great is about to happen. There's no such bliss as nature, which can provide serenity and calmness in mind. Take a long walk to a sea shore and observe the beauty of nature, the rising sun, the chirping birds, the waves forming, and the seagulls catching worms and flying away. Observe how the small dew-drops on shrubs and grass evaporate and disappear with the rising sun. Our worries and stress are just like that!

You may have read or heard of an Italian folktale called "The Happy Man's Shirt". In this tale, a prince fell into despair due to excessive worrying and fretting about life. He strongly believed that wearing the shirt of a happy man would make him happy too! So he sent their soldiers in search of a shirt of a happy man so that he could wear it too. The soldiers questioned thousands of people who were leading good lives and appeared happy, but unfortunately none of them were genuinely happy.

When they were interrogated, soldiers found that they were living a happy life in society and family's eyes, but deep inside they didn't feel content. At last, after a long hunt, they were able to find a happy man with no shirt. This man was happy because he worked so hard that he had no time to be unhappy. Even though this is just a story, most of us realise that to keep oneself happy and calm is to be busy in things that you like most and that which needs your attention most. Troubles are almost inevitable in everyone's lives. Blessed are those who find peace and ways to stay happy.

There are several methods for a person to get happy by engaging and indulging himself in various activities of their choice. Some take regular breaks from their busy lives and responsibilities by flying to their dream destinations in order to find joy and to revive themselves.

A very uncommon, yet essential piece of advice for a calmer you is to:

"Nurture your mental peace"

Its importance can only be realised when we face wars between two nations, stress between neighbours, conflict between two parties, discomfort between family members, etc. In your childhood days, you might have at times witnessed conflicts between your parents or extended families over something really silly. Do you remember how they behaved just after the conflicts?

The peace of the whole family gets affected and the tensions between them grow. Funnily, the affected family members would even go to the extent of having hunger strikes and not communicating for days. Peace is not an absence of violence or a war. It is the situation that creates the optimum level of joy and happiness in each one of us.

How do you exactly maintain your inner self? Can mental peace be attained by the satisfaction of maintaining your outward appearance and improving your hygiene alone? Is it because you believe that this is what society gauges you on? How much daily care do you put into maintaining your inner self? Do you take enough time to actively maintain your inner peace consistently?

Meditation is the best healer and only needs a few minutes on a frequent basis as consistency is the key. It's an art of knowing your inner-self, spending a few minutes alone with yourself by taking a break from the rest of the world! It makes you focus on your inhale-exhale processes, thereby helping you control your thoughts, putting you in relaxation mode while making you feel at peace. Next is to feel gratitude and contentment, which is a positive vibration you can experience, if focused on a daily basis.

Self-care is a most important factor to maintain your inner peace. If you neglect your needs, you are bound to lead a stressful and frustrated life when things get busy and difficult. No matter how hectic your schedule is, take enough time to take care of yourself. Take a power nap when you feel low or go for a walk.

Reward yourself for any tasks you've completed. Nurturing our own mental peace is really important, especially in today's world, as the violence that we experience in today's world is an expression of inner conflicts in human hearts.

The final piece of advice is not to force yourself to fit into someone else's box. In many cases, most people hesitate to say 'no' which leads to situations unavoidable and brings along unwarranted stress. This further snatches away the beauty of life itself and creates unnecessary chaos and panic. Also, procrastinating and keeping things for the last moment also steals away the mental peace.

Most commonly students who study at the eleventh hour of their examination or the ones who keep homework and tasks to be completed at the last moment will constantly feel stressed during their student lives. This also affects their overall performance, quality of their works and sometimes might negatively reflect on their results too.

In one of the organisations I worked, the things were mostly left for the last moment. With the auditor's visit imminent, the authorities, feeling pressured to complete a backlog of work, descended into panic mode, frantically scrambling to arrange everything needed for the impending review. Leaving things to the last minute always brings unwanted stress, anxiety which all can result in the poor delivery of tasks. Such habits can undermine your career by restricting your potential. So avoid procrastination at all costs and don't forget to take timely breaks, refresh, relax and take care of yourself.

Conclusion

Observing nature for half an hour everyday in the morning will relieve your stress and help you start your day with a positive mind-set. Secondly, get busy in life doing the things that you love most. The more a person is indulged and industrious, the more easily he will find calm and happiness. So it's true saying that work is worship!

In order to attain peace and serenity one must learn the art of relaxing and refreshing the mind by taking regular breaks out of his busy schedule. A peaceful, forgiving and sensible life creates a peaceful world. To attain peace, it is compulsory to comprehend the true meaning of it.

Be grateful that we are alive and have a chance to experience living as a society and enjoy the beauty of this divine nature. Energy healing is the best and effective way to maintain your sense of inner peace. Spending a few minutes every day to take care of your emotional health is more than worth any investment.

You should not only be grateful for the things you possess, but also focus on the non-material aspects of your life, including creativity, talents and the valuable people in your life.

Monitor other individuals around you, especially those closest to you. They might be likely stressed just like you. Ask them about their day and how they manage stress. Think about how you might help them in a meaningful way. Practice serving out of love and understanding.

Any small act of kindness goes a long way, not only will it serve them but will lift you morally as well. Do things that make you feel good and proud about yourself. It doesn't necessarily need to be done for the whole day, but doing it in evenings will help you feel relaxed and to bounce back after a tough day. Finally, avoid procrastination at all costs.

> *"Your mind can achieve everlasting peace*
> *when you stay positive with a calm mind.*
> *So take breaks, recharge and refresh your mind"*

3.3. "STABILISE YOUR FINANCES"

The Power of Money

Money is a powerful tool that can bring comfort, opportunities, and financial security. However, when given utmost importance, it can also consume and corrupt minds, leading to a destructive obsession that prioritises wealth over human values, relationships, and even one's dignity.

The Importance of a Mindful Approach to Money

It is essential to approach money with balance and wisdom. When money is controlled by us, it can be a valuable tool. But when we get controlled by money, it can lead to a destructive mindset and obsession. A mindful approach to money involves recognising its value and role in supporting our goals and well-being, without letting it define our worth or happiness. There are many things money can't buy; time and happiness are just two of them!

Treating Money as a Loyal Attendant

Think of money as a loyal attendant, dedicated to serving your needs. Just as an attendant ensures a smooth journey, money facilitates your path to success. It's a means to an end, not an end itself. When you treat money as an attendant, you:

- Make money a tool, not a goal or an objective in life
- Stop chasing wealth and instead focus on true passions
- Develop a positive and respectful relationship with finances
- Recognise that true fulfillment comes from purpose, not profits
- Make mindful money choices that meet your needs and priorities

- Focus on the blessings you have, rather than the things you lack in life
- Break the chains of financial stress and live a more balanced life with joy
- Invest in deep associations and memories, not just accumulating possessions

The Benefits of a Mindful Approach to Money

By adopting a mindful approach to money, you'll find that money becomes a tool for empowerment, not enslavement. You'll be more intentional and alert towards your finances, directing them towards your experiences and activities that bring personal growth and happiness.

Examples of Mindful Money Management in Indian Culture

Indian culture has several examples of mindful money management. For instance, the concept of "dharma" emphasises the importance of living a virtuous life, which includes being mindful of one's finances. The Bhagavad Gita also teaches us about the importance of detachment and living a simple life, which can help us avoid the pitfalls of excessive materialism. When we detach ourselves from being over-materialistic, we can lead a more harmonious and contented life.

Conclusion

In conclusion, handling your money wisely is essential for achieving financial security, peace of mind, and a sense of fulfilment. By treating money as a loyal attendant and adopting a mindful approach to finances, you can break free from the chains of financial stress and live a more balanced life with joy. Remember, true prosperity lies in living a life that aligns with your values, passions, and purpose.

"Use Money, Don't Let It Use You"

3.4. "BE MATURE, YET ADAPTIVE"

Through this chapter look at what maturity truly means and why being adaptive to this changing world is important for our success and survival. Being mature in thoughts, but staying updated to the current world and its changing technologies can help you think innovatively and keep you focused. This attitude of updating yourself from time to time will help you understand the changing world and its demands better. It can help you succeed and stay on top of whatever field you're placed in. It will give you undue advantage over your competitors.

Having the ability to adapt quickly into challenging and new circumstances or situations is important for a person to be successful. The situations can be for example the entrance of a new competitor in your field of business or a global pandemic like the one we experienced very recently that can disrupt the proper functioning of your activities.

Irrespective of what hurdles or bad circumstances you might face, you should be prepared to find strategies and adjust your plans that can help achieve your goals. This flexibility in your attitude is a unique skill to possess while navigating through uncertainty and difficult situations.

Remember that maturity certainly has nothing to do with the number of candles you have blown. Some attain maturity at a very young age, and some never attain it at all. In a biological sense, youth is a term to describe the period between adulthood and middle age of our life. The human body and mind is at its best during this period. A person should be fit and healthy both physically and mentally to lead a happy and successful life.

The individual can keep himself active and mindful like a youth, by engaging in positive activities such as meditation, yoga, and physical exercises like aerobics, athletics, or even dance. He can improve his state of mind by being creative and cultivating great imagination, generosity, openness and spontaneity etc, into their life. This is a period when one has a creative mind with lots of ideas, resources and energy to fulfil all their dreams with least support. The specialty of any youth is the energy and resources he possesses to excel in his passionate field and with the right attitude and hard work, nothing can stop him from achieving these goals.

Age and health are always inversely proportional to each other. Many people lose their jobs as a result of declining body functions. Aging often leads to cognitive impairments like dementia and poor memory. A report says that people across the world suffer from it every three seconds, which is alarming for mankind.

These symptoms can possibly be delayed if we find ways to connect with your body early on by engaging in various activities. In various multinational companies related to IT sectors, you can see people working there from early morning to sometimes late night, spending hours sitting in front of the computer. Studies have shown that compared to an active individual, inactive men and women have high rates of depression and anxiety disorders.

If you look at the physical and psychological aspects, you can see that there are many differences between a youth and an elderly person. One needs to cultivate and develop certain qualities within him at a very young age to maintain his youthful mind, so as to keep himself updated in this drastically changing world. He needs to develop positive habits like reading informative books, news and articles, and engaging in talks and debates with the new generation.

Youthfulness completely depends on one's maturity and attitude towards life. There are two different ways of looking at how life works and how people find their paths. One way is you take your time and explore different options before finalising your path and the other is that you immaturely choose to settle at a very early age. I remember a famous quote by Albert Einstein:

"There are only two ways to live your life. One is as though nothing is a miracle. The other is as though everything is a miracle"

You should also learn to be optimistic and explore ways to change your ageing mindset with new habits, approaches and strategies. By maintaining optimism, one shall maintain his youthful self and show maturity in every field of his life. The great boxer, Mohammad Ali once said:

"I hated every minute of training, but I said don't quit. Suffer now and live the rest of your life as a champion"

Swami Vivekananda who inspired youth of all generations, stressed on the importance of character building. He once said, *"Character is the foundation of everything"*. He emphasised that for a student, strong character and staying disciplined is more important than any academic achievements, as one's character plays an important role in the overall growth of a person. It builds a strong foundation to a great future.

Conclusion

Choosing to be adaptable in any situation, can help you to grab opportunities, plan changes, and in mitigating risky situations, thereby contributing to your overall success. You should cultivate positive thinking and stop blaming others for your present sufferings. You should always have a clear and positive approach towards life and greet others with a happy face. This quality of yours can make other people stay humble and polite, reflecting the same positiveness towards you.

People respect those who respect them, so stay positive, charismatic and energetic. You should try helping and accommodating others in their bad situation whenever it's possible. Avoid being a pessimist who attributes bad life events to permanent and pervasive causes which results in believing that good events are temporary, impersonal, and specific.

True youthfulness and character are not measured by age or time, but by the vitality of your spirit, the willingness to be adaptable, the wisdom and maturity of your hearts, and the integrity of your actions. By nurturing these qualities you may continue to cultivate a timeless youth and character that inspire others and leave a lasting impact in this world.

"Let Inner Radiance and Virtue Be
The Keys To Your Eternal Glow"

3.5. "BE DECISIVE"

As we journey through life setting goals and working towards achieving them, it's essential to think about the impact that it will have on those around us. When we focus solely on our personal goals, we can become isolated and disconnected from the world around us. We forget that our actions, big or small, have the power to make a difference in someone's life too. Let's look at 'decisiveness', which is an essential skill to have, especially in emergency situations and challenges faced while working towards your goals.

Being a good and prompt decision maker will require you to look at the different options to deal with the challenges and opportunities, but not necessarily compromising your health or the lives of people around you. By incorporating the habit of fair decisiveness and giving back, we not only enrich the lives of others but also our own.

Giving back to others and leaving a legacy of love and kindness is a vital aspect of living a fulfilling life. While indecisiveness often paralyses a person's ability to fulfil their dreams, one's decisiveness and firm actions will certainly act as a catalyst to their success, thereby contributing to their overall growth and progress.

What factors do we need to consider while making decisions?

There are minor as well as major decisions one needs to take in his life based on his circumstances and situations he might face. Knowing which option to prioritize and how to decide effectively will contribute to their successful and happy life. Depending on our day to day needs, there are times when we need to make minor decisions like which job offer needs to be accepted, what to wear, whom to meet, where to go for shopping, what to eat for lunch, whom to visit or invite for dinner, whom not to invite and if a person can be taken into your circle or if he is toxic enough to be removed from your circle.

Mostly at workplaces, employers give much importance to the key ability of 'decisiveness' while looking for people with leadership skills to take up their managerial and senior most positions. For a leader to have this ability is important while gathering information to avoid unnecessary cost and poor choices, executing major plans and taking the tasks to its successful completion. Most people, sadly, are not capable of identifying and managing their own emotions well and will make poor judgement and decisions based on that impulsively.

On the other hand, smart and successful individuals will always check the intensity of their emotions and the impact that will have on their behaviour before taking any crucial decision. They understand that their bad emotions can affect their morality and sometimes their overzealousness can make them impulsive and overconfident.

Successful people know how important it is to stick to their morals while making important decisions. They know that when emotions are pulling them in all the wrong directions, their morals are the most trusted companion which can resist the negative emotions, and guide them to the right path. They will make sure to not get carried away by their temporary emotions, and will possibly make their decisions looking into the situation and circumstance as rationally and objectively as they can. So always remember the wise old saying:

"Don't make permanent decisions based on temporary emotions"

Sometimes, having to make too many decisions can be stressful and leave you feeling exhausted and lead you to a stage called 'decision fatigue'. It can make you ineffective for the rest of your day. The best way to deal with this stage is to incorporate the minor decisions as a daily routine, so as to free up your mind for the complex decisions that you might need to take later. Practicing this daily and implementing this to our daily routines will increase our ability to make effective and good decisions.

This has been proved as the best strategy to deal with the 'decision fatigue' and has been practiced by some of the most successful people. Another important thing to notice about 'decision fatigue' is that it is always at its peak at the end of a hectic day. That means, you are likely to experience 'decision fatigue' and chances of you making wrong decisions mostly at the end of the day is high. Keeping this in mind, it's better to take complex and most important decisions in the morning when your energy level is highest and your 'decision fatigue' is at its lowest.

Similarly, it's advisable to take minor decisions later in the evening after your work and when your 'decision fatigue' is at its peak. When in a dilemma and uncertain of how to deal with a complicated task or taking a crucial decision, practice this trick of waking up early in the morning while your mind is still fresh, and before you deal with heaps of minor distractions like friends calling over phone and children making noises.

Similarly, try finishing off smaller tasks like choosing outfits for the next day and distracting chores like returning a call to a distant relative to discuss a non-urgent matter etc., before going to bed. This will take some burden off your shoulders the next day and you can wake up feeling much more relaxed and ready to take up complex tasks and decisions.

Conclusion

It's always recommended to mindfully check and evaluate the options objectively when it comes to making effective decisions. When feeling confused about making a decision, it's advisable to check the pros and cons of different options available and compare them with any predefined set of criteria that it needs to meet.

Let's look at some examples of sensible criteria you can check against. Will this decision actually benefit me and people related to it, if so how? Will taking this decision harm me or anyone related to it, if so how? Will I regret this decision later in my life, or will I regret not making a decision later at some point in my life? How will this decision affect or reflect my values?

If in doubt, give it time and if it's urgent, sleep well at night before making any hasty decision. Waking up the next morning all refreshed and with a clear focused mind and emotions will help you make a better decision. By applying these tactics will help you make your complex decisions more effective, easy, fair and much more reliable.

Most successful and smart people also know the importance of fair analysis before making complex decisions and for that they gather resources and information as much as they can. They also give importance to fighting stress when it comes to making decisions. They exercise regularly to retain their mental clarity, and their ability to think rationally. Unwanted stress can result in the production of cortisol, which can hinder a person's ability to think clearly. Studies have shown that exercising regularly can improve the overall functioning of brain cells that are responsible for making decisions. So when in stress, try hitting a gym!

Often people make a decision first and then think of collecting information, resources and evidence needed to support their decisions, whereas goal-oriented and smart people when in dilemma and at difficult times, beat this 'confirmation bias' , by gathering the information and supporting evidence that's needed first before fixing their option.

They take valuable advice and opinions from other reliable and knowledgeable people, so that they can analyse the situation in a different perspective. This helps them to tackle irrationality and make decisions more objectively and fairly. It's also important to remind yourself of the wrong decisions that you made in the past. For a person to be successful, he needs to be aware of his past shortfalls and decisions, so that he can benefit from those mistakes while making decisions again in a similar situation.

Keep in mind that whatever decision you make, the repercussions resulting from that particular decision can linger there for long and can affect your future and the future of other people directly or indirectly affected by that. So make sure to keep the above mentioned strategies in mind, and take decisions wisely while making the whole process of decision-making worth your time and effort.

PLATO

"
A good decision is based on knowledge and not on numbers.

"Embrace the power of decisiveness, even in uncertainty!"

3.6. "PROCURE WISDOM AND KNOWLEDGE"

This chapter will enlighten you about the importance of being observant to gain true wisdom. A person with wisdom will always be enthusiastic to know more in depth by observing their surroundings and situations. There is a clear distinction between acquiring knowledge and attaining wisdom.

To attain true wisdom one should observe more to come to a convincing conclusion; whereas to attain knowledge one has to learn what's already been found and written in books. Knowledge is defined as "justified true belief." But we can still increase and widen our fields of knowledge through observation. Many scientists and researchers find and invent things by observing and building upon their already existing knowledge.

There are great personalities who set an example for us. Whenever you find anything for your studies, you should procure quality-based knowledge out of them. Whenever you watch television, a cell phone, and a computer, you should gain information by collecting valuable articles and reports.

> *"To acquire knowledge, one must study.*
> *But to acquire wisdom, one must observe"*
>
> Marilyn Vos Savant.

How can we be more observant and how would it benefit us?

If you look around you can observe that our mother nature in itself is a comprehensive collection of various sources that provide some or other kind of knowledge. You should have that enthusiastic and positive outlook to it so as to find the spiritual, technical and scientific meanings of similar and dissimilar things. Whatever food we eat or intake is not preserved in the form of food materials in our body after a certain period.

Instead, it becomes a portion of our body in the form of fat which then converts to energy and power for us to live and survive. Similarly, knowledge can be considered as the food of the human mind that shall enrich you with the information needed to create ideas. Always remember that all-powerful ideas come only from a beautiful and determined mind.

You can achieve great things by transmitting ideas. That's how extraordinary things evolve. One single idea can lead to another and so on. Individually, no single person can fully put to fruition or complete an inspiration without it eventually needing others to complete it or to help realise it. With kindness, moral support, compassion, and belief, a person can obtain their best results.

Here you do not have to become a lawyer or a politician, to make millions by cheating, bending, and stealing the truth to make others agree with you. There are many ways you can find to acquire knowledge. In our quest to find the purpose of our lives, we strive to procure knowledge from intellectuals, professors, scientists and their works or from informative books and knowledgeable videos.

Sir Isaac Newton also developed the laws of motion, which stated that an object in motion will continue to stay in motion until and unless an external force acts on it. These laws of motion are used in different fields like car manufacturing, car testing, aeronautics, etc. These laws also have provided a basis for many innovative innovations like parachutes, trampolines, diving boards, etc. When a person is driving and suddenly sees someone or a hazard in front of him, he immediately hits the brakes, so as not to cause damage to the person/thing on the road or to himself in the car.

Also, when he hits the brakes, an opposing force acts on the car's forward motion, which in turn stops the car from moving. There's an incident related to these basic laws of motion that I would like to share. I remember, back in my twenties, riding a bike too fast with my friend in the backseat.

After a few miles, I wanted to slow down so that I could get off the bike, but mistakenly I pressed on the brakes, which resulted in my bike stopping abruptly and me flying off the bike. I flipped over the handlebars and landed on my head first with considerably serious injuries all over my head, face and body. As soon as I applied the brakes, the fast moving bike stopped, but my body didn't lose the momentum, and I was thrown off because of that. Ouch! It was rather a painful and rough lesson to have ever experienced!

When Newton discovered these laws, it was not for anything other than just his enthusiasm to explore the reason why things happened the way it was and how it happened. Whatever knowledge he gained was purely for his understanding as he didn't try to find meaning or purpose for his life from these discoveries.

But later through these discoveries, many scientists found the meaning and purpose of this knowledge.

Similarly, medical professionals (doctors, dentists, veterinarians, etc.) who have learned medicine, anatomy, biology, etc. use their prior knowledge they acquired to understand how animal and plant bodies work, and use that knowledge further with a purpose to help examine, treat or cure any injuries or illnesses that their patients may have.

Conclusion

The whole point of acquiring knowledge is to produce both meaning and purpose to our lives. It helps us find the answers we were looking for and to grow the enthusiasm to know even more. Having good observation techniques are really crucial when it comes to acquiring knowledge in a particular topic we might be interested in. We need to cultivate our observational skills too to fully understand and engage with the individuals and the circumstances we come across. We have to think critically and pay close attention so as to improve our awareness and observational skills. Developing these skills isn't that hard and there are some easy yet effective and proven methods to improve our observational skills.

"Knowledge makes a man a human, without it he is a beast"

3.7. "BOOST YOUR ENERGY LEVELS"

This chapter explains the ways of eliminating fatigue from your life by bringing small but regular changes in your routine. Oftentimes we feel tired due to several factors, like age, ailments, our eating habits, not having proper sleep or being overburdened by work that seems never-ending! Whatever the reasons might be, feeling exhausted and tired often can affect your productivity and quality at work. It can stress you out, and every easy and small task will look more complicated and even seem unattainable.

One of the common reasons for feeling tired is not getting enough sleep. Often due to the lack of proper time-management, unavoidable circumstances or unwanted distractions, the tasks that you plan to finish get stretched out to late night. Chances are that you might get used to this irregular pattern of stretching the tasks late into night every day, thus reducing your sleeping hours. You might be well aware of Charles Darwin's theory- "The survival of the fittest! " This world belongs to the people who are motivated, energetic and who possess strong determination. In order to be your most productive self, you always need to prioritise your physical well-being.

Some proven helpful tips and tricks to fight away your fatigue:

- **Fuel up your energy levels:**
  - As you all know, the food that you eat is the fuel your body converts to as energy for its day to day activities. This energy makes you feel good, helps you to stay focused in your work, thus contributing to a successful life. You should never stay hungry and work on an empty stomach.

- Try eating often in small portions at regular intervals. Avoid consuming high content sugary beverages and alcohol if possible. Cut down on your tea and especially coffee consumption.
- Caffeine can sometimes help you to stay awake for a certain time but it will contribute to unhealthy sleeping patterns and other health issues. Also, doctors recommend that taking naps at regular intervals or during lunch breaks will make you feel fresh and energetic.
- Sleep well at night and take regular naps in between your tasks. Taking power naps do charge up your brain and body. Another factor which contributes to an increased energy- level is having regular physical exercises.
- There is research that suggests that adding more physical activity into your day-to-day life could also contribute to an increased energy levels and reduced fatigue.
- Physical activities can help you get fit and motivated throughout the day. It can help you in maintaining a healthy weight thereby making you feel more confident and good about yourself.
- **Connect with yourself:**
  - Are you an introvert or an extrovert? If you are an introvert, you tend to feel energised following some alone time. You will be least bothered about mingling with others or spending time with others. If you are an extrovert, you will feel revitalized by speaking or connecting with someone else.
  - You also prefer to get connected with your friends through various social media platforms. Consider if you were somewhere in the middle, that is, you are an ambivert, then you should try mixing the two. You can find many ways to boost your energy levels, either by

listening to music if you are into it or by engaging in any physical activities you like.
- People say that doing cardio or any free-hand exercises helps them to get back to their normal selves. Have you ever thought of why you should get more connected with yourself? You shall get a proper answer if you ask it repeatedly. If you love yourself, you will never get trapped in unwanted thoughts or negative feelings.

- **Take a break in between work:**
  - You will know what to do when you feel that your schedule is very hectic. You have to find a real break from your busy work if needed. If you feel overloaded, then it will hamper your entire task. Take breaks often following a 10:10:10 rule.
  - You will feel relieved and revived when you head outside for a while, and break away from sitting for long hours in front of your laptop.
  - Many of you might feel your eyes getting tired or depleted after a long hour of work or after a journey. Here a 10:10:10 rule works where you have to look at a 10-foot-long distance in each 10-minute gap at least for 10 seconds duration.
  - This will refresh your eyes with an improved vision and helps defog your brain. Give it a try from today, and benefit from this unique method.
  - You will see an improvement in your productivity and experience a more powerful brain. So what's stopping you? From now on, get yourself moving with this technique!

- **Embrace a workday shutdown ritual:**
  - In the realm of time management, a shutdown technique serves as a precious instrument for enhancing work-life integration, balance and maintaining the well-being of a

person. A shutdown method basically places its space to create a division between work and personal life.
- This helps you to disengage yourself from the demands of the workplace both mentally and physically. While applying this technique, you don't have to bother about all the disturbing stuff revolving around your family!
- Practising this method daily will equip you with an overall knowledge of incorporating a shutdown ritual thereby enhancing your productivity at work and a happier you.

Conclusion

One of the large and often overlooked contributors to your tiredness and low energy levels are the food that you prefer to eat or to not eat. So eat well, drink plenty of water, and get enough sleep to boost up your energy levels. You should first understand and learn about yourself to manage your energy. Try to take some time to connect with your inner-self.

The journey to success is a marathon, not a sprint. Always be mindful of what you feed your mind with. To maintain your momentum, boost your energy levels frequently by celebrating small wins, taking breaks, and refuelling with positive self-talk. By doing so, you'll stay motivated, focused, and driven to reach your destination.

So you see the personal benefits of developing and building up your energy levels are enormous. If you look at the professional aspect, an increased level of energy will enable you to have an improved productivity at work thus improving your professional relationships with both your superiors as well as subordinates!

"Renew your energy levels to find a revived self"

3.8. "DISCOVER YOURSELF THROUGH NOVEL EXPERIENCES"

'Destinations are achieved by those who travel a lot'- were written somewhere near the toll while I was traveling in some past days. While watching YouTube, I found some shorts in which when interrogated by an Indian actor Ashutosh Rana, they said - 'People who travel more, earn more.' At first I thought about how it could ever be possible! Thinking a lot, I realized that it was true. Earning knowledge is something different, that is, earning through experience and mingling and talking with people from different walks of life.

This unique blend of experiential learning and social interaction helps you develop a deeper understanding of the world and its complexities. It allows you to see things from different perspectives, challenge your own assumptions, and grow both personally and professionally. By investing in this kind of knowledge, you'll reap rewards that far exceed any material wealth, leading to a richer, more fulfilling life.

Nobody is untouched by tension regardless of whether he's a student, working professional, homemaker or an entrepreneur. All of them need to spend a valuable time along with their family apart from their hectic schedule somewhere to their dream destinations. When I was young, my parents would often plan to visit places that they wanted us to explore in India, and mostly our visit would be to our hometown in Kerala. The best part about traveling for food was that moment when we stepped our foot outside in different parts of India. Here we were taken by surprise with the extent of varieties that we never heard before.

During our stay in those places other than our native hometown, we would try the delicacies that were popular in those particular localities. We would often hunt for the locally sold ingredients that gave those foods their peculiar taste. Whether it be chilly oil with steamy momos or some perfect tasting curry prepared with coconut milk, the sheer taste of food available in our country is truly amazing!!!

My mother, when she gets hold of the ingredients, would try preparing them later back home. I'll definitely not brag about it, but my mom's dishes almost always ended up tasting like the delicacies just the way they tasted back in the places where they were originally from !

Conclusion

Whenever possible, try taking some time to explore this world and the variety of food each and every country has to offer. The food that the world has to offer is as vibrant as the food that avails within India. Try finding activities that those places are popular at providing. Getting in a nature hike or snow sport could also maximize your holiday happiness. These physical activities during vacation improves our wellness levels and in building stronger relationships and life long memories. There are few who would like to enjoy their vacation just by lying along the poolside, simply stretching and moving their limbs.

There are many things other than food to know about by travelling. We can utilize these opportunities to learn different cultures, and their life-styles in general. Learning and knowing these through enriching travel experiences can be taken as an integrated part of our life journey. There can be a lot of experiences and lessons that can be learnt from these paths while traversing through life. It's not necessary that you need to visit posh places to experience these.

Each and every experience that we get through our journey can be shared with others, and we can learn from other's experiences too by hearing about their travel stories. Journey is something that feeds our soul and gives us immense happiness. So take some time out to visit places, experience new cultures and foods and share those experiences with friends and family. Live with no excuses; travel more and sometimes it's better to be alone... Nobody can hurt you there!!

"Life begins at the end of your comfort zone"

3.9. "EMANATE CONFIDENCE AND CHEERFULNESS"

As you step into the vibrant tapestry of life, remember that your attitude is the master weaver, crafting a narrative of either tribulation or contentment. Confidence and cheerfulness are the golden threads that can transform the fabric of your existence, illuminating even the darkest corners with alluring and resilient radiance. By cultivating these luminous attributes, one can unlock the doors to a life, where challenges become opportunities, fears transform into courage, and every day begins with a purpose and a promise! At times, just being confident enough doesn't work! To achieve a level of confidence does take time and skill.

To lead a happy and contented life, we need to take time to prioritise our emotional, mental and physical well-being. These factors if taken care of properly will positively impact almost everything in our life. There are times when we all feel not being good enough! We struggle a lot with confusion, lack of confidence and self-doubt. We at times compare ourselves with other successful people around us, and somehow get convinced that we aren't as good as them. But do you think that us not being better than them is the real problem? The real problem is the self-doubt and the negative self-talk that we constantly feed our minds with. With this self-doubt and negativity, we turn down every opportunity that comes our way and never recognise our strengths and capabilities to learn new skills and overcome challenges.

At times we get so overwhelmed pushing ourselves forward in life, running after achieving something and providing comfort and happiness for others that we rarely notice our own sufferings. We always try to prioritise others needs and expectations before our own, often juggling between tasks and finding time to relax for a bit. Our hand becomes too full that we get so confused to know which one to focus on and which one to be left behind.

There comes a point in life where we might feel to be transformed into a completely different person. Taking up a new job, career changes, marriage, having kids these all evolve us into a new changed person. We develop a new identity with the new responsibilities and often forget about our own individuality through the process. We forget about the importance of self-care and finding ourselves, which results in self-doubt and a huge dip in our confidence and our main purpose in life.

To overcome this problem, the first thing to set right is your self-talk and mindset. Whatever you feed your mind with will contribute to your happiness and wellbeing. If you are constantly self-doubting yourself and questioning your abilities, you will subconsciously fall into the trap of failure. On the contrary, if you feed your mind with positive thoughts and believe in yourself, then you can flip the results around and make a positive difference in your life.

Practice meditation daily to manage your anxiety and stress. Calm your mind and body with breathing exercises. Take regular walks to freshen your brain and keep yourself healthy and fit. Stay away from phones and social media. Find your time to read knowledgeable books and articles. Eat properly, drink enough water, exercise regularly and most importantly sleep well. These habits will definitely help you achieve a great work-life balance and keep you motivated.

Oftentimes when you feel less confident, you might think of faking it until you make it! But it's never a long-term solution; rather it will hinder our ability to work towards attaining our set goals. To feel confident, one must constantly work towards improving their skill sets. It might be time-consuming and equally frustrating at times while learning new skills, but believe me; there will be light at the end of the tunnel. You will feel much more accomplished and motivated when you are confident in your abilities. With this trait vested inside, you can develop the strength to face any challenges that come your way. The skills developed will give you the confidence to push yourself through the difficulties and to lead a successful life. A famous quote by Henry Ford says:

"Obstacles are those frightful things you see when you take your eyes off your goal."

Conclusion

Confidence comes with consistent self-care, learning from past mistakes and taking accountability, reflecting on your past achievements, taking challenges, keeping optimistic and positive perspective towards life, practicing simplicity and leading a disciplined yet purposeful life. To build your level of confidence, practicing self-care is a must. Keep track of both your progress and failures while taking challenges. Reflect on your mistakes and achievements alike. Don't be afraid of taking challenges and setting personal and professional goals in life.

Think positive and be optimistic about the challenges you have set for yourself. Let no one's negativity influence your optimistic approach. Stay away from anything that drains your positive attitude. Believe in yourself and your ability to achieve your goals and never lose sight of your final destination. Be humble, knowledgeable, disciplined yet cheerful at all times. These right attitudes will help you sail through almost all the difficulties that life might throw on you. Always remember, challenges are inevitable, but succumbing to it is a choice.

Feeling satisfied in life and being cheerful at all times brings in much positivity and reduces unwarranted stress and other ailments. Count your blessings. See the sunshine, not the shadow it creates. Feeling dissatisfied in life brings unhappiness and negative consequences. Avoid it at all costs! Lead a healthy lifestyle, allocate your precious time wisely, spend time with your loved ones, cultivate a hobby that you like most, motivate yourself and the people around you, set higher goals and work towards achieving them. A great mathematician, and a known public intellect, Bertrand Russell, revealed another wise secret to avoid stress:

"The secret of happiness is this: let your interests be as wide as possible, and let your reactions to the things and persons that interest you be as far as possible friendly rather than hostile."

3.10. "ELEVATE YOUR PASSION WITH A PURPOSE"

In this chapter, we will see how elevated passion and purpose go hand in hand for the successful completion of a task. We as human beings are all capable of living at higher levels rather than just existing. We are capable of living a contented life full of purpose and passion. In this chapter, we will explore why and how working with a genuine purpose will help you succeed in life. Some necessary practices that you should practice daily to find your real purpose in life are listed below:

We need to follow certain methods every day that can help us live our best lives. There should be decisions that need to be made on what we want to get and what all steps we need to take in-order to achieve it. This is where the importance of elevating and igniting your passion with a purpose comes in.

So what is it like to elevate your passion with purpose?

It's something that gives satisfaction and benefits not only to you but creates greater value for others too. For this, you have to take small steps strategically, one at a time. Some necessary strategies that you can practice and implement daily to find your real purpose are mentioned below:

- It's highly recommended that you should have the habit of reading books or articles of your interests daily.
- The road to success is always under construction. So always try to learn some skills daily or explore new ideas of your interest.
- Self-motivation is a must. So keep motivated to achieve smaller tasks that lead to greater results.
- Keep yourself organised, make a to-do list and try finishing the set tasks daily. Don't delay or keep it for another day.

- Give priority to your needs first and that's not at all selfish. Never try solving others' matters without solving yours first.
- Daily practice is a prolific workout for a healthy, balanced and stress-free life.
- Make a practice to walk daily. A long walk in nature will keep you fresh for the day and help you concentrate on your daily tasks well.
- Know who is right and wrong for you. Choose your circles and relations wisely. Make good friends who shall inspire, encourage and lift you.
- Get inspired by great men from history and around you. Watch motivational and inspirational videos to boost your inner strength, morality and productivity.
- Always practice good habits and keep yourself away from any kinds of distractions or unwanted medicines and drugs. Bad influences can come in any form. Stay clear from those.
- Your state of mind is everything, so make yourself mentally capable and fit to make the right decisions at the right time.
- Don't pretend to be perfect (even if you are) as it will unnecessarily make you overconfident and hinder any scope of personal growth or further development.
- Always try to create a better tomorrow than what it is today. Remember that you shouldn't judge each day by the harvest you reap today, but the seeds that you plant for tomorrow.
- Learn what kindness is. Kindness reciprocates kindness. Be always kind to everybody; even to animals. Practice it in your day to day life.
- Learn how to be true and honest to yourself. You will realise the importance of it in the long run. Your heart might ask you to do things your way, but society will demand differently.

- Don't get immersed in social media. Keep a distance from it if it's heavily influencing you and is deeply embedded in your life. Avoid overly using your social network and internet unless your work is dependent on it.
- To experience growth in your life, you have to do things and leave your comfort zone. Do what's needed and necessary even if you don't fully like it at first.
- You have to stop shortcuts. Patience, resilience and harmonious hard work will lead you to success even if it's a long journey.
- Show your gratitude to God every morning as he has granted one more day to your life. Show gratitude to the food you eat and to everything and everyone who has at some point helped you grow.
- Avoid getting tempted. Always remember that nothing is permanent in this temporary world. Temptations and impulsiveness will later become a reason for depression and unhappiness.
- There is nothing noble to be superior to your fellow man; true nobility is being superior to your former-self. Evolve yourself and change the wrong approaches or bad decisions you might have made in the past.
- Never stop learning, growing, evolving and turning into the best version you can ever be.

Conclusion

So in-order to elevate your purpose for your personal growth, you have to be passionate and mindful of the tasks you choose to do every single day. You have to understand where your passion lies and lift yourself up to become the best possible version you are capable of.

Your elevated purpose along with your passion will create something that's beneficial for the community you live in. Thus you will create an impact and make a difference to the people and the society that you are part of.

"If you have a purpose, spark it;
Ignite your passion and fan the flame"

PART 4:

Relationships and Communication

4.1. "BE GRATEFUL"

This chapter focuses on the importance of practicing gratitude in our day to day life. One of the most important qualities a person needs to get successful is 'practicing gratitude'. When I talk about practicing gratitude, please bear in mind that being grateful is a choice that we need to make and is not a result. Mostly we have seen people showing gratitude when they do something exceptionally well. They show gratitude when everything goes right for them, whether it be a successful career, a good relationship, winning an award, being able to buy expensive and luxurious things. So you see it's easy to show gratitude when we achieve or accomplish something that we have always wanted. Being grateful for your success or achievements is great, but being equally grateful for the lessons that your failures and struggles brought to you are important too. Lessons learned the hard way and the successes resulting from those are sweeter than the ones that were gained easily!

Since we live in a society where human relations are of great importance, practicing gratitude is a powerful way to build strong relationships, trust, and bring positivity into our lives. Gratitude brings with it a feeling of appreciation, love and respect. Your relationship will be strengthened and will always remain fresh and vibrant when you are thankful for even the smallest things that they do for you, when you treat them with the respect and affection they need. Remember, respect should be mutual; a one-sided respect is never mutual if it is not reciprocated. Respect when not reciprocated well, results in relationship failures.

Gratitude is like a boomerang that once released; will surely come back to you. It is good karma that will bring respect back to you. This positive feeling of showing gratitude prompts personal growth and soon you will see an evolved self. So you must express genuine gratitude, not only in your words, but in your actions too. This generates happiness in the people you interact with and encourages them to reciprocate in a similar manner. So practice and develop the quality of thankfulness and gratitude in your daily life.

Practicing gratitude daily will make you feel better as a human, increase self-awareness and will aid you in fulfilling your responsibilities too. Oprah Winfrey once said:

"Opportunities, relationships, even money flowed my way when I learned to be grateful no matter what happened in my life."

You need to give importance to your focus too to cultivate gratitude. Try to focus on the good and positive deeds of people around you. Your thoughts and feelings whether positive or negative will also depend on what you focus on initially. How you feel and think about things and situations will be the way it will be manifested outside. It's better not to be negative about everything and complain constantly about the glass being half empty.

Rather, if you look at the positive aspects of things and appreciate that the glass is half full, it will give you a sense of satisfaction and happiness. Focusing on brighter aspects of situations and having a positive approach towards unfavourable situations will help you immensely to improve your life, career or your business. Your personality will be of someone who can be positively approached and who is optimistic about the people around him and life in general.

Your positive personality and attitude will be contagious and will rub on to the people who come in contact with you too. When you feel a sense of gratitude, you tend to forget about your insecurities and fear and all you see is opportunities. You will feel more confident and optimistic about your approach. So it's important to focus on the right and positive aspects of things or situations.

It just takes the same amount of energy and effort to be negative about things as it does to be positive about it. Your focus and attitude determines which one you'll choose. Charles

Dickens said: "Reflect upon your present blessings, of which every man has plenty; not on your past misfortunes, oh which all men have some."

In this modern era, there are too many ways of showing gratitude or sending thank you messages through various social media platforms such as e-mail, WhatsApp, Messenger, Twitter, Instagram, or through a phone call. I still remember the good old days when people used to show gratitude by sending a nice handwritten thank-you note via mail or by post. It can still be practiced in this modern world. The receiver who receives it will take this as a positive gesture when he knows that you took extra effort and time to write a thoughtful card and drop it through post, taking much care of his feelings.

The main thing that is lacking these days is the effort and genuineness one puts into expressing their thoughts, as many people these days look for the easy way which in turn adds up to their failing relationships.

If everyone takes responsibility and sets a benchmark for their gratitude towards their family, it can contribute towards repairing even the most strained relationships with one's family.

The term thankfulness is a matter of great enjoyment for the giver as well as the receiver. In the case of friendship, showing gratitude can make the bond stronger and the relationship more valuable and successful. Concluding this let me quote a famous saying by Norman Vincent Peale:

*"The More You Practice The Art of Thankfulness,
The More You Have To Be Thankful For"*

Conclusion

One of the key factors in experiencing real success and happiness is through gratitude. Human relations can further be strengthened and improved with love, care and showing gratitude. Gratitude is one of the most important virtues you can cultivate for your meaningful existence. Just be grateful and know that the necessities and luxuries that you enjoy are deprived of many. Being grateful for the things you have, the things you do, and for the people in your life, that will make you feel happier and content.

When you stand in front of the public to show our gratitude towards them or to your teachers and your friends, it spreads similar happiness to them too. Practicing gratitude will shift our focus from what we lack to what we already have. Just look around - at yourself and your life! You can see a lot many things that normally go unnoticed that you can be grateful to. Be grateful to the universe in which you are now, be grateful for it to provide you sunshine, good health, fresh air to breathe, food to eat, water to keep you hydrated, a place to live in, a supportive and caring family, and for all your needs that are being fulfilled.

"Gratitude begets happiness; practice it daily"

4.2. "CHOOSE YOUR CIRCLE WISELY"

This chapter will help you understand the genuineness of the people you surround yourself with and help you re-access their influence and contribution towards the formation of your character and your way of thinking.

You might have heard people saying that you'll eventually show traits of the five close people you mostly spend your time with. So it's really important to be selective of people you wish to surround yourself with daily, as it plays a crucial role in your life's success or failure.

If you befriend winners, they'll become an active catalyst in your success, and on the contrary, if you are spending more time with losers, their negative traits and habits will rub on to you too. So it's important to keep this in mind while choosing your inner circles. By inner circle, we mean the closest friends and family whom you spend your most time with. You have no choice in selecting your biological family, but you can definitely make wise choices while selecting friends, life partners and connecting with business partners. The better your inner circle is, the better your opportunities will get.

Grouping up with people of similar interests and common goals can help you to attain your desired results in a much lesser time and as you will be working towards it with a more consistent approach. Surround yourself with like-minded people, who will benefit equally with the efforts you all put in. Having study partners with similar interests in certain subjects, getting a mentor for guidance in the workplace, going out with friends who equally value healthy eating and fitness, will encourage and motivate us to keep on track and in adapting their habits that can benefit us too in the long run.

Similarly, getting along well with people who have similar financial goals and business interests will help you to progress in life. There are other goals too which might influence people to get together, like spiritual growth and recreational activities. Whatever goals you and your inner circle envision, always keep a check on your accountability, and on who contributes to what. Having an accountability check is good, but timely accessing if they are doing things that can harm or uplift you and regularly checking if they stick to their vision as promised is important too.

We all are social beings, and we know the importance of having true friends. We need friends to have fun with, who can motivate and uplift us, and be there equally for our good and bad days. They are the anchors that keep us steady and strong during the difficult storms that life brings.

The most beautiful and powerful quality of a true friendship is to be able to understand and to be equally understood. They should possess the qualities of generosity, trust, understanding and unconditional love for one another. They should be able to make connections based on shared values and experiences, support one another and accept each other unconditionally.

True friends know and understand each other better than anyone else. They have the power to make us laugh, cry and help us grow. It's a platonic yet intimate bond that is strong enough to withstand any kind of emotional separation, no matter how far away they might be. They are our confidants, our partners in crime and our safest havens.

As you grow older, wiser and mature, you might notice that your circles have shrunk down or are no longer as important as they were to you once. You might notice that they are not the same people you admired before. The change happened because you got to see their actual faces, and you filtered them and chose to have quality friends over quantity.

Always value people who believe in showing you the mirror and who make you introspect yourself, when you stay away from reality. Your inner circle should be these people who can help you make a better person. These are the relationships that will potentially last forever.

As Stephanie Lahart says:

"Strive to build a friendship that doesn't consist of competition, comparison, jealousy or drama. Make friends that bring out the best in you, celebrate you and that genuinely like and love you. Genuine friendship is life!"

Having too many friends is not a great achievement as some people these days do on social media like Instagram and Facebook. But to have a meaningful relationship and to make a healthy trustworthy friendship is a very difficult task. Making friends especially in adulthood seems very challenging as there are less structured ways to develop faith that can develop into true friendship.

Most of us will be sceptical and judgmental about making friends and connections as people at times can be hideous and we will be unsure if we would like to take the relationship seriously or not. Unlike the school life where children easily make friends, adults don't have the same opportunities to build friends.

As we grow older our needs change and people's perspective and intentions change too, depending on the past circumstances they have been through. Making meaningful relationships and friends at this stage is a challenge. This is the time when you should look out for people who share the same interests and aspirations as you or have been through the same experiences as you have. Finding mentors who work in the same field as you will help you progress your career.

Getting genuine advice from friends, family or colleagues can give you the boost needed to solve a problem or to get out of a rut you are in. There is an art of taking time to listen to a person's problem properly, understanding it deeply and working out different ways to solve it, before giving any advice to a friend. If you put an effort and time to learn on how to communicate and receive sound wisdom, you will be able to build everlasting friendships.

> *"A friend is someone who knows everything about you and still accepts you with love."*
>
> St. Augustine

Moreover, a true friend wishes for your welfare and walks with you through the difficult phases of your life. They will never leave your side in distress and put you in despair. So remember the aforesaid principles and set these life rules when it comes to selecting and recognising a true genuine friend. Sometimes, a knowledgeable and experienced friend's wisdom brings valuable and objective insights that might help you overcome your life challenges and move away from distress and confusion.

At times one might feel scared even to take an opinion from their true friend as they feel vulnerable or even embarrassed in certain situations. At those times, seeking advice might feel like bruising one's own ego or stirring up feelings of shame. But remember that asking for advice from a genuine friend doesn't necessarily make you less confident or not self-assured. A true friend will think of you asking his advice as him being valued and trusted by you.

Your friend might be able to give you valuable insights, his own perspective and suggestions to solve your problems. Knowing different and new perspectives and opinions will stimulate learning, exchange of ideas and information, or even deeper connections which are proven to be the building blocks of any healthy relationship.

Conclusion

In today's world, I want you to know that it's very rare to find true and real friends. Nowadays with increasing use of social media, friendships can be maintained or destroyed with just a click of the mouse or swipe of the screen of your cell phone. Contrary to this, during good old times, friendships used to be everlasting, intimate, sober, committed, and almost stable.

Friendship should be a relationship that needs to be developed on compatibility of several attributes like mannerisms, behaviours, feelings, attitudes, experiences, skills, personalities, cognitive abilities, trustworthiness, mutual respect and regards, humility and selflessness and so on. A true friendship is built on foundations of trust and mutual understanding. It is considered as a sacred bond that transcends time, distance, and adversity, providing a lifelong source of love, care, comfort, strength, and joy.

So it is really essential to cherish and nurture such relationships, for true friends are the rarest gems and treasures you found in life who will never leave your side and will stand through every triumph and tribulation, offering a shoulder to lean on, a listening ear, and most importantly a supportive heart. These true friends will help you navigate life's journey at difficult times, thus providing a sense of comfort, security and belonging with unwavering loyalty and unconditional support.

"True friends stand by your side even in tribulation"

4.3. "BE A GOOD LISTENER"

Through this chapter, we will understand how important it is to be a good listener in every phase of a human life. As a person who wants to improve his chances of success in life, he should possess a good listening skill too. Your job effectiveness and your personal relationships can be adversely impacted if you have poor listening and communication skills.

In the workplace, you might have to listen properly to the tasks set by your superiors, or your team mates for the successful completion of a project. Sometimes you might need to carefully listen to any feedback or remarks by your stakeholders or clients to figure out what they want and ensure that you are providing them with their desired results. But don't hesitate to ask for clarifications if needed, as it will showcase your interest in knowing more and understanding the thought process deeply.

Once you are sure that you understood the whole concept, you'll be ready to work on finding the right solution avoiding any potential errors. People use their listening skills to understand things as it is, to obtain as much information they might need, for learning and for gaining knowledge and insight about certain topics. Sometimes they use this skill to lighten themselves up through entertainment like listening to songs and music of their choice.

Some of you might have heard of General Adolfo Rodriguez. He was a famous commander of the Argentinean army with many victories in the battles to his credit. The people of Argentina considered him as a national hero and highly commended his war techniques and military plans.

Once, a press reporter in an interview asked him about the secret behind his achievements, but he didn't respond immediately. Instead he paused for a while and responded in one word that it was 'silence'. The reporter, perplexed by the response, stared at him for some further clarification.

Then General Rodriguez pointed out several notes that were stuck on his office wall, of which some read as follows:

- Do good deeds silently.
- Love God and humans silently.
- Do your prayers silently.
- Adhere to your duties silently.
- Accept God's will silently.
- Be happy with others silently.
- Conceal other's faults silently.
- Wish and aspire secretly in silence.
- Look towards heaven silently.
- Attain the virtue of effort silently.
- Persevere until death silently.
- Embrace your last breath silently.

He further emphasised on how practicing these qualities of silence helped him tremendously to set appropriate goals and to achieve great victories in his life. It helped him to think and analyse the situations deeply before coming up with useful military plans. Whenever we think about charismatic leaders, we often think about great orators who have mastered the art of speaking. The subtle trait of charismatic speakers is that they are more comfortable with their own silence.

On the stage, a moment of silence allows you to hold your audience's attention onto what you'll be saying next, creating suspense for whatever you are going to say. It gives you enough time to structure your own thoughts into words. The infamous dictator of all time, Adolf Hitler was rather famous for such qualities. He was known to captivate his mass of audience with mystique and suspense whenever he stood in silence before addressing them.

As a famous quote says:

"Be silent in two situations. Firstly, when you feel no one can understand your feelings from your words; secondly, when someone can understand you without any words."

Conclusion

Mostly in any conversation there are chances of not getting through or receiving the information as it intended to. To avoid this, we can practice certain methods and techniques like adapting active listening into our day to day life. You need to first pay attention to what the person is talking about without any interference or interruption from your part. This shows them that you are genuinely interested in whatever they are talking about.

Then after listening, provide them with feedback of what you understood from your perspective, and ask for clarification if you're not sure of what they meant. Avoid any judgement if at all possible and respond with the appropriate emotion that's needed for the situation. Show them validation and sympathy if necessary, which will further enhance their relationship and trust in you.

Sometimes silence is empty but can be full of answers. Give more importance to what you understand, think, and what actions you might take for every situation in your life. From a physiological standpoint, silence is good for overall physical health and mental well-being. It helps lower your blood pressure, boosts your body's immune system, can enhance and uplift your mood, and there are many more benefits added to it. So practice effective listening from now on and know when to keep silent and when to speak up!

"Actions speak louder than words; execute in silence"

4.4. "PRACTICE TOLERANCE"

Intolerance is the absence of love and kindness that mostly result in disasters like family estrangement and war. So you should maintain a different approach like tolerance towards triggering factors so as to avoid any unwanted disasters. For me, tolerance is accepting vivid cultures, religions, opinions and other essential factors to maintain a beautiful life and to spread the fragrance of diversity. In other words, tolerance means treating others the way you would like to be treated.

Various types of tolerance include:
- Spiritual tolerance
- Age tolerance
- Racial tolerance
- Gender tolerance

The creator of this universe has given us a diverse world just like how a garden with a variety of flowers makes it look more beautiful. We can compare our planet to a garden as it has different continents, territories, religions, languages, cultures, costumes, racism, age groups, etc. We should understand that every being in this world is born with the right to exist in this world, treated with love and respect. We should give reverence and respect to all, so diversity should never be considered a curse; but be taken as a blessing to mankind. If every person on this earth understands and practices this basic rule, it will make our earth a much more peaceful and beautiful place to live in. Tolerance is usually invoked as an object to which people should aspire; mainly when diversity is increasingly a feature of our ultra-modern democracy.

Spiritual Tolerance

Spiritual tolerance is something that is related to patience, and to accept, respect and appreciate various spiritual beliefs, practices, and traditions.

It involves recognising and respecting the diversity of spiritual experiences and perspectives, by being open-minded and non-judgemental towards others' spiritual paths. The main characteristics of spiritual tolerance is acceptance, which means to respect, value and welcome the diversity of people's spiritual beliefs, traditions, experiences and practices. People should respect each other's spiritual ideas and perspectives and should be given a freedom of practicing it in their own comfort without being judged.

Spiritual tolerance doesn't mean that you should force your ideas onto someone who doesn't have the same perspective as yours. Everyone should be non-judgmental and empathetic by avoiding criticism of others' spiritual beliefs and also by understanding and relating to others' spiritual experiences and struggles. To construct a modern society, we all need to apply tolerance in this form. Nothing stirs more than a conversation related to one's religion. So avoid religious talks if it's not necessary and is not a threat to humanity. One's religious beliefs and the way he treats others that are different to his own, will speak volumes of his character and upbringing ! The more you know about other religions, the more easily you can shed the myths and misconceptions that you have ingested about other faiths.

Age Tolerance

It refers to the ability to comply, regard and value individuals of different ages with different life experiences. It also includes recognising that people of all ages should be treated with love, respect, importance, and support to help them make progress. Not only teenagers, but adults too have to understand that people of all ages have different choices and may like or enjoy different food types, music, and may even dress differently as they wish . You need to be open to accepting those differences. Unfortunately, not many people are that tolerant and that's when our society comes under unnecessary stress and pressure. Ultimately, cultivating age tolerance requires a multifaceted approach that promotes inter-generational understanding and environments where individuals of all ages can thrive and contribute.

Racial and Political Tolerance:

Being tolerant is mostly a good thing; countries in Asia are accepting a lot of refugees. Refugees are flowing into India on a large scale because they aren't safe in their own country. India is very tolerant in many ways and gives equal rights and liberties to all its citizens. It has been accommodating major refugee populations from Tibet, Sri Lanka, Bangladesh, Pakistan, Afghanistan, Myanmar (Rohingya) etc. Nepal too saw a lot of refugee influx from Bhutan and other places, but recently had to close their borders, due to the policy being misused for being too tolerant. Each country has its own policies as per the 1951 Refugee Convention or its 1967 Protocol for restriction of such population. Some countries like Malaysia and Thailand were not signatories to such a convention but Indonesia has accepted a lot of refugees. But a nation alone can't feed and take care of too many refugees when its own people are facing challenges accessing basic rights and services.

Gender Tolerance:

Promoting gender tolerance is an essential part for creating a strong society where everyone can express themselves freely, without fear of discrimination or judgment. Gender tolerance is not only a fundamental human right, but also a crucial step towards achieving equality and empowerment for all individuals, regardless of their gender, identity or expression. If we discuss gender tolerance, women are seen as more cooperative and social than most of today's men.

Most modern women know family values and respect for others. This doesn't mean that all men and women are respectful and tolerant these days. Aggression in both genders is very common which steals away the joy and peace in most of the modern nuclear families these days. Studies have shown both men and women being mentally and physically abused at all stages of their lives. We can see gender intolerance in big corporations and small companies too. The main intolerance is the difference in pay-scale. Women with her multitasking abilities, still get paid less than their male counterparts.

Conclusion

Practicing tolerance is a journey, not a destination. It requires effort, understanding and an open mind. Tolerance makes you free from sufferings and pains. In other words, we all can lead a harmonious life ahead by practicing a peaceful and tolerant approach. Every parent should try instilling the quality of being tolerant and having a peaceful approach in their children at a very early stage itself if possible.

It can contribute to a brighter, accommodating, empathetic and more compassionate society in future. Remember that a tree is not measured by its branches, but by its roots. Similarly, a person is not measured by their differences, but by their good manners that were instilled in them by their parents and their abilities to tolerate and accept others. A tolerant approach is the best, for it allows us to grow strong, like a tree with strong deep roots, and to nurture a world where everyone gets a chance to bloom.

"Tolerance builds bridges, not walls."

4.5. "COMMUNICATE EFFECTIVELY"

In this chapter, we will look into the benefits of effective communication and how it will aid us in leading a successful life. Investing time daily to improve your communication skills can significantly boost your confidence and productivity in both your professional and personal lives.

What exactly does effective communication mean, and how can we achieve it?

By effective communication we mean one's ability to hold and engage in conversation with another individual in a consistent and focused way without losing the purpose.

It can involve two or more than two people expressing their views, opinions or intentions without losing the purpose and focus of the conversation, while giving chances to each other to express their views or feelings too.

We all as social beings need to communicate and interact with others effectively in various levels including personal and professional. If we look at the professional side of communication, having an ability to hold a conversation effectively with much clarity and conciseness is the most important skill a professional should possess.

For efficient communication, the first and foremost skill one needs to develop is active listening. Let's look into the methods for achieving this and the importance of having effective communication at the workplace first.

Habits to practice for effective communication
- Have good observational skills
- Listen actively and ask for clarifications if needed.
- Have emotional intelligence with understanding, compassion and empathy

- Showing confidence while sharing details and information. At workplaces, this skill is considered very valuable and important as it helps people to express themselves and their needs and to properly understand the responsibilities and tasks assigned to them. This skill is an essential one to have if you are working in sales or customer services.

Benefits of effective communication in the workplace

- Engage your team to work collaboratively on a specific task.
- Avoid and resolve unnecessary conflicts and confusion.
- Build trust among clients and teammates with constant support and empathy.
- Demonstrate your understanding on the matter and help improve your and your team's productivity as you all have a clear vision of what to attain.
- Identify challenges and engage team members in discussing potential solutions.
- Clearly and concisely express opinions and concerns to your teammates and vice-versa.

In today's modern and digital world, there are plenty of platforms available for you to gain the skills of speaking. In order to make friends, or find mentors and employers, you just need effective communication to be made with them. When it comes to building a social circle among your friends or society, conversation plays a vital role.

Many of you may not know how to begin with, where to start from and what exactly to say to get your listeners attentive and interested. Once you get comfortable and attain that momentum, you will feel easy to converse with them.

"One of the greatest pleasures of life is conversation."

Dr. Johnson

There are several speaking skill courses you can find on downloadable apps, which you can carry in your phones and use at your own comfort, pace and free time. You can connect to various people across the globe, which will help you grow confident in holding conversations with people who don't share the same language as yours. During the period of Covid-19 and isolations, I enjoyed and learned a lot speaking with various people through online speaking applications. These tricks and methods can definitely help you improve your conversational skills.

Everyone has their own way of speaking, some with low subtle tone, some very loud and others with different accents depending on the countries and places they belong to. Some people can sound very boring and monotonous while they speak. Some speak as if the whole world revolves around them- too self-centered and egoistic. Some tend to put forward their problems and discuss their worries which leave the other person listening too to feel depressed.

So observing and indulging in conversations with people who have different mindsets, emotions, mood and styles, these emotions and styles can effectively get passed on to the listeners too.

Effective communication requires one to be an active listener too. Then, it's essential to clearly articulate your thoughts using a combination of verbal and non-verbal cues as needed, to effectively communicate. You can practice this by reading informational books on communication, participating in public speaking groups or even simply engaging in more meaningful conversations with your friends and family members daily.

Communication is one of the most inevitable factors for your existence. Some of its key roles in personal development are:

- **Wider influence:** By getting your ideas and thoughts across, you can create better opportunities for yourself.
- **Career Development:** How well are you able to communicate and explain your thought process through? This can help you in an interview thus enhancing your

chances of getting a job and in the development of your career.

- **Strengthening your Relationships:** Understand that communication is to a relationship, what oxygen is to life. Without having transparent, honest and sincere communications, any relationship can die. By working on and practicing effective communication will maintain and keep your relationships healthy.

- **To make wiser decisions:** By communicating effectively with other experienced people, you will be able to make better choices and decisions in your life.

- **Increase in Productivity:** Any sort of miscommunication and misinterpretation of tasks or ideas can potentially hamper your team's efficiency. When you communicate effectively, you eliminate misunderstanding between your teammates, which creates a chance for increased understanding and productivity.

- **Quality of Life**: The way we communicate with others, both personally and professionally will determine the quality of the personal and professional lives we will be living. So communicate efficiently

"Communication doesn't take place,
if it's not carried out effectively and efficiently."

4.6. "RECIPROCATE RESPECT"

Respect is a universal language that's been proven to be effective and transcends words, cultures, and boundaries. It is the way of treating someone that makes him or her being valued and special in any relationship. The willingness to give respect should be genuine and should be received gracefully. It is something to be earned by a person not just for a short while, but over a long period through their constant effort and good deeds.

When you give respect to others unconditionally, your thoughts and emotions will also follow that positive path. Most of the people who are immune to giving respect have difficulty to understand and will only consider giving it, if they receive it. But being respectful and grateful needs maturity in thoughts and a person who is truly capable of that will consider giving respect to even the people who might not be worthy of it. They will be kind and respectful to others even when it's not reciprocated well. Giving respect is something that should be practiced in our day to day lives. It's a quality that should come naturally whenever we have to interact with another human being.

Reciprocating respect and understanding is not something that can be equally gauged, as the understanding and the ability to respect varies from person to person. Some people do well anyway, without longing for respect or being valued, but some give more value and emphasis on how people reciprocate respect and love. Reciprocating respect, love, understanding and cooperation are considered as precious qualities for a good human to possess. It feels good to receive and give respect, as it shows how valued you as a person is and your efforts! So it's really important to recognise people's efforts and to reciprocate respect and understanding where needed in order to have a successful relationship and a career.

Respect reciprocates back is not a casual statement in any way but it plays a significant role in everyone's life. Just like a boomerang that returns to its sender, respect will always come back to us. The greatness of a person depends on how they treat others with respect and kindness, irrespective of one's position and value in a society. It gives a sense to others that they are being treated genuinely and equally, and thus a trust will be formed between the giver and the recipient. Sometimes the ability to give respect is about one's choice or character. It is also human nature to get attracted to that person from whom they receive respect.

Not only does a person older than us deserve respect, but a child also deserves the same. Respect is also a form of keenly listening to someone when they speak. It is seen that most people speak more and listen less. The greatest mistakes we humans make in most of our relationships are that we listen half, understand a quarter, think a little, and just react double. The problem is that when most people start talking, they try to impose their ideas on others and thus forget to pay attention to what others want to express. Our creator has granted us two ears and one tongue with a genuine intention of listening more and speaking less. To listen to others with genuine interest means to understand the inner feelings of a person and to accept him and his opinions with respect.

In most relationships that are unsuccessful these days, are usually due to the lack of respect for each other and their feelings. When in a relationship, if a partner behaves and believes that they or she is superior and should be controlling the relationship, disregarding the other person's opinion or feelings, then it's already a failed relationship. That relationship will be stunted as there won't be any scope for developing and maintaining it, if one constantly decides not to give respect to the significant other and to the relationship itself. There are some people who are highly egoistic and will be highly self-centered that they will not be willing to understand and learn reciprocity in a relationship.

Reciprocating, understanding and giving respect to each other's views and feelings require them to be willing to cooperate with each other, and take individual opinions into consideration before making any major decisions in life. This gives the other person in the relationship a sense of belonging and validation. When this happens, a person will be willing to reciprocate with the respect that he or she received. In any relationship that's too controlling, there's no place for cooperation, respect, mutual understanding and independence. So in order to achieve a committed, lasting and a successful relationship, both parties should respect each other and their respective opinions and differences, respect their efforts and time that they choose to give each other, and reciprocate the love, feelings and support that they have for each other. When the respect is given, the respect is earned too. This is what the reciprocation of respect means in the true sense.

> *"There is one word which may serve as a rule of practice for all one's life-reciprocity."*
>
> - **Confucius**

Conclusion

If you want to show your respect and gratitude to others then you will have to keenly listen to what they want to express! Secondly, you should be very kind and respectful to even the ones that don't reciprocate the same. Suppose the person you are dealing with is evil-minded, then you shall keep yourself away from him or be silent in a respectful way. To respect humanity and brotherhood, we should treat everyone alike. After all, respect is that emotion of humans that comes even from the heart of a stranger when we meet. Also, it's our nature to talk to those people who want to listen to us. Everyone deserves to be treated equally, fairly and with respect! Let it be a hard-working garbage collector, a farmer who works in his field to produce our food, a bus driver who gets us to our destination every day, or even a beggar.

I want to admire the greatest entrepreneurs of all time, Mr. Ratan Tata who dedicated his whole life for the nation, was a soft-spoken person known for his selflessness, professionalism, liberal outlook, and for being an active philanthropist who also contributed the majority of his wealth through their trusts towards charity and upliftment of poor and destitutes till his last breath. He adopted stoic silence in many situations of their life and possessed a humble gentlemanly behaviour with great empathy, respect and humanity for all living beings. By choosing to respect others, we create a world where empathy, understanding, and compassion thrive and where people on the receiving end will understand the value of reciprocating with equal respect and compassion. We build a world where everyone feels valued, understood, heard, and seen. So, let's give and embrace respect without hesitation. Let's send it out into the world with kindness, empathy, generosity, and humility. And let's welcome it back with open hearts and minds, knowing that love, empathy and respect always reciprocate back.

> *"Respect is the most important element needed for any relationship to survive and develop, but sadly it's the most ignored one too"*

4.7. "TAKE ROLES & RESPONSIBILITIES SERIOUSLY"

Through this chapter, let us understand why taking our roles and responsibilities in life seriously and maturely is important for a successful life. Life is a grand play, and we are all actors on its stage. Life is nothing but a walking shadow; this was what the famous William Shakespeare's thought of life was. So, life is like a role play primarily set for us to decide who will play what part in it.

Each participant has to perform well and do justice to the character that they or she is playing, so as to give maximum entertainment to their spectators. Like that each of us in this world has a unique role to play, with our own script, props, and audience, both in society and in relationships. As we navigate the twists and turns of our journey, it's essential to remember that our role is not just about ourselves, but also about how our role will impact others related to us too.

Just like how a play requires rehearsal, dedication, and teamwork, our lives require effort, commitment, and collaboration by each one of us. We must work together to create a harmonious and meaningful story of our lives, where each person's role is appreciated, valued and respected. You don't have to be in the spotlight every time playing a central role in people's lives.

You sometimes just need to support and play your role in a rightful manner and just do the right things that need to be done. Playing your role carefully means being empathetic and mindful of your thoughts, words and actions. It not only means to take roles, but taking responsibility for your mistakes and learning from them too. So what exactly does it mean to 'play a role' in life? As mentioned before, it's not about playing the most important and central part in relationships and in your society.

It means to be honest, authentic, sincere, and true to yourself and others. Practicing these principles in your day to day life and in your interactions with others, will increase your worth, value and influence among the people around you. Similarly if every single person on this planet took practice and implemented this in their lives, this world would be a better place for all of us to live in.

How important is it to set our life goals?

Setting your career goals will help you to stay focused, determined and will act as a driving force generated by the genuine wish to achieve them. It can only be possible when you set your mind to your goals and tasks without getting distracted by any external or internal factors. Mostly, people tend to get easily distracted without putting in much effort or leave midway when things go a bit deeper and difficult.

This is a rather dangerous trait as it shows your 'taking lightly' attitude towards life in general and that you are an inefficient person who is not willing to put in more effort when it's greatly needed. If you are a student then keep in mind that the efforts that you put into your studies everyday will accumulate over the years and will reward you with success and happiness. So never lose focus and just concentrate on whichever career path you have selected for yourself and the desired results will just follow..

There are some expectations that people in your life or family put on you. Firstly, you should recognise and understand those responsibilities, roles and expectations so as to provide them with the value that they anticipate successfully. Having responsibilities and roles increase your efficiency and enhance your focus. These qualities not only add value to you as a person but to your family and the organisation you work for too.

Earning bread and butter and providing the necessities for their family is a responsibility that almost every adult has to take. I'm not implying that money means everything, but almost everything depends on your ability to provide for yourself and the people who matter to you. There will be practical needs in day-to-day life that will require money. A famous quote by George Bernard Shaw says:

"There is no love more sincere than the love of food."

If you are unemployed, it's your responsibility to help yourself find a job. For this you might have to create your profiles on different job portals to attract any potential employer's attention. There might be chances that you haven't updated your resume for quite a long time.

Upgrade yourself with the skills that are desirable in your preferred job market. When you make the necessary changes and do the required additions to your profile, you will be able to bag greater career opportunities.

Setting the right career and up-skilling to the job demands and requirements is very much needed for a professional to be successful in their field. Whatever career path or business ventures you choose to follow, the decisions you choose to make or not make, will impact your life to a greater extent. In addition to your lifestyle, your career or success in business will define your status and value in the society. In other words, your career, your success and your economic status will determine your social circle and relationships. It's very important to choose the correct career path. During childhood and teenage years, mostly getting inspired by public figures or people around us, we dream and aspire to become something or the other when we grow up. Someone wants to become an IAS officer, while someone aims to become a doctor or an engineer. Your career choice depends on your academic abilities, your subject interests, your exposure to that field and your ability and willingness to delve deeper into that particular subject. So you have to consider all the factors including the above mentioned before choosing a career path. Know that your success is your own responsibility.

Conclusion

Success doesn't come overnight. You must take your responsibilities seriously and work willingly along the way to accomplish your set goals. There is always scope for success if you have the willingness to work and feed yourself with positive thoughts. There is always a chance of improvement at any stage of life if you have the right mindset and the attitude of getting things done. Hope that everything will turn out good in the end with constant effort and there will be light at the end of the tunnel. You first need to feel optimistic about any adverse situation. Being optimistic gives you the ability to think and decide efficiently and you work and hope for better results. In these situations a pessimist will lose all hope and panic to the extent that they will become redundant and will believe himself to be a failure. Sometimes being realistic doesn't necessarily allow you to have enough hope and to look at the possibilities. It's the roles and responsibilities of a person which allows him to keep moving forward even in adversity. It influences the decisions you make, and the efforts you take. For a potential win, you have to keep your hopes high and your responsibilities with much sincerity.

"You are not a clairvoyant to predict or see what will happen in the future; play your role carefully."

4.8. "GRASP THE POWER OF LOVE"

As normal humans, somewhere deeper down in our hearts, we all want to feel loved, connected, valued and heard! There will always be a spark of love inside us, waiting to ignite the flame of love and hope. It's that promise of hope in darkness, the gentle touch that heals the soul, and the unwavering acceptance that sets us and our wounded hearts free. As we learn to harness the boundless energy of love, we'll discover that it's not just a sentiment, but a force that can reshape our reality, rewrite our stories, and awaken us to the limitless potential that lies within and around us. We are in constant search of happiness and love from others. Oftentimes we tend to check on other people like our family, friends, colleagues or acquaintances. We rarely ever check on ourselves and our needs. But in this chaotic journey of life, we need to understand the importance of self-love, and embrace it every day.

There is a huge impact self-love can make to transform our life through psychological uplifting, something which we never will experience with constant self-criticism, neglecting our needs and negative perception of ourselves. To make our dreams and goals come true, we need to take some time to care for ourselves and our feelings. We should never neglect and ignore our physical and mental wellbeing. Showing self-care and compassion will help us increase our confidence and our ability to make things work. By self-love, we mean to know the importance of taking care of our needs first, while working towards a goal or better life. It is opposite from the concept of people pleasing and sacrificing our own needs in order to prioritise others happiness, comfort and convenience.

There are times when we need to approach the world with empathy, love and compassion too. Many wars and battles have been fought here on the face of earth, but none of them succeeded in establishing peace. All these wars and its consequences have made life hopeless and terrible for many innocent people across the globe. With technological advancement these days, it will only become worse and harder for every living being to be affected by these. War only snatches away resources, and peace from everyone's life. Contrarily, love has the power to unite human hearts and subsequently establish peace and harmony.

> *"A flower cannot blossom without sunshine and a man cannot live without love"*
>
> **Max Muller**

When your heart is filled with the power of love and when you feel the depth, delight and ecstasy of this extraordinary power, you will find and see the good in every genuine person you come across in life. The only thing that matters will be the genuine and unconditional love towards them. You have to set them free to experience their true love towards you. There is always a saying that- 'If you love somebody, let them go, if they return, they care for you. If not, they never cared to begin with.' You should also have the strength and courage to love your enemies too, as love is one universal language that everyone is capable of understanding. Expressing that language of love is what most of us hesitate to do in our lives? Our personal relationships, our family lives and even the relationships between two rival countries can all be possibly mended if we use this universal language and power of love.

> *"If I had a flower every time, I thought of you... I could walk through my garden forever."*
>
> **Alfred Tennyson**

As I said earlier, war only creates nuisance and with technological advancements, it's the main threat that today's mankind and the world as a whole are facing. Only if the representatives and diplomats of nations sit together and talk through any misunderstandings, with kindness, empathy and love towards each other, will humanity avoid the pitfalls of the war. It will protect the generations to come from many sufferings. It's us humans who have the power to turn this world into a hell or heaven. Love is that magical wand which has the power to turn our life and world into a beautiful paradise.

"When the power of love overcomes the love of power, the world will know peace."

Jimi Hendrix

One should be aware of the pitfalls of blind love too. Not all love can be true love. This world of affection has seen many sacrifices too in the pursuit of true love. Sometimes wicked love can disguise itself as true love too. If someone's love wants you to strip off your individuality, then that love is not worth keeping. If you have to prove someone of your love by sacrificing your needs, wishes, opinions, desires, plans, etc, then know that you are blind in love.

A blind love for someone is like a red signal light. You might mostly be forced to make decisions that might not be in your best interest. It can also make you unable to spot major issues like differences in values and thoughts, manipulations, lack of transparency and trust.

In today's fast-paced hectic life, we often get confused when dealing with our emotions and at times we feel overwhelmed. Mostly this state of confusion and stress occurs due to immense work overload, expectations from family, friends and colleagues at work, family responsibilities, social obligations, sufferings due to illness, daily chores, errands and so on.

This is where the importance of self care and self love comes in. When faced by these difficulties, try to steal some time to find the inner-self. Indulge in activities that help nourish your mind and soul. Read your favourite book, do your favourite hobbies and discover yourself again. Find time out of your busy schedule to enjoy and do the things that you love to do.

Conclusion

Find time to do the things you have always enjoyed doing, it clears up the confusion and helps you keep your mind focused. It helps you connect to your inner self, rediscovering your purpose of life and protects you from overthinking. Self-care, kindness, empathy and passion definitely plays a pivotal part in the journey towards our success! Love doesn't believe in false-self, ego, attitude and power.

The world where love rules there will be an absence of power; and where power exists, love can never coexist! Even in the workplace, where no ego-battles exist, and where each individual has love and respect for each other, the productivity and dedication of each one of them towards their work increases too. So be the authentic you, and gift yourself and the world the unconditional love, acceptance and kindness of your heart.

> *"When we choose the path of self-love,*
> *we become the best selves too in the process."*

4.9. "PRACTICE LOYALTY AND FAITHFULNESS"

Faithfulness means to stay loyal and committed. You should be faithful in every aspect of life, irrespective of how they seem. Without faithfulness in character and actions, it's impossible to gain trust. Being faithful in every relationship means caring and helping each other, easing their burdens, and remaining loyal and supportive even in hardships. This trivial faithfulness will prepare you for greater things in the future. As you use the opportunities and talents that God entrusts to you in a good manner, trust him, he shall give you even more. If you behave dishonestly even in little things, how you can be honest with bigger responsibilities?

Small things can add up to make a big impact in our lives. As Norman Vincent Peale said, "Little incidents form the life of a person." To achieve our goals, we must be faithful to ourselves, prioritize our own growth, and regularly assess our progress.

Here, I suggest everyone be faithful to themselves. Put yourself first and others a close second. You should assess your own progress periodically. Try to memorize or recall any incident that changed your life. Many incidents occurred and changed my life. I want to recall an incident from the past. When we were traveling from my native where my parents live to my present location in central India, my little nephew accompanied us along with his parents who were on vacation from the UK. One gentleman who was pursuing their MBA from Symbiosis was found observing our young lad. My curious nephew who liked reading books, was keenly reading an encyclopedia related to the Milky Way Galaxy.

The gentleman interrogated him about various stars of the Universe, and asked too many questions from that book so as to puzzle him, for which my nephew gave the correct answers instantly. One of the questions was about the number of stars we can see with our naked eyes. The little boy spontaneously replied that there are over 1400 potential visible stars; out of which approximately only 900 are visible and due to temperature and other atmospheric extinction that dims the rest of them to be invisible. I noticed how enthusiastically he explained things further soon after answering those questions. In the mood of teasing, again he asked the little boy to play some games instead of reading that book. Also, the gentleman as a piece of unwarranted advice further went on to say that when he was at this age, he used to play with pebbles and so should my nephew too.

He then asked my nephew to join a game to which my nephew politely replied that he wanted to finish off what he was keenly reading then! This incident opened my eyes to how faithful he was to his passion even from his early days! He has proven himself to be a no-quitter and his self-confidence, pure dedication to his work, and focus on self-development have always inspired us. He always engages himself in acquiring knowledge, and seeking out new skills and learning opportunities. As a good observer, I started preparing myself to quit my depression and hopelessness. I got a lesson from him.

> *"If your self-confidence is high, you can win half the battle."*

Majority of people these days complain about lack of time and give excuses for their incompetencies and dedication. People spend more time talking about their neighbors, binge watching movies and soaps instead. They are least bothered about planning their life, developing a skill or pursuing their passions and often end up living without a motto. If they reflect upon their lives, they can see how wasteful their lives are without proper time-management or dedication to a work that can be quite satisfying later in their lives. Moaning and complaining won't solve your problems, or change your current situations, but evaluating and discussing various solutions can definitely bring positive changes. As John Lennon sang *'Life is what happens to you while you are busy making other plans.'* We must avoid excuses; stay focused on our goals, utilise our time wisely and prioritise on self-development. Remember, faithfulness requires integrity and from time to time, the creator uses little things and challenges to test our integrity and dedication.

Conclusion

In conclusion, being faithful to your work, life goals and self-development can bring positive results in your life. By taking care of even the slightest everyday tasks and pursuing our passions, we grow as individuals that can inspire others. This commitment, faithfulness, dedication and persistence in our work can have a lasting impact on others too around us.

> *"Whoever stays faithful to simpler things, will also be faithful to the complex ones."*

4.10. "JOY VS. PLEASURE: KNOW THE DIFFERENCE"

This chapter illustrates the meaning of joy and pleasure and the differences between the two. One can find peace and joy in acceptance, knowing one's own worth, and standing true to themselves. There will be circumstances where people might not hesitate to judge you, beat you with their experiences, imposing their limitations and biases onto you.

It's human nature to judge people unnecessarily, so try to ignore them and instead try to focus your mind on building yourself up. Joy conceptually can only provide your mind with some positive emotions such as gladness, elation, and to a small extent amusement.

But what is true joy?

True joy can vary depending on person to person and for different situations in life. For some like saints, babies and toddlers it's limitless. But do you know where the purest form of joy can be found? It can be found in ordinary moments, and those moments can happen in any place where gratitude is alive! Joy can truly be called the emotion one experiences during a particular moment. For some getting attached spiritually to God is the purest form of joy and love. Love and joy can be seen as interconnected in most situations.

Love brings one immense joy, fulfillment, and a sense of belonging. It enhances a person's overall well-being and contributes much to that person's happiness. Now let's look at what happiness means. Happiness is something that we choose to feel irrespective of our circumstances. A person can bring happiness into their life by following a balanced mindset, a better understanding, maintaining beautiful relationships and a healthy lifestyle.

A person can choose to be happy in adverse situations too. You can feel happy even in the absence of dopamine. You can only feel happiness or joy when you consider yourself in a safe state. You feel more indulged, connected, contented and satisfied when you are happy. So being happy is a positive mindset to have, and practicing to be happy is the key to a content life.

Normally people get confused between happiness and pleasure as both make them feel good. Our society, the increasing exposure to social media and the culture that we are brought into plays a significant part in instilling this confusion even more.

This wrong belief often makes people look out for one, when in fact it's the other they might need. In this modern world and marketing media, people are groomed into believing that life is all about seeking pleasure so as to be happy.

We must understand that pleasure and happiness cannot be the same as they have different foundations and physiological effects. Pleasure is often stoked up by dopamine and can easily be converted to addiction, whereas happiness often makes us feel connected. When you feel safe, dopamine can increase your overall confidence and connection. But this same dopamine, when in the state of threat, will trigger us to violence, aggression and unnecessary conflicts!

Joy and happiness have a profound impact on one's overall well-being and quality of life. It supports a better immune system and enhances your mood to keep you healthy, energetic and moving. If you choose to keep yourself happy from within, you will be more resistant to diseases and other ailments. There's an incident that I want to share at this point.

While running my contracting business, there came a situation where three of my employees had to be hospitalized after they met with a severe accident due to my supervisor's negligence inside a cement factory. It happened at the fine coal hopper which they were supposed to poke externally through an inspection door.

Soon after poking for a minute or two, fine coal that was burning inside the hopper gushed onto the chest of four employees who were working near the door. One worker sadly succumbed to death as they somewhat gave up their hope of surviving and was feeling less confident of their chances throughout the treatment. Even being devastated myself, I tried my best to motivate these three men back into life, and fortunately for two of them the treatment miraculously worked well! I'm thankful that they chose to trust my words and the doctors who treated them! Their hope for survival and the choice of being positive and happy even when they were going through severe pain is something that still inspires me!

Though they were struggling for their life, their positive mindset and their wishes to survive surprisingly healed them both within one and a half months! Instead of crying and giving up hope, they both chose to be grateful and happy that they were alive, which helped them to heal faster and the medications to work better. So, happiness is the kind of satisfaction one chooses to experience even when one undergoes a phase of difficulty and finally gets through something that wasn't expected.

What exactly does pleasure imply?

Now let's get an insight of what pleasure actually means. Pleasure for most human beings is something that is related to the fleshly desires of their body and mostly has nothing to do with happiness or inner satisfaction. It is a satisfaction one gets for a few moments which later on leads to discomfort and annoyance. It has nothing to do with intellectually satisfying activities in life. Pleasure even leads someone to suffer from pain and poverty.

So it's better not to indulge yourself to a luxurious life so as to attract discomfort due to an unhealthy and financially poor life. When I began my professional career, I was about to buy a sports bike. My friend who accompanied me uttered silently – 'Drive as a means, not for pleasure or as a hobby!' which was thought-provoking for me and eventually I decided to drop the plan.

Conclusion

If you have to spend two hours of your precious time watching movies, what kind of movies do you prefer to watch? An inspirational biopic or movie that will make you feel immoral? If you have to read a book to uplift your mood, what kind would you pick? If you have to spend some time which can give you mental satisfaction, what would you prefer? Spend quality time with your family and parents, or to attend a drinking party?

Your decisions depend on how maturely you can think, and your maturity will lead you to the life you experience. Pleasure is always derived from some external sources, while joy arises from within when you bring your full awareness to the experience. Eventually a person's level of maturity helps them decide to prefer joy over momentary pleasures. Now knowing the difference between joy and pleasure, you as an individual and as a part of your society, can try applying these tips to attain a healthy and happy life.

"Pleasure Is Naive, Whereas Joy Comes With Maturity."

PART 5:

Positive Mindset and Habits

5.1. "THINK AND ACT WISELY"

If you are hurt by someone's comment for what you are not, it's the turning point of your life to think about your hidden powers and take necessary action. Try not to take others' views and comments too personally, as they have not walked your path and they will never understand your perceptions. To get out of this negative mindset and never ending loop of hatred, you need to practice self-love at first, and see yourself through your own eyes and experiences.

Watch motivational documentaries, read reassuring stories and self-help books which might help you become less attuned to others' opinions about your life and what others might think of you. In practical terms, it might look a bit difficult, but properly training your mind on how to keep your thoughts and emotions in check and validating those with your actions can help you in the long run.

By boosting your confidence too, you can stop yourself from taking things too far and avoid getting hurt personally. When you start seeing yourself as a competent and worthy person, all the negative perceptions of you that others have created to diminish your worth will fade away from your mind. It will help you recover from the trauma and the outlook you have about yourself because of others' negative opinions, will eventually change too. Try to credit yourself for the amazing strength and qualities you possess. Practice positive habits daily that will help you to increase your knowledge, and eventually you'll see that those negative opinions of others don't even matter to you anymore! This will help you to self-validate and understand yourself better, rather than constantly looking for other people's validation, or getting affected by other people's ruthless judgements.

Set a goal in your life and have a visionary outlook. Your power of thinking and enacting accordingly will turn you into a man of sense. This action will stand beside you in good stead in your struggle for a win. In critical situations, this will give you the confidence and willpower to take risks and you won't hesitate to give it a hundred percent effort for overcoming it. But while leading a normal life, if there comes a situation with any risk involved later for which you were unprepared, there will be people around you to discourage you and beware of various risks involved and hidden in the course of action. If you are brave enough to continue and take up the challenges life throws at you, which will make you a true winner!

I want to highlight a beautiful poem written by one of the great poets of America, Robert Lee Frost which is titled "The Road Not Taken." When they went walking together with their friend and a poet Edward Thomas who was chronically indecisive about which road they ought to take- but was often confused. As both the roads looked similar, yet one was appearing to be the most used one. First one was covered with grass and the second one was clean, which the poet thought was because it might have been used mostly by the people. They somehow thought of trying their luck and took the path that appeared to be full of grass! Robert Frost chose the first path that was least used by many which led him to write the famous poem.

Conclusion

The power of thinking calculatedly involves being able to plot actions that lead to getting the best results. The only thing you have to do is to ensure that your actions are executed in a certain way apt for the situation and at the right time. You must enhance your power of thinking and take necessary measures in order to achieve your objectives much efficiently. You should have a clear vision of the possible risks that come in the way of your course of action.

You should try to analyse the risks and find possible ways out early on if possible. It's not always the final result that matters but the willingness of one to take risks, the journey that they took, the adversities that they faced and the decisions they made that led him to success that matters the most. When you think and act wisely, no matter what life throws at you, that's when you can truly be called successful.

> *"Nurturing and developing wisdom itself can be daunting at times, but acquiring it to a great extent
> can help you elevate your life"*

5.2. "MINDSET MATTERS"

In this chapter we will look into the ways to develop the right mindset, as it's one of the crucial steps to success. It's the way you think and view your habits and traits that forms your personality. It gives life an entire direction that leads to your dream goals and destination.

How can the right mindset be achieved?

Mindsets can be of two types: The fixed mindset and a growth mindset! Let's look at the fixed mindset. This refers to your belief that the inner qualities like your personality, character, charisma, intelligence and abilities are fixed qualities from the time you were born. Whereas, the growth mindset is your belief that the above inner qualities can be further enhanced and improved by constant efforts and practice. With the fixed mindset you feel less motivated, unwilling to change yourself and trapped in your beliefs that you have limited abilities.

Doing multiple things at a time might lead you to fail in all the tasks due to the lack of concentration and the inability to dedicate and focus on even a single task. With passionate conscious goal statements, you can convert an accidental pattern of thinking into a structured pattern of thinking. Always remember, your mind stores all information that helps you to achieve your goal. With much determination you can set your distant goals and reach your destination within a short timeframe. You have to cultivate a growth mindset.

Don't try forcing determination as it's a natural instinct, but setting small goals and consistently achieving it will bring unbelievable results. If you have a goal, smash the hell out of it and do whatever is needed to chase it. Only dreaming doesn't work, you have to desperately work on your abilities to achieve those. If it was that much easier to achieve something in someone's life, you could have found everyone successful. Keeping in mind, your uniqueness and making persistence your forte you can mould your life in a better way. Here you have to sweat a lot, putting aside all your negative emotions and unfruitful habits which can create obstacles to your path to success.

A sailor, when he sails through the sea, has to face rough waters, but never loses sight of his destination and adjusts his course to navigate through those rough tides and challenges. Remember the quote by Franklin D. Roosevelt, "A calm sea never made a skilled sailor." This is a great analogy for life's journey!

Some long term agents like passion and hunger for success plays an important role too when you possess a fixed mindset. When you really love your work, you will be keenly working on it, setting your soul ablaze.

Other elements that cater your determinations are:

- **Create your definition of success:** You have to create your success story. For each person the definition of success is different, so you are here to find yours!
- **Set short term goals:** This one is definitely going to help you a lot by making a "to do list" to achieve smaller goals in a short-term period.
- **Day dream about what you want to be:** Where are you now? What do you want to become after 3 years? Where do you want to find yourself by then?
- **Build self- confidence:** 'Self confidence is a must. Try to acknowledge your personal strengths and talents and remind them often'.

- **Untag yourself from your past failures:** Don't at least tag yourself as an unwanted, loser, coward, cheater or anything that makes you low. Forget about your past and learn from your past mistakes.
- **Challenge yourself for a better you:** You have to challenge yourself regularly or on a daily basis so as to see some spontaneous changes in a dynamic process.
- **Set some realistic goals:** Stay focused on your goals. You don't try to follow anyone but with at least having some dream to see yourself in a position in your field, you have set it. Be like Swami Vivekananda as he wasn't a blind follower.
- **Adapt to changing circumstances:** It is a vital skill for success and resilience. Adaptability is a key to turning obstacles into opportunities!
- **Chart a new course when needed:** Be willing to pivot and adjust plans. You have to explore new options and opportunities. Sometimes, the best way to move forward is to change direction. Don't be afraid to chart a new course and explore new horizons!
- **Reach your destination, stronger and wiser:** The journey is just as important as the destination. Enjoy the process, learn from it, and keep moving forward. You got this!

Conclusion

The willingness to achieve something and not stopping even if the odds look like they are not in your favour is what determination is!!! The higher the determination, the higher will be the chances of your success. Trying to find what your determination is? You need to follow your dreams relentlessly with passion and with single focus, without giving in to temptations and distractions.

Functioning at your most optimum level needs a turbo power of good health. Having a growth mindset means to believe and enhance a person's inner abilities to achieve what he wants from his life. Remember, a determined and growth mindset is like a muscle that can be developed and strengthened with practice and dedication. Now it's time to transform your dreams into reality!

"If you have a purpose in life, you will be determined too"

5.3. "NURTURE A POSITIVE ATTITUDE"

This chapter explains the importance of nurturing a positive approach towards life in general, to attract better opportunities and possibilities . A person with a positive attitude has an ability to gravitate others onto them. He'll be uplifting others, being very optimistic about situations, and will never feel hopeless in adversities.

Practicing this positive attitude is highly desirable in any part of this world. Positivity is highly infectious and contagious too. So if it is that desirable, how can we cultivate it in ourselves? Or is it an inborn skill that we all are naturally gifted with?

With mostly negative news coming from around the world nowadays, it can be difficult for us humans to keep a positive mindset. Overcoming negative thoughts and trying to stay consistent in the way we feel and act can be much harder. If you can learn to keep a positive mental attitude through all the hardships that come with life, you are setting yourself up for a peaceful and a successful future. 'Failure is the stepping stone to success'- a common motivational quote of all time.

Most of us consider failure as something that stops us from achieving something great. But a person who shows much courage and strength to accept and reflect on it will try even harder with each failure that comes along. You might have to face a lot of hurdles on your journey to success, but feeling exhausted and giving up is the actual failure. Most people find it easy to give up at the last moment when all they need is to be consistent in their efforts. As famous Paulo Coelho once said:

"Don't give up. Normally it's the last key on the ring that opens the door."

The great scientist of all time, Mr. Albert Einstein failed the entrance admission to college. The great poet Rabindra Nath Tagore never took an examination in their life. The great entrepreneur Bill Gates dropped out in their first year of college. There is one thing that's common in these above-mentioned personalities. They became great because they trusted their capabilities and put effort and passion in their work. So there's no need for you to feel unworthy or envious of others' success.

Remember that every single person's life is filled with possibilities and opportunities. You just need to point or focus in the direction of your goals and dreams. No matter what others think or say, or what your situation in life might be at present, whether it is related to personal, family, social or financial- you can always turn your life in a positive direction, only if you try harder.

So always try to develop and practice a never-give-up approach and simultaneously nurture a positive mindset. So whenever negativity comes to your mind, remind yourself that you are much smarter, stronger and knowledgeable than you believe. These daily positive self affirmations can help you to push yourself forward with greater confidence and focus.

Humans have incredibly powerful minds and thinking capabilities unlike any other living beings. Our minds can influence the emotions we feel, our thoughts, perceptions and opinions, and thereby our behaviours. Practicing meditation too can help you feel positive and better about the situations that you are facing. It will help you to be in the right mindset, where you can find reliable solutions for your problems. When you keep a positive outlook for everything in life, you will experience a much more profound change in your life.

Do not focus on just being better than your predecessors or contemporaries, but try to be a better version of yourself. Once you know your current self, you need to push those limits further consistently. With those consistent efforts, you will be surprised at how far and beyond you have come. You can do miracles; no matter your current circumstances, what you are, or what you were in the past. Always try to develop yourself by bringing that positive change in your attitude and setting an example to others on how to improve themselves even in adverse situations. With the right attitude you can make a positive impact, whereas with a wrong and negative mindset, nothing fruitful can ever be achieved. Try to bring that positive change in yourself, that you want others to follow. As once Thomas Jefferson said:

"Nothing can stop the man with the right mental attitude from achieving their goal; nothing on earth can help the man with the wrong mental attitude."

Conclusion

With a right mindset and a positive outlook, you can transform a negative situation to a favourable one. This can be done only if you interact and surround yourself with like-minded and positive people. With this you create a positive environment where your thoughts will be heard and you get others' perspectives and ideas to overcome those negative situations. It would be wise to understand the fact that no fingers in our hand are the same, and so are others ' opinions and thoughts. A true friend can't be found if you try to find a person with a replica of your character and thinking. A wise man will always find people who have better ideas and opinions than himself.

You should be able to interact with different people with a positive attitude and paying attention to what they have to say, while respecting their opinions. Paying attention when others speak is also a way of paying respect to them. Also, it shows the positive side of you and how you treat people with kindness, humility and politeness. Giving kindness and respect is a rare quality that one can possess, and believe me, no matter what, it will always be reciprocated and appreciated.

If you want to get respect from people, you should have those qualities within you too. If you are receptive and respectful to individuals' opinions, they in return will be more open to what you have to say. It is important to take control and responsibility for your own feelings, thoughts and actions. Nobody can make you feel in a different way that you don't want to experience. So stop making excuses that people influenced you into the actions that you decided to take.

In conclusion, cultivating a positive mindset and having control on your thoughts is crucial for achieving happiness and success in your life. Positive thinking can develop both mental and physical wellbeing thus increasing your self-esteem and confidence level, improving personal relationships, and helping enhance your problem-solving skills.

> *"Cultivating a strong positive mental attitude will create miracles in your future."*

5.4. "KEEP POWERFUL, POSITIVE THOUGHTS"

As we navigate the tapestry of life, our thoughts weave an intricate pattern of possibilities, like a master artist, our minds brushstroke and portray a reality. In this majestic art of living, positive thoughts are the vibrant hues that illuminate our journey, infusing every moment with meaning, purpose, and unbridled potential. By accepting the kaleidoscope of positivity, we spark a symphony of hope and triumph.

Positive approach can be helpful and can resonate to all aspects of our lives, whether it is personal relationships, professional lives, your health, your career and dreams, you name it. To overcome the fears, challenges and shortcomings that we face in life, we should adapt to a change in our thoughts and beliefs.

Have you ever observed the fact, when your life is without any troubles and is running smoothly? During this phase, mostly everyone around you will be gravitated towards you and will even give you high hopes of achieving more accomplishments in your life. But, in reality, the depth of your confidence will mostly be tested with sufferings and setbacks in your life.

At this point in life, these same people will get an opportunity to judge whether you can withstand this situation and overcome your pains and sufferings. Have you ever thought how you should withstand these adversities or hardships in life? Here is when the magic of powerful positive thoughts work!

Keeping your spirits high by positive thoughts can help you face even the worst circumstances. It's true that you might have the least control over your destiny, but you can definitely turn the bad situations in your favour by being powerful in your thoughts and actions. If you carry positive thoughts; you shall not lose your heart and confidence for every little problem that comes your way.

As a community or society too, if we implement the same sort of solutions to our problems every time, with no positive outcomes, it's high time that we start to change our approach to the problem. Next in your personal relationships, if the weakness was the lack of communication, you shouldn't expect a positive change if you are not willing to put any effort in improving your weaknesses.

If you don't communicate in an effective way, it will further damage your relationship, making you and your partner feel more drifted and disconnected from each other.

Nurturing the same old habits and approaches won't help anymore rather than damaging it further beyond repair. By incorporating powerful positive methods- such as understanding, mutual respect, friendship, unconditional love, patience, and empathy- you can drastically change your relationship with your partner.

Next, let's focus on your health. Consider this scenario: you're striving to break a harmful habit that's damaging your well-being! Maybe you are addicted to an unhealthy lifestyle like alcohol or cigarettes which are damaging your internal organs. If you really want things to improve, you will try to get rid of the habits that brought you down to this condition.

You will need to look at different ways to stay fit and bring changes into your harmful habits. Next let's look into your dissatisfaction in your professional life or in your career. If you think that nothing is changing for you, and no career progression is happening in your life for quite a long time, then it's time to consider changing your perspective and look for advancing your skills.

You better know what life is, and cultivate the skill of turning critical problems into noncritical ones. Try hard enough not to lose, but if you do, remind yourself that if one door closes, many doors with numerous opportunities will open for you along the way. Never confuse self-confidence with overconfidence. How can we differentiate them? When a person has self-confidence, he'll be aware of their powers as well as weaknesses. They will be very sure of their capabilities and will have the power to make the right decisions in their life.

On the contrary, an overconfident person has a wrong perception of himself. They will only concentrate and focus on their abilities that will boost their ego, completely ignoring the fact that they need to work on their weaknesses too. As they don't care to rectify their mistakes or hesitate to work on their weaknesses, everything goes further down the drain and they fail miserably in life.

But even with this wrong decision, if they keep up their hopes and practice a powerful positive attitude, they can save himself from further loss and a potential depression. While facing these defeats, if they can find a purpose and a dream to focus on, their life can drastically improve. Many people do their best in the beginning but they lose consistency, patience, control and persistence, which lead them to become unsuccessful. They lose their self-confidence and will appear like empty sacks that cannot stand on their own!

Conclusion

Positive thoughts are very powerful as you can concentrate much on finding opportunities with an optimistic outlook even in the toughest times. The power of positive thinking lies in its potential to reformulate circumstances and impact your sensations. The power of positive thoughts has great benefits on your health too. It can lessen the risk of cardiac arrests by practicing positive thoughts in a very calm and peaceful way.

Think of setting an uncommon success by having an uncommon dream of achieving something different. You should set an uncommon dream to achieve uncommon success because the day you stop dreaming you start dying. Here the uncommon dream can be met with proper planning and action along with a little sacrifice. You will fulfill your dreams when you follow this rule.

"A well-planned action is always a great action towards great success!"

5.5. "BE OPEN TO NEW IDEAS & PRINCIPLES"

This chapter reinforces the need to stay updated and to be open to new ideas and principles to succeed in this advanced and ever-changing world. If you want to see progress in your life, you should always be open to criticisms, take guidance and listen to people who have walked the same path as yours. Listening to others' perspectives and taking their advice doesn't necessarily mean being open and accepting it blindly. Take your time to process the idea, think and reflect on it before making your mind to accept it.

They could be of some value; of course, as that might be the first time you discovered a reliable solution to that particular problem. Remember that success and defeat depend on how you think or modify your thoughts and approaches. Acceptance is defeat whereas determination is victory. You can either succumb to your troubles or decide to fight them with all means. Imagine you are having a tough time at work, or you're looking for some new ideas, or simply want to take a second opinion on a colour you chose to paint your office.

As a human, it's our tendency to give advice to others out of our own experiences or accepting others' ideas at the time of indecisiveness at a crucial time. Developing your interests and researching something new can be an exceptional and excellent way to expand your horizons or skills, and make your life much more amusing.

How can we stay updated with new skills and adapt new ideas into our lives?

Let's look at some recommendations for flourishing your skills:

- **Think about your interests:** Getting to know your true self will help you understand your interests, set a clear goal based on your potential and help you work towards achieving those values and interests.

- **Explore various possibilities:** There is infinite hope to discover new passions and learn new things in your life. Reading knowledgeable books or watching documentaries related to new topics will give you better ideas. You can even try attending various workshops and get valuable ideas from experts and mentors to improve your knowledge in that particular field.

- **Be up-front to new experiences:** First of all, you have to leave your comfort zone and give it a try. Unless you do so, you can't experience progress in your life. Procrastination and self-doubt will only help to drag you down. So give it your all to experience success in life.

- **Set some realistic goals:** Start achieving short-term goals and gradually put in extra effort to gain something big. Set time-frames to set those small goals and you'll see a drastic change in no time. If you are interested in bodybuilding, you can either join a gym, or follow progressive overload training, or you can set small workouts and can gradually increase the intensity of the workouts and its timings.

- **Make genuine friends:** Surround yourself with genuine people who share similar interests and who will keep you motivated, engaged and determined to achieve your dreams. Surrounding yourself with unmotivated and negative individuals will only help you to drag yourself down to their levels. So select your friends wisely, avoid the ones who drain out your energy and won't contribute to your happiness.

- **Do good deeds**: To flourish your fortune; you have to water it with noble deeds. Grass will only remain green till you water it regularly. For us humans and any living being on the face of this planet, death is inevitable. But just like some incredible beings that we still remember; only our noble deeds can keep us alive in people's hearts.

- **Check your abilities**: Never depend only on luck but achieve abilities in life which can contribute to your success in life. As you know a paper can be flown by luck; but to fly a kite, creativity, ability and experience are required. So keep a check on your knowledge, update it in a timely manner, and enhance your skills or abilities to succeed in life. Your skills and knowledge can never be stolen and will always stay with you.

- **Make time for holidays**: Apart from your hectic life and vast schedule, you have to sometimes take a break and spend some quality time on yourself and your family. Plan for a holiday or visit an amusement park. It will enhance your life and is proven to be good for people with a stagnant mindset or depression to overcome it. At times you have to be alone too to reset your mind, reflect on self and to just focus on your ambitions in life. It's observed that new ideas come to mind when you are calm and alone!

- **Make it fun**: Find ways to create a fun atmosphere to learn something new from engaging in enjoyable activities. You engage in creative activities that will help you to train your brain and to put your mind at ease. A creative mind is always a progressive mind.

- **Take risks in your life:** Sitting idle and moaning in situations will gain you nothing other than despair and pain. By constantly trying and working your way out through hard work will make your dice of fortune roll towards success. So, don't give up hope, and just keep trying!

- **Get a reward for every progress:** Celebrate your accomplishments, however small it seems along the way. Every attempt matters and every progress should be celebrated. By doing so, you will motivate yourself to achieve greater results. A self-reward habit will boost your confidence and productivity.

- **Be a powerful visionary:** You should have a vision on how you can mould things for a better tomorrow. Know your inner strength and believe that you are capable enough to build your future in a better and meaningful way. When your vision for your life is clear, you will sense an inner strength to attain it and will use your fullest potential.

- **Avoid selfish behaviour:** The most cheap and inexpensive thing is 'advice'. Ask from one and there will be thousands that'll be offered. Coolest thing in life-cooperation; ask from thousands and only few will be ready to offer. People often find it easy and better to give advice than to help. Don't think of your gain only, but also think of helping others in life too. Their success will be the greatest profit you will make. But make sure whom you help too, as a person who is not willing to put effort or to help themselves will certainly not value your efforts or time.

- **Always stay positive:** Never feel bad if someone hurts you with their actions or words. Always remember that people will only throw stones on a fruit bearing tree with sweetest fruits. However, it's equally important to acknowledge constructive criticism and work with integrity to eliminate harmful habits that may be holding you back. So, know your well-wishers and stay positive to any negative criticism by your opponents who will only criticise you to make them look better.
- **Be patient:** No results come sooner as you have to give time to acquire knowledge and develop a skill. With much patience, constant effort and persistence you can enhance, grow and develop yourself as a knowledgeable person. Always practice a never-give-up policy. No matter whatever hurdles and obstacles come your way, never give up hope and just keep working towards your dreams. Remember, working slow and steadily will definitely help you win the race.

> *"The person with the new idea is a crank until the idea succeeds"*

5.6. "SELF-EFFICACIES ARE IMPORTANT"

In this chapter we will see why self-reflection and continuously reassuring ourselves of our abilities and potential is a crucial part for our success. You can be your own best cheerleader or your worst critic. The difference between two options matters a lot. Believing in your own abilities is very crucial for a successful completion of any task. For this firstly, you have to look into yourself and understand the techniques of self-discovery. Knowing yourself reflects that you are more mindful in setting the goals that are just right for you and your abilities. You won't have to rely on extrinsic motivation to move towards your goals.

Self-efficacy in a deeper context:

Ever wondered why some people hesitate to take a relatively hard task, while some others are willing to take up difficult challenges? There's something called 'self-efficacy theory of motivation', which was developed by a Canadian Psychologist Albert Bandura. In his book, 'Self-efficacy, the exercise of control', he explains this theory of motivation. This theory of motivation through self-efficacy, explains how it can be a strong predictor of an individual's high performance in a task.

You might be comfortable doing a certain task as you feel confident finishing it, but you might hesitate if someone asks you to do a task which is relatively difficult and new to you. Always remember that self-efficacy is not general, it is specific to tasks. According to this theory of motivation in his book, he explains about the four factors that are determinants of self-efficacy and in turn affects the performance of a person in that particular task. The first and the most important factor is your 'experience' or your past experience of completing a somewhat similar task.

You are likely to be more confident to finish a particular task to its highest standard in future, if you've had experience of finishing a similar task in the past. The next factor that he mentions is the 'vicarious experience'. He says that you can develop and increase self-efficacy vicariously through observing other people similar to the inexperienced you, performing a task and then succeeding in it. Contrarily, your self-efficacy can be negatively impacted if you see someone similar to you taking up a particular task and failing in it.

The third factor that he mentions is the 'social persuasion'. These are the encouraging or discouraging words that the influential people around you can give.

Depending on the encouraging or disparaging remarks that you receive from certain people, your self-efficacy to do a particular task can boost up or decline respectively. The last but not the least factor that influences or impacts your self-efficacy is the 'physiological feedback' that you sense and experience from your body when confronted by a particular task.

Depending on how you interpret these signals that your body sends will impact your self-efficacy of doing that task. These signals can be excitement and feeling thrilled that can increase your self-efficacy, or else it can be anxiety or fright which can negatively impact your self-efficacy. Let's say for example, you have been asked to sing in front of a large audience at a big cultural event in just two months! When you were asked to do this task, you felt butterflies in your stomach.

If you interpret this signal of your body as excitement, then your self-efficacy will increase and you will confidently look forward to the day of your performance. On the contrary, if you interpret your body's signal as anxiety or stage-fear, then possibly your self-efficacy to do the task will decrease. So we can say that the more ease you feel with a particular task, the greater your self-efficacy for that task will be.

Based on the above mentioned factors in this model, you can take four approaches to increase your or your team's self-efficacy. The first approach you can take is to master the particular task that you are assigned to. Based on your current knowledge, set a realistic yet challenging goal to begin with. Once you achieve that short term goal, set yourself a bit more challenging goal and build on it overtime. These short term achievements will eventually grow and help build your self-efficacy for that particular kind of task.

As mentioned in our previous example, if you are not a confident singer and you have been told to perform in two months before a large audience, you might feel anxious at first. To build your self-efficacy, you might start with watching other's performances and then over the period you might like to perform in a small but safe environment, surrounded by your family and friends.

Once your self-efficacy grows and is high enough, you can feel more confident in performing in a much more pressurised environment with a large group of audience. The second approach that can be practised is to 'model behaviour'.

It's where you find a role-model whose self-efficacy is high in that particular skill or task you are looking to excel in. These role-models can be really motivating if they have started off building their self-efficacy from the same position where you are standing now. Now let's look at the third approach, which is 'social persuasion'. Social persuasion is to find mentors or coaches who themselves have been mentored by other skilled people in the past, and who can understand your journey of learning a new skill.

These mentors or coaches will guide and help you build your self-efficacy rapidly than you can achieve with your own initiative, by working directly with you in every step you take. The last and final approach is to work on improving your emotional state. We all interpret the signals that we sense from our body based on our past experiences. We can sometimes misinterpret these signals. Let's take our previous example of singing on stage in front of a large audience. Imagine that you get too nervous and anxious before singing on stage, which is a completely natural feeling. You strongly believe that you are terrible at singing to the extent that sadly it actually affects your singing.

Now because of this poor performance in the past event, your mind further believes that you are not a good singer at all, and makes you more nervous for the next performance too. This wrong belief is so harmful that it can bring down your confidence and self-efficacy. It might not be that you are bad at singing, but you might have misinterpreted the signals so wrong and negatively that it diminished your confidence and willingness to try to sing on stage. Only when you learn and practice to interpret these signals positively over time, can you improve your self-efficacy and win your confidence back.

Every person has the ability to execute specific plans to produce specific performance attainments. For this, you have to discover yourself and have to bring the possible changes to transform yourself from the old to a new you. Through many hurdles of daily life, you'll always have your own back and only you know what it's like walking in your own shoes. Whenever things get tough, you are the first responder. No one else knows what's going wrong with you or your life. Learn to forgive yourself first and move forward for a better life. Our education system never teaches us on how to tackle the day-to-day hurdles that we face.

In the books, you weren't taught how to face those real-life problems, what necessary steps you have to take to rectify the errors you made knowingly or unknowingly, and how to get rid of the consequences it might have brought.

Remember that no one is perfect and you can't claim to be one too! You can't satisfy everyone or change each and every person's perspective in this world. There may be many critics around you, so why blame, curse and beat yourself up? Who are others to judge you when they haven't walked the same path that you were on? Even when facing those life challenges alone, believe that you can do much more for yourself than what others will. What you need is to have confidence and willingness to work on yourself so as to bring some drastic changes within you.

Many of us don't have this mindset of changing 'self' and expect the world to change for us instead. As mentioned in one of my other chapters, be the change that you wish to see in others. This change in you will eventually bring lots of positive vibe and goodness in others too. This attitude of changing and evolving to be a better self will help you to distinguish yourself from others.

Conclusion

'Self-efficacy' or your willingness to believe in yourself is a stepping stone to any successful life. It's a belief that you have to put in yourself and your capabilities to perform a particular task or to achieve a specific goal. The strongest factor for success is self-esteem: to believe that you deserve it, to believe that you can do it and to believe that you can get it. Irrespective of people's unfair criticisms and negative attitude, you will have to stand up for yourself and build up your confidence level slowly and steadily, and one day people will accept you just the way you are.

Never lose your uniqueness for the sake and comfort of others and put yourself in a back-bench leaving your dreams unfulfilled. Give yourself time, energy and resources that you have needed to find yourself, nurture your talents and dreams. Keep in mind that nobody can understand and play your role better than yourself, so believe in your abilities to achieve those dreams. You have to show faith in your potential to deliver the best and you can see the wonders as days pass. You can create history: no matter how big and tough the task seems to be!

Self-efficacy and self-esteem both play a vital role in your life as both are related to each other in several domains. Self-esteem is a matter of fact to achieve something in your life whereas self-efficacy is how you feel your potential to perform in various situations of life. As most people can achieve and benefit greatly by increasing their self-efficacy for the tasks that are necessary for the successful completion of their job, sometimes having a high self-efficacy can be disadvantageous too.

You need to be very cautious not to have an overly sense of self-efficacy, as that might result in over-confidence and poor performance. As a result of high self-efficacy, you might believe in your capabilities to an extent that you abstain from putting in the necessary effort that's needed for the successful completion of the task. To summarise, self-efficacy is proved to be a strong predictor of a person's or a team's performance. By improving on self-efficacy, you can help raise yours or your team member's confidence to finish a task effectively.

"Believe, act, achieve, and repeat"

5.7. "GROW YOUR EAGERNESS AND ENTHUSIASM"

A normal person may do what they want in their life, yet lack drive and purpose. In contrast, successful individuals or entrepreneurs are often extremely passionate and enthusiastic about their work, driven to excel in their pursuits. They will do things with absolute delight, without losing confidence, energy, patience, hope and excitement throughout the journey, equally inspiring others around him. It is applicable to each and every area in our society, whether it be for students, employees or an institution.

Being enthusiastic means possessing no ego or attitude while seeing someone succeed. They possess a child-like heart where they get inspired by other's success stories and learn from it. Being enthusiastic makes you more creative, active and helps to take up challenges in a more positive approach. An enthusiastic person will be more concerned about the progress, the quality and truth of ideas and knowledge.

A person gets frustrated and tired in their life when they face lots of failures one after another, hesitating to analyse their own bad decisions or judgements, wrong attitudes and lack of motivation after each failure. They become blind to their own mistakes, unable to take any criticism or judgment on themselves. Instead of learning from their past mistakes and knowing where their true passion lies, they doubt their calibre, their abilities and their willpower to make a change.

Gradually they start hating themselves and slide into the stage of depression leaving all hopes of recovering from the loss. They further spoil their life with a lack of motivation and do not consider giving them a chance to cultivate their passion instead. There are effective methods to overcome this weary situation. Every successful person has tasted failure at some point in their life. But it's the willpower and the determination to keep up the enthusiasm and passion alive that keeps him moving forward.

As the great English-born American political activist and philosopher Thomas Paine once said:

> *"You can buy a man's time; you cannot buy a man's physical presence at a given place. You cannot buy enthusiasm, you cannot buy loyalty, you cannot buy the devotion of heart, mind and soul; you have to earn these things."*

What do the above words indicate? The attributes mentioned above are not something you earn from outside, but contrarily; these are the qualities you have to develop within you. You might have read William Shakespeare's famous quote, "Our bodies are gardens to which our wills are gardeners". By this they meant that we have to overpower our emotions and not to become slaves of our emotions. Deep inside you have to cultivate the way of generating and maintaining enthusiasm to become a man of victory.

When you think you are more powerful you can generate more power to do different things in a very different manner. Try to have a solution-oriented approach and focus on the possibilities and advantages. Be optimistic in any situation and associate yourself with positive, likeminded, uplifting people with the same interests and passions as you do. The positive circle will help you move forward, keeping you motivated and inspired to accomplish your dreams. In order to maintain your enthusiasm, you have to consistently be motivated, active and inspired.

Enthusiasm makes your confidence grow and helps you overcome challenges that you might face. Enthusiasm is highly contagious too! A person who is enthusiastic and excited about his goals radiates positivity, drawing people in and inspiring attraction. As he shares his passion, others will be inspired to contribute to his journey towards success. People around him will view him as an optimistic person which will keep him motivated, boosting their confidence to continue.

Conclusion

Awaken your inner spark, be positive and passionate about the things you do, and your enthusiasm will start to flourish. Give yourself a greater opportunity to grow your passion and make a positive difference. But how will you increase the power of enthusiasm to attain greater results? The most vital and enduring form of inspiration is the existence of the goal itself.

The goal should be something that interests you. If it's not something that interests you and still you want to hold on, then take some time to research about that new subject and acquire knowledge and resources related to it. There are always ways to make things more humane. Always remember that enthusiasm and guidance can contribute to the creation and progression of a keen person.

When your passion and desire for work is non-existent, the urge to improve yourself gradually fades away.

But as you reignite your inner flame, you'll begin to approach life with a renewed sense of purpose, motivation and energy, tackling challenges with much confidence and resilience.

Your warmth and eagerness to achieve something becomes contagious, inspiring others to follow your footsteps, thus creating a ripple effect of positive energy that spreads far and wide. By arousing your eagerness and warmth, you'll unlock a transformative power that will revolutionise your life, uplift and make you much more productive.

You'll discover a sense of fulfillment and joy that comes from living authentically and your presence will become a signal of hope and inspiration to those around you. Welcome this journey with open arms, with a child's enthusiastic curiosity and let your inner optimism shine bright for the world to see!

"There is only one success mantra to be successful, and that is: to love the thing you do or to do the thing you love without losing motivation!"

5.8. "CHOOSE A HEALTHY LIFESTYLE"

In this modern world when most of us give too much importance to luxury, convenience, comfort and improving our living standards, we give less importance to the benefits of some healthy practices that our past generations were forced to adopt. We all are aware of the importance of eating healthy, and exercising, but still will prefer comfort over healthy practices. With the growing culture of fast food and dependency on processed foods, people are increasingly becoming more prone to obesity, diabetes and other diseases. Most of us in-spite of having good transport systems in place and most workplaces favouring 'cycling to work', would rather prefer to drive to work.

We prefer taking lifts, when there's still an option of climbing stairs. As our desire for comfort and luxury grows, we become unaware of the consequences that it can bring to us and our families. Today in most workplaces, they provide healthy breakfast and gyms for their employees to stay fit and healthy.

Practicing regular exercise or indulging in any kind of physical activity like running, walking, swimming or sports exerts a strong influence on the quality of an individual's physical as well as mental health. These physical activities, reducing stress-anxiety levels and good eating habits will help us prevent chronic diseases such as diabetes, heart diseases, autoimmune disorders etc. It also helps improve our physical endurance and learning capabilities. It further helps reduce depression, anxiety and a lot of other health benefits. Physical exercise such as walking, cycling, or swimming for more than 4 hours per week is highly recommended. It can significantly decrease the risk of developing artery diseases, cholesterol and prevent cardiovascular diseases. Also, regular exercise (mostly cardiac and some free-hand) induces a drop in systolic and diastolic blood pressure.

Most of the diseases today are associated with obesity and unhealthy diet. Keep your body-mass index and weight on check. To achieve a certain weight goal, you might have to undertake strenuous exercises for considerably long duration at a time or as suggested by your gym trainer or physician. Practising yoga can help you calm down your body and mind. It will help you relax, focus and reduce your stress levels and anxiety. Yoga is well mentioned in ancient sacred texts known as Rig Veda. Performing yoga also contributes to increasing patience, flexibility and a peaceful life.

There are several asanas in yogas (refer to any book of any yogas) and several breathing techniques (long inhale and exhale) that can cater to your needs. You can find remedial meditation techniques that can keep you disease-free. Yoga is thus considered a reliable tool for better living.

Arthritis is one of the leading causes of physical disabilities in older individuals. The most common form of arthritis in the elderly group is osteoarthritis. In today's fast paced life, most of us have to depend greatly on unhealthy processed foods and have rarely got any time for physical activities, which altogether makes us more prone to destructive health issues. We get so addicted to junk foods or street foods and other highly processed carbs which can make us feel sick and tired.

Obesity brings us laziness, brain fog, depression and other ailments. Obesity generally is calculated based on our body mass index (BMI). BMI gives us information about our exact body fat. By knowing the BMI, we can further assess the risk involved with the increased fat and can work towards reducing it through exercise and other medications. Most people experience muscle weaknesses, imbalances and mobility issues that can develop to major physical disabilities during their fifties.

Exercise improves learning ability and thus improves the mental performance among the children. The one who does exercises regularly has a good intelligence quotient (IQ) level along with logical and perceptual skills, verbal and mathematical skills and other abilities. Depression and anxiety can also be reduced by practicing regular exercise. The benefits are low for those who perform low-intensity physical exercise.

Researchers have suggested that there is a positive relationship between exercise and decreased anxiety. One can achieve their goal of physical transformation through exercise by either selecting a short-term or a long-term exercise plan depending on their goals. Thus a combined version of moderate and vigorously intense activities can be performed to meet the desired goal of weight loss. This change in weight will make the person feel good about himself and their confidence grows.

Encouraging healthy habits in the younger generation like toddlers, students, teenagers and young adults are important too. It's better to implant the good habits at a younger age so that they get used to it and will continue practicing it throughout their life. Make them practice meditation at school and home; teach them the importance of keeping good postures and the strategies to follow healthy attitudes and positivity.

For adults who are healthy, they perform well at workplaces. Their ability to learn, adapt, develop and implement skills will be higher, and so their productivity will be higher too. Healthy individuals will be highly motivated, enthusiastic and optimistic in their approach to challenges. Being healthy will bring job security, good career prospects and will help enhance employability.

Conclusion

When we embrace a lifestyle of wellness, our bodies become temples of high vitality, reflecting the beauty and wisdom of our souls. The person who is physically fit with increased confident levels will be less likely to suffer depression or other health ailments. A gain in confidence, strength and overall wellbeing will always make him stay more enthusiastic and motivated.

By nurturing our physical health, we honor the sacred gift of life that was given to us, realizing our inner strength, and delivering each day with purpose, immense energy, and joy.

Let's celebrate the incredible journey of our physical transformation, where every step towards our fitness goals, every choice towards attaining wholeness, and every moment of self-care is a testament to our unwavering commitment to radiant living.

> *"Having a sound mind in a sound body will bring real wealth in your life!"*

5.9. "YOUR TIME IS PRECIOUS - VALUE IT"

This chapter explains the importance of valuing and utilising your time as a precious asset. Nothing is more precious than time! Time is the most valuable resource you possess. It's a limited and expensive resource that once lost, can never be regained. Every moment counts and how you spend your time determines the quality of your life. Time is finite as we all have a limited amount of time on this earth. There's so much uncertainty revolving around our time on this planet. As the famous quote says - "Time and tide waits for none", it fits into the narrative of everyone's life. Time once gone is gone forever, so the value of time in everyone's life is of immense significance. It's more precious than health, wealth, and almost everything. You can regain your lost health with proper medication and you can recover your lost wealth, but time once lost can never be recovered. So value your time and treat it carefully.

Why do we need to value time and how does it influence our productivity?

Every successful person in history has made the best use of time and energy. The prosperous people of the world are very conscious about their time and how to spend it. Most of us common people have been seen killing their time and not utilising it wisely.

Whereas, some people on the other hand, cry about their lack of time, without knowing how to work efficiently by properly planning their time. Mostly they don't have time for their loved ones because of their tight schedules. Indeed, sometimes it seems like there aren't enough hours in a day. Especially in the new norm, people feel the strain on time as they are pulled into more directions than ever before.

But this problem can still be sorted out by having a systematic and arranged time management. Planning your day's work ahead and having a proper work schedule can save you much time for your loved ones and for extracurricular activities. But for most of you, time management is an aspiration and it's something you're all working on to improve.

To achieve this you have to increase your productivity within a stipulated period. For this, you will have to have a greater vision for life and value your precious time. So make the most of every moment, cherish every second, and live every day with a purpose and intention, because time once lost is forever lost, and only memories are left with us.

There is a short story from my life that I want to share with you all. During my childhood, my maternal uncle used to be very ill and mostly bedridden. I remember him saying,

> *"I can buy you any toy you may want to play with, but unfortunately, I can't buy time to play with you."*

While being away from him in Bhilai, there wasn't a single day I wouldn't have thought of him.

His unexpected demise shocked me, I wept and missed him a lot, remembering what he suggestively told me in the past. He was implying that his time was very limited and he was helpless about it. He was also highlighting the value of time and how it is a limited resource, unlike material goods that can be easily purchased. In the same way, one day you will realise how limited and precious your time really is and just because someone is here today doesn't mean that he will be here forever.

You should realize the fact that arguments are merely a waste of time and that each moment spent with loved ones should be cherished forever in your heart. In the end, it's not the wins or losses in our arguments that we'll remember, but the love, laughter, and moments we share with our loved ones that will last forever.

Conclusion

Never spend time on unnecessary things and put aside your work for tomorrow, else you may never find time to finish it. You will get into a habit of procrastination and will find yourself helpless with your accumulated and unfinished tasks. By ignoring your daily tasks, roles, and responsibilities, you will only overburden yourselves later. But if you can delicately do your work on time, you will feel more accomplished and satisfied at the end.

Remember, success is not just about achieving your goals, but also about living a life that is fulfilling, contended, happy, and impactful. Let us choose to invest our time in nurturing our relationships, creating memories, and cherishing every moment with those who bring joy into our lives. For in the grand tapestry of life, it's the love we share, not the arguments we win, that will be our lasting legacy!

"Time, once lost, will be lost forever"

5.10. "CULTIVATE UNIQUENESS IN YOUR THOUGHTS"

In this chapter we will learn how to create uniqueness in your character and actions through unique ideas and thoughts. Every person on this planet has their own unique experiences that make him believe and act the way they do. But to know what to cultivate and what not to, is what makes him unique and desirable. There are some skill-sets and approaches you need to learn to create uniqueness in your life. Let's look at some of them:

- Always be cheerful and practice positivity irrespective of your situation and circumstances. Your magnificent aura will help you and the people related to you to keep calm in adverse situations. Remember, a calm mind can help you find solutions to your problems much more efficiently.

- Whatever you set your eye on, try working on it with great passion, and enjoy the journey through the process. By stop being a perfectionist, you will rather be focusing on the baby steps that you put forward towards achieving your goals. When you make the process enjoyable, you won't feel exhausted or bored through the journey.

- Whenever you feel awkward and anxious around people or situations, try engaging in interesting and important discussions on topics that attract them. By doing so, you show your inclusiveness and willingness to know people and their opinions. You give the impression of valuing people and their experiences.

- Not all think and act the same. Each of us are unique on our own and different from each other in our behaviours and beliefs. When you understand that people have different perspectives and opinions based on their experiences or situations, you willingly accept them as they are. So try forgiving your enemies and set yourself free from all the grudges that you hold against them.

- Never go astray when it comes to your mission in life. Stay focused, and remind yourself that you have to keep going forward no matter what. Take timely breaks, but when you sit to do your work, just keep on pushing yourself to finish your tasks for the day. When you finish the set tasks, reward yourself. When you haven't, punish yourself by not getting involved in routine activities that you enjoy doing at the end of the day. Cut away your entertainment, and finish off the pending work for the day before going to bed. Keep notes on your progress each day, and it will help you stay on track.
- Always be ready to fight away your fears and set your focus on your mission. By overcoming fears, you become more courageous and confident in yourself and your ability to achieve your goals. So be courageous and confident when you set your challengingly high goals and expectations.
- Try not to be too serious all the time. Find ways to lessen your stress levels and anxieties. Get fresh air by stepping out and doing your favourite activities. Mingle with friends and family whom you enjoy spending time with. Be childlike and playful sometimes and revive your innocent self. Let your inner child be free sometimes.
- Always try to resolve issues and conflicts in your life and relationships. Leaving it as it is will only help worsen it! Avoiding talking about it will help the resentment grow stronger and unresolvable later on. So improve your conflict resolution skills, so that you can help yourself and the people around you to better understand and compromise, whenever difficult situations arise.
- Always act confident. Haven't you heard people say to fake it until you make it, when it comes to confidence?

Reflect on the way you carry yourself and your body language in general. Once you know how to carry yourself confidently, practice it every day until you are truly confident!

- Acquire knowledge on basic human psychology through reading or watching videos related to it, so that you can understand better on how people think. This will help you to understand the people and their feelings better. It will make you more empathetic and understanding of their needs or perceptions.

- Always acquire new transferable knowledge and skills. Take up online or in-person lessons or courses to increase your skill-sets and improve your chances in life. Know that learning has no age limit. The more you learn about things, the more wise and knowledgeable you become. It will influence the way you think and improve your personality in a unique way. So always be willing to learn something new.

- Be ready and prepared to accept whatever life throws at you. Life is full of challenges and surprises, so be ready to face them with strength and determination. Never get discouraged and depressed by the challenges. Remember that with persistence and dedication you can overcome this. Not every challenge will be the same, so you have to prepare yourself to overcome it with different approaches. There comes sunshine after rain too!

- There's no harm in being a little skeptical about everything. Precaution is always better than cure. Having intuitions and being skeptical will help you judge the situations and their outcomes better. It will help you play safe and protect you from unfortunate consequences. By being skeptical, you will gauge all the pros and cons of a certain situation or object, and take your decisions accordingly.

- You need to be fully aware of what is right and wrong in a social setting. You need to be aware of your own right as a human and the ways it needs to be protected. There are sets of basic rules and regulations that a human must follow, which makes them different from the other species. To cultivate uniqueness in your personality, you need to practice and protect these set rules and boundaries.

- Give importance to your spiritual development. You can spiritually prosper by engaging into certain positive habits every day. The positive habits that you can cultivate are meditating, reading knowledgeable and informative books, taking time to pray or practicing gratitude in day to day life.

"Be bold, be different, be you"

PART 6:

Overcoming Obstacles

6.1. "PREVENT HAZARDS AND OBSTACLES"

In the pursuit and search for success, obstacles and uncertainties are inevitable. We all know that success always comes with various challenges too. There's no one who has never experienced hurdles and challenges on their way to success. It's not the presence of challenges that defines us, but our resilience and ability to navigate through effectively, that matter.

By adopting a proactive approach to risk management and developing the resilience to overcome adversity, we can transform potential threats into opportunities for growth and innovation.

In this journey, we'll explore proven strategies to anticipate and mitigate risks, and how to cultivate a mindset of resilience and to develop the skills needed to turn challenges into catalysts for success.

Let's look at some common challenges that people often face in the path to achieving their dreams. It's really important to recognise, understand and find ways to avoid and overcome these challenges, to help reach our fullest potential and goals. One of the common hurdles is the 'self-doubt' or fear one has before taking initiative or setting their mind on a particular path. There can be fear of judgment by others, fear of facing consequences or failures and other factors that hinders them to move forward. This self-doubt holds people back from trying something new and thereby reaching their fullest potential.

At this stage, it's important to understand that failure is just a stepping stone to success. Having this positive attitude and moving forward no matter what will help you overcome these obstacles. It's a great trait that experts call 'resilience' and something that a progressive human should always possess. The person who has the quality of being optimistic leads a hopeful life.

In every walk of our life, you can notice that it is filled with hidden and potential dangers. Just observe your surroundings and imagine what worries you most when you walk on your streets. While walking through your streets you might be worried about protecting yourself from stray dogs that are not vaccinated and might harm you, if it chooses to bite you. Only 20% of the whole population of dogs can be termed as 'domesticated pets'.

You might have noticed the owners mentioning "Beware of Dogs" on their gates to protect their families from predators and to protect their genuine guests from unnecessary damage as a precautionary measure. Preventing an obstacle or problem by foreseeing it and making plans to mitigate it by taking necessary steps is something that should always be considered. Planning a remedial approach beforehand will help you overcome the stress and any adverse consequences that a problem might bring along.

So, how to overcome these obstacles that come in our way to a successful life? How can we prevent these and how to overcome them? We rarely see anyone who is born with a magical power and ability to overcome setbacks with much ease and comfort. It's a skill that comes with observing and understanding how things work in this world. A little fire if ignored or not handled with proper care can cause mishap that can cause risk of human loss and financial damage.

You might have noticed how the high raised buildings, apartments and institutions have security measures like surveillance systems and fire safety measures put in place! They add security features, fire fighting systems and teams to prevent and protect the inhabitants and public, in case a fire outbreak occurs. This is a very intelligent and positive approach of taking precautionary and preventive measures before something actually happens. So taking effective precautionary steps will always protect you from unnecessary worries, thus saving your energy and time.

'Negative self-talk' is another major reason that hinders our progress and success! The way we motivate or demotivate ourselves by self-talk can really affect our ability to succeed in life. Talking to ourselves negatively will damage our confidence and our ability to take appropriate actions and risks.

Whereas, when we constantly feed our mind with positive thoughts and approach tasks with a 'I can-do' attitude and self-affirmations, it will magically improve our ability to focus and complete our tasks in the best possible manner.

We should also surround ourselves with people who can believe in us and our abilities, rather than people who will drain our energy by constant criticism and unnecessary judgments. So practice 'positive self-talk' and mingle with supportive and progressive people.

Another common hindrance to success is to give too much importance to perfection. When we look at things with that perfectionist perspective, we can slowly slip into inaction and procrastination without even noticing it. Sometimes to get things done effectively and on time, we need to give much importance to progress rather than shifting our focus on perfection. Procrastination hinders progress. So identifying the main reason for it and eliminating it will help your process to improve things faster. There are some great methods and effective strategies to overcome procrastination and inaction.

Try breaking down your tasks into smaller, manageable and attainable ones, be realistic of your approach, set yourself realistic deadlines to finish each stage, and once those small tasks are accomplished, reward yourself by doing your favourite hobby or spending quality time with your friends, or a movie night. Embrace a growth mindset, acquire knowledge, seek feedback from knowledgeable people and try learning from your past mistakes. Develop your skills that can help you solve your problems. Pat your back at times, try celebrating your small wins and learn from the setbacks. You don't need to experience failure to learn from it, you can learn from others' mistakes too and avoid it at any cost.

People try numerous methods and techniques to improve their habits so as to experience success in their life. In order to get successful one should always cultivate habits that will differentiate him from others. Not being consistent with your approach and not having discipline in life is a perfect way to failure. Setting a proper schedule for your goals, working towards attaining them each and every day, holding yourself accountable for your actions or inactions, and reflecting upon them will help you to achieve your objectives in the set timeframe. There's no doubt that the foundation of success is built on these good habits of being focused and staying disciplined.

You can even see cases where people find it hard to achieve success even after several attempts to resolve their problem. Most people like these will be hesitant to set healthy boundaries and suffer from long term relationship problems or traumas which often leaves them depressed, helpless and frustrated. This mental state of being depressed affects their social and professional lives too. Success in business studies and career can only be possible when you slowly begin to unstuck yourself from being gloomy or depressed. But at the end of the day, you should not forget that the most successful people have experienced the worst in their lives.

Surprisingly, most people handle failure much better than they handle success in life. This is because success is indigestive for many, as it starts giving them a sense of superiority and strength. They suddenly feel so accomplished and put no effort to maintain their success, which makes them unable to handle complex challenges thereafter.

With success, there comes an ego and negative attitude that makes some successful people arrogant and self-centric. You might have seen many athletes ruining their career once they acquire fame and popularity through success. It can happen to anyone who is immature in their thoughts, completely forgetting their roots and has never learnt the art of foreseeing and preventing the difficulties and challenges that may arise in future.

Conclusion

You should try to recognise the purpose of your life in order to set your path right. Once you are successful in determining the objectives of life, you will have to consistently work hard towards achieving it. You will also need to be aware of the potential risks and challenges that are associated with it. Recognising these problems, and finding precautionary measures to avoid the situations that create those hurdles and difficulties are the first step towards success.

On the contrary, those who aren't able to determine their purpose will always face a state of ups and downs in their life. If you choose yourself to be stuck in your ineffective wrong habits and stay addicted to bad behaviours, then there is no escape. You will either stay redundant or fall even deeper to your lowest, making it even harder to overcome your struggles.

Always remember every step in the journey of your life is uncertain; so don't forget to carry your sensory precautionary tool of observation, to encounter the hidden dangers and potential challenges.

"Proactivity turns obstacles into endless possibilities of success"

6.2. "AVOID TEMPTATIONS"

This chapter will help you understand why staying focused, holding on to your morals and not getting distracted by temptations is the ideal way to lead your life. Temptations are all day, all around and you will encounter it in many instances of your life! It comes in all forms - big and small, many and little. It has the power to make you work against your own goals, morals, and even your health. It can make you do things that can mess up your routines that you have set for yourself. It can even mess up your ideal life that you imagined with someone special. It can make you sacrifice your long-term goals for short-term pleasure.

Just imagine a teenager glued to his mobile screen to feel happy and gratified when he has an important exam to attend the next day! Imagine a businessman trying to dodge paying taxes to maximize his profits. These are examples of short-term temptations that can result in long-term pain and trouble later on. So how can we stay away from getting distracted and falling into temptations? What are the ideal principles one must follow to control and save oneself from these tempting situations? Let's look at some methods that might help us achieve this!

Most human beings experience unhealthy and worldly desires that try to detract and shift their focus from something great to something that will further add up to their stress later on. It could be a love of unhealthy food, or more harmful things like an addiction to toxic substances like alcohol, cigarettes, drugs, etc. If you love a particular kind of food that is not deemed beneficial for you, try keeping it out of your sight. Remove the temptation from your mind by focusing and engaging yourself in good habits like planning a schedule, getting involved in your favorite activities like gardening or singing, sharing your feelings with your true friends, and discussing various options to handle it, etc.

Believe that you are more disciplined than you think and that you have the ability to overcome any temptation. Avoid negative self-talk and silly excuses that you're not capable of controlling yourself. Focus on your good qualities and abilities. Think about what makes you proud of yourself. You might be surprised to find too many positive habits in yourself that you never thought were good enough to be proud of. Your punctuality, personality, character, importance of hygiene, respect for others, protection of vulnerable people, great dressing sense, your empathy for others all are good qualities that you would never want to compromise.

Always think about what you want from your life. Having a clear purpose and knowing what you are as a person and what you want to achieve from this life will keep you away from unnecessary distractions and unhealthy thoughts. At this point, when you are faced by any tempting situation, you will ask yourself if risking your goals, your future and your goodwill is worth the momentary temptation or not. Will falling for this temptation ever let you live a peaceful and fulfilling life? If it's not worth it, then it's simply not!

Plan your daily activities wisely. Choose a good habit like reading books or doing hobbies that will make you feel better about yourself. Don't over-exert yourself, and take one step at a time. Slowly increase your time limit day by day. This will help you concentrate on that task and spend more time getting that right rather than feeling the urge to check your mobile or getting tempted by any damaging habits like smoking or drinking. This will increase your ability to control your negative urges and develop self-control over the period.

You should also be aware of the fact that indulging in too many things that you consider good can also bring in adverse effects. Getting too busy socialising with friends and people, spending too much time on hobbies, sports, and exercising can also turn to temptations which can steal the joy and happiness from any meaningful relationship that you might want to keep. It has the power to destroy the feelings and intimacy needed for any strong relationship.

Try finding the root cause that makes you feel tempted and get that issue sorted by every means. What makes you feel stressed out? Do you consider yourself to lose self-control and get into temptations when you are stressed? Work on methods that can relieve your anxiety and stress. Do you sleep well and on time? Are you able to find time to exercise regularly to avoid depression and to stay fit? Do you eat healthy and properly at the set time intervals?

Have you got the habit of skipping breakfast or meals which results in low levels of blood sugar? How much time do you spend on your phone and social media? Excessive usage of phones and social media will lift your mood and give you instant gratification, but can also be easily turned into temptation that can damage your health, career prospects, and relationships in the long run.

Conclusion

Surround yourself with people who have similar goals, and who possess great values and morals in life. Find honest friends who won't hesitate to criticize your negative actions or thoughts, just like how they appreciate you for your good deeds. In this way, you'll constantly feel motivated and be willing to work towards a quality life and career.

Don't fall for other people's wrong ideas, however convincing it may sound! If it's wrong and immoral, it shouldn't be followed! Temptations are natural, but falling for it is your choice and only you are responsible for that decision! Remember that your decisions and your life choices will decide your future and the future of the people belonging to you.

If you can't find ways to overcome the temptations or to come out of the destructive habits that you fall into, get help! Asking for help from a friend or a family member who has been through a similar situation will give you the courage and confidence needed to get out of any addiction on time. Practice meditation and get involved in spiritual activities, if you consider yourself a spiritual person.

Practicing spirituality or indulging in your favourite hobby is a great tool to overcome such unwanted thoughts and confusion. It provides you with inner consciousness and mental strength to remind you that no trial, tribulation, or any form of temptation can be greater than the goodness that resides within you. Do some charity work and help people in need, if that helps you stay empathetic and improve your morale.

"When it comes to temptations and addictions, it's much easier to abstain and stay out of it than to get out of it."

6.3. "DISTRACTIONS ARE DESTRUCTIVE"

Distraction is undoubtedly a major roadblock to achieving success. Have you ever wondered why 'distractions' happen? Before diving in further, let's look at what 'distraction' actually means. There are mainly two types of distractions: the internal ones and the other external ones. Internal distractions are often related to your thoughts or emotions. It can also be related to your physical state like hunger, anxiety or tiredness.

Whereas, external distractions are often related to anything you are overly interacting with, like technology, social media, romantic relationships, friends or family. Though these Internal and external distractions are good to have a balanced life and will give you immense momentary gratification, sometimes when overly indulged, it can turn to be immensely distracting and annoying too.

For any person with a set goal, uncontrolled distractions can be destructive! Distractions not only provide temporary escapes from uncomfortable feelings or situations, but can also prevent you from confronting and resolving them in a healthy and constructive way.

Distractions become addictive when you consider it to be more enjoyable than being focused on your goals that demand strict schedules. So now when you know why distraction happens, let's look at the ways to get rid of the thoughts that lead you to these distractions.

The first and foremost is to stay disciplined and have a fixed routine. Eat healthy at the right time and get enough sleep to avoid feeling tired the next day. Start your morning with scheduling the tasks for the day, and set the most challenging and critical one for the most convenient and productive time of the day. This includes creating a conducive work environment. Stay motivated and try breaking down your tasks into manageable and realistic small chunks.

Do those small tasks one at a time, and take breaks after finishing each task. Set a time to finish the task and use a timer to achieve this. Have a clear idea of the things you want to accomplish and why you want to achieve it. Knowing what you want in your life, setting those goals right, and assuring yourself of the benefits that you'll accomplish in the future, will motivate you and make you committed to the tasks.

Know your limits and capabilities, and set tasks accordingly. You might sometimes want to do it all, but it will make you less focused on one particular task, thus resulting in a lesser quality of work and a more negative and stressful experience. So avoid multitasking, which can altogether be tiring and can lead you to finding destructive ways.

Here it leads you to reduce your focus, lower productivity, increased stress, decreased quality, burnout, etc. Try focusing on a single task at a time. Group similar tasks together and complete them in one session. Practice mindfulness approach to set tasks.

There is no harm in taking small breaks, but try to stay away from devices and social media during those breaks. If possible, try connecting with real people, children, nature or animals around you during your break. Or just go for a short walk or for an exercise routine in a gym.

Turn off the phone notifications and tools like website blockers to avoid getting tempted looking for messages and posts until you have done with your tasks for the day. Let your friends and family know the best time to reach you.

Reflecting on the power of focus, reminds me of the incredible story of Stephen Hawking. Despite being diagnosed with a deliberating motor neuron disease at the age of 21, Hawking refused to let distractions derail his dreams.

Confined to a wheelchair and communicating through a speech-generating device, he wrote bestselling books, delivered legendary lectures, and pioneered groundbreaking research in cosmology.

Hawking's wholehearted devotion and focus serve as a testament to the human spirit's capacity to overcome even the most frightening difficulties and challenges. His achievements are an inspiration to all of us who want to minimize distractions, maximize our potential, and achieve greatness, no matter what challenges we face!

May Hawkins's remarkable journey motivates you to stay focused, persistent and committed to your goals. So, silence away your distractions, and let your inner brilliance shine through!

Conclusion

Keep personal goals outside your relationship goals and set healthy and clear boundaries between the two. This will help you to maintain your individuality and sense of purpose. You can bring back new experiences and excitement back to the relationship. At the end of the day after accomplishing your daily goals, don't forget to reward yourself with an activity of your choice.

This will motivate you to stay focused and productive. It's a way to celebrate your accomplishments and provide a sense of closure, helping you feel more fulfilled and satisfied with your day. Feed your soul with positive thoughts and do activities that will make you happy and alive.

Indulging in creative activities like cooking, sewing, gardening, or reading books and spending time with friends and families are all good to keep your spirits high. Staying focused and avoiding distractions is a skill that takes practice but trust me, it is worth the effort!

"Your life goals are worth avoiding distractions for"

6.4. "RECOVER FROM PAST TRAUMAS"

Have you ever thought of what a human life encompasses in general? It is the combination of happiness and despair. Pain and suffering is a judgement that you have placed upon the conditions of your life. A mother takes unbearable pain to bring a child into this world, yet most women want to experience the state of motherhood!

Every mother takes unendurable pain to deliver a child, only to experience the joy of seeing her child. If we consider every pain and suffering in our life as a lesson or hardship before experiencing the joy of success, it will make the painful journey more bearable. There is a stark difference between such sufferings and unnecessary sufferings. Believing human life is a bed of roses that has no thorns is neither enlightenment nor possible. In other words, it's a combination of a bed of roses and a bed of thorns. It's simply what we call life!

The one who wants to cherish the sweetness of roses will have to tolerate the presence of thorns in their life. The happiness of human life is so entangled with the sorrows that nobody can imagine one without the other. It's just as impossible as separating light from the flame or stealing fragrance from a flower!!!

Furthermore, one cannot imagine a life separated either from pain or happiness. In the beginning, the hurdles in the way of life might appear exasperating. The change happens only when we start to feel the pleasure in finding ways to conquer them.

Physical sufferings such as illness, pain and other forms of ailments can be treated by proper medications and precautions. Disabilities or physical weakness can also be treated to some extent. There are other forms of suffering like hunger and poverty, that can be seen in our society. There are mental sufferings that are caused by prolonged frustration, grief of loss, anxiety; loneliness, heartbreak, and hatred that can hardly be cured by medicines.

These people and their loved ones should possess immense patience and should have an empathetic approach to help them overcome these sufferings of guilt and self-pity. Moral sufferings are caused due to human errors and evil actions that include taking someone's life, war, and violence. Natural sufferings have nothing to do with any human actions and it normally includes natural disasters like floods, tsunamis, earthquakes, etc.

See the significant damage and loss caused by the ongoing Russo-Ukrainian war between since February 2014. Such geographical and non-ethical damage result in massive loss of human lives that includes innocent women and children, loss of infrastructure, destruction of agricultural land, loss of electricity or other natural resources, and a reduction in private consumption of more than a third relative to pre-wars. These destructive wars not only impacted the lives of those living in these countries, but also adversely affected the global markets. The impact of the armed conflict on food exports including grain has worsened a global hunger crisis with catastrophic impact on poor nations throughout the world.

Conclusion

When faced with a challenge, look for a way to go ahead and not a quick escape. Keep on going, as miracles will never happen spontaneously as results will come to you at the right time. In the beginning the hurdles on the way of your life will appear to be very troublesome. Those who fear will suffer, and will keep on suffering as a result of their constant fears. Never forget that the pain you feel today will be the strength of your bright future.

At this moment I remember, what George Bernard Shaw once said:

"A life spent making mistakes is not only more honorable, but more useful than a life spent doing nothing."

6.5. "ELIMINATE YOUR TIREDNESS"

Tiredness can be a heavy burden, weighing us down and sapping our strength, both mentally and physically. But what if we could shed the exhaustion and unlock a newfound sense of energy and purpose? Imagine waking up each day feeling revitalized, refreshed, and ready to tackle the day with enthusiasm and passion. It's time to break free from the circle of fatigue and adopt a more vibrant, dynamic life. In this tour, we'll explore the secrets to transforming tiredness into vitality, empowering you to reclaim your zest for life and discover your full potential.

One of the best methods to get rid of tiredness is to maintain a healthy lifestyle. Tiredness can be because of two reasons. First one is that you are not having a fitness level equivalent to the intensity of work you are doing. And the second one is that you have some malfunction going on in your body. Exercise can bring back efficiencies by double. It is true that the fittest body yields the fittest brain. It has an immediate impact on the productivity and interpersonal performance at your work.

Your mind also plays an important role in stress relief as your mindset brings complex problems in the brain functioning. Stress is the mother of exhaustion, it doubles your mental load and you easily feel tired. Live free, free from the burdens of this world, you can't control them, all you can do is to act with an open mind. Focus solely on that only. Keep taking tiny breaks in between, leave your body free during those moments with no stress and emotions.

Meditation can get rid of fatigue as it seriously affects people's moods and behavior. Shut your eyes, relax and take deep breaths. Feeling incapable, useless, low self-confidence also makes you tired. Respect yourself, your work, livelihood, existence, responsibilities and achievements doesn't matter how small or big they are.

Always appreciate your efforts irrespective of results- 'I am trying hard, I respect myself.' Repeat it daily for better results. Learn to handle moments that create pressure and don't let them exhaust you. See life above them, realize the entire story of your life and that there's a life beyond this situation and then feel light and start acting. Don't force concentration, don't act in rage, relax and do your work, don't attack but calmly finish off things one after the other. Tiredness depends on psychological affect and results in the lack of action.

Such conditions require immediate attention which stops one from performing effectively. Here is a famous quote by Swami Vivekananda:

"Tell your body that it is strong, tell your mind that it is strong, and have unbounded faith and hope in yourself."

Conclusion

Boost your energy level and make your goals manageable. Lack of goal can also make a man tired which incur suffering a lot. Burnout is a result of setting unrealistic goals and taking too much stress. Self-talk is a good habit which I suggest to all, especially positive self-talk. You shall create an action plan and recognize your accomplishments along the way. As we embark on this journey of transformation, let us remember that our ancient Indian wisdom has always emphasised the importance of balancing body, mind, and spirit. By adopting simple yet powerful habits, we can eliminate tiredness and discover our full vitality. So let us take the first step today, and discover a more energetic, vibrant, and joyful version of ourselves.

"Cast away all your tiredness, for that will bring you a fortune."

6.6. "AVOID SHORTCUTS LIKE THE PLAGUE"

In this fast-paced world, most of us constantly look for ways that can save us our time and efforts. People nowadays find it harder to be patient, and mostly hesitate to follow the right path and process that's needed for a successful life. They always look out for shortcuts to achieve success, power, money and fame. So what allures us to take shortcuts? It's the greed of achieving goals quickly, without putting in the hard work that's needed to attain it.

This need for achievement without the long and stressful process is what tempts us to take shortcuts. It comes with the promise of easy success and instant gratification. Although it makes us feel better, relying on shortcuts brings severe consequences too. It stunts our growth and hinders our ability to learn and progress in the long run. A shortcut often involves taking the easy way out, bypassing the learning process and the hard work required to achieve the true mastery of a work or subject.

When we take shortcuts, we miss out on a valuable experience that comes with making small mistakes, learning new skills, and knowledge that are essential for success. Shortcuts might help us achieve our goals much faster, but we won't possess the foundation that's needed to sustain the success in the long run. We often don't realise that the success that we achieved easily today will not withstand the challenges that we might face later in life. By taking shortcuts, we are rather shortening our beautiful career, future and our happiness in life.

The people who rely on shortcuts will eventually have to struggle in life and may even have to start their journey all over again with twice the effort and the fear of failures compared to the people who took the hardships and long journey to achieve their goals. The youths and students who are not ready to work hard, though they want to achieve their best might consider taking shortcuts like malpractices and other illegal actions.

They are merely lazy who want everything in life without any effort on their part. They never understand that the things that are easily achieved never last, and if they truly want to achieve something that lasts forever, then they need to be prepared to work harder. Most of them fail to see and understand that there's no quicker way to knowledge and perfection, especially the ones that come with life experiences. There are no shortcuts to true success, but there's always a shortcut to failure.

You can see that there are many many shortcuts to failure which eventually ends up taking longer than usual time to recover and rectify before attaining true success. So we must learn and practice doing the right thing at the right time, to avoid the risk of rectifying the wrong thing at the wrong time.

Have you ever heard the life story and struggles of J.K Rowling? The renowned author of the Harry Potter series is a perfect example of someone who avoided shortcuts and achieved immense success through hard work and dedication inspite of the struggles and challenges she had to face one after the other. Before being branded as a world renowned and bestseller author, Rowling was a poor single mother struggling to meet her needs just by living on welfare benefits. She wrote much of the first Harry Potter book in local cafes while her daughter was asleep. Rowling's journey to her present day success was not easy.

She had to face so many hurdles and rejections from twelve publishers before Bloomsbury Publishing agreed to publish her book. However during the rejections too, she didn't give up. She continued to write, honing her craft and learning from her mistakes. We all take shortcuts once in a while during a busy day, and sometimes it makes sense. For convenience and to save time, we mostly use modern day technologies like Google maps and other navigation systems to find the easiest routes to our destination.

We sometimes use calculators to figure out a time consuming calculation to avoid confusion and to save our time during work. These shortcuts can help ease our stress in day to day life, but the problem arises when we try to find shortcuts in each and everything in our lives. When we apply shortcuts in everything we do, it creates more problems than solutions for our future making us less efficient, more dependent and lazier. It leads us to disappointments and failures.

So for long-term and everlasting success, the key is to take necessary steps that lead to steady progress without skipping any of the necessary processes involved. No matter what, always try to keep integrity, high morale and discipline, with an honest approach towards life. Be patient, highly motivated, focused, loyal and committed to your work. With this right attitude and approach, success will surely come your way at the right time!

*"Never Take Shortcuts Bypassing
The Necessary Steps and Experiences"*

6.7. "RULE OVER UNCERTAINTIES"

Life is a journey filled with twists and turns, uncertainties and challenges. It's a path that requires courage, resilience, and determination to navigate. As we journey through life, we encounter numerous hurdles and obstacles that test our resolve and push us to our limits.

The Power of Confidence

Confidence is the key to overcoming uncertainty. When we have faith in our abilities and talents, we're better equipped to handle the challenges that come our way. Talents can be converted into victories by ruling our doubts and fears. The higher the level of confidence, the higher the chances of achieving success.

The Dangers of Overthinking

Overthinking is a major obstacle to success. When we think too much about our lives, we create tension and anxiety that can lead to depression. Many people get caught up in comparing themselves to others, which can lead to feelings of inadequacy and low self-esteem.

The Importance of Self-Control

Self-control is essential for navigating uncertainty. It is the ability to regulate our thoughts, emotions, and actions in the face of adversity. When we have self-control, we can make better decisions, stay focused, and avoid getting bogged down by negative thoughts and emotions.

Embracing Challenges

Challenges are an integral part of life. They help us grow, learn, and become stronger. When we embrace challenges, we open ourselves up to new experiences, opportunities, and perspectives. We must learn to view challenges as opportunities for growth and development, rather than as threats to our well-being.

The Art of Decision-Making

Decision-making is a critical skill for navigating uncertainty. It is the ability to make informed, thoughtful, and timely decisions that align with our values and goals. When we have the art of decision-making, we can navigate uncertainty with confidence and clarity.

Conclusion

In conclusion, navigating uncertainty requires confidence, self-control, a willingness to embrace challenges, and the art of decision-making. By cultivating these skills, we can overcome the obstacles that stand in our way and achieve our goals. Remember, uncertainty is an inevitable part of life, but it is how we respond to it that truly matters.

"Trust your inner strength to triumph over uncertainty's challenges."

6.8. "BREAK AWAY FROM LONELINESS"

This chapter explains why breaking away from loneliness is very important for our mental well-being. Everyone on the face of earth might have experienced loneliness at some point of their life. Especially as we grow older, we believe loneliness is more likely to hit us than the much younger ones. But astonishingly, many young people these days choose loneliness as a way of their lives, especially to cope with the problems mostly created by external factors that are out of their own control.

These youngsters take drastic measures like drugs, alcohol and abuse of other substances to cope with their loneliness and depression. Knowing how to handle problems maturely and identifying if one is going through depression at the right time is crucial and often helpful when dealing with loneliness.

So how will you exactly know if you are lonely?

We as humans are naturally more social. Socialising with other people makes us happier and gives us a feeling of belonging, connection, confidence and being wanted. It sort of gives us a sense of identity and inclusion. At times most of us enjoy our 'me time' too to revive and rejuvenate, but constant solitude can result in us being emotionally and physically down and disconnected to the outer world.

We will often find ourselves dealing with poor sleep patterns, unhealthy eating habits, negative emotions, mood swings, lowered self esteem, low self confidence, uncaring behaviour and even feeling sad, miserable and misunderstood. People often hesitate to ask for help when they are isolated and cut off from an actual connection with the community they are living in, rather they will be more dependent on digital mediums, or find solace in digital and virtual connections which ultimately cannot feed their emotional needs.

Loneliness is a particular stage of our mind when someone lacks a genuine connection towards others and the society in general. It can bring along the pain unexplainable, suffocate our souls and make us feel sick. It's a feeling of disconnection, a sense of being isolated from the world around us. But we know that loneliness is just a temporary visitor if we don't give it a chance to stay in our life permanently. We should never give it a permanent residence in our life and should never hesitate to show this temporary visitor its way to the door, if it's bringing in more damage to our lives.

There are so many negative consequences loneliness can cause. It always makes us feel helpless, and more impacted by the hurt that others might have caused you. It feeds on the negative emotions of our mind and we slowly slip into the stage of depression. Try not to succumb to loneliness and thereby to this kind of negative thinking which can do you more harm than the hurtful situation itself.

When you give way to loneliness in your life, you are letting it steal the beauty of your life. Those who feel lonely for a long time will be deprived of all the means of happiness and contentment in life. Sometimes people who feel lonely for a relatively long period might mentally or physically hurt themselves and can cause harm to others too. During this phase, they will seemingly become more distant with people, preferring to spend most of their days in a dark room with some bad memories haunting them every second.

Do you know that the feeling of loneliness for a long period is a kind of mental illness? Do you want to know how to overcome it? Psychologists always recommend that intense loneliness needs attention and should be quickly taken into medical and psychological consideration. This is an alarming stage in which a person will have a significantly low level of self-esteem and will constantly think of taking negative decisions that can destroy the very beauty of what life might have to offer.

At this stage they can have a tendency to break out of their present situation by concentrating on all the negative solutions they can imagine. To overcome this problem that loneliness brings us, we must first acknowledge its existence. Try to analyse what you are going through, and what emotions you carry deep inside. Do you feel void and empty inside your mind most of the time? If yes, then initiate small steps to fill it. This is the time when you should reach out for help and guidance, maybe from a friend, or a neighbour, or a close family member. We all know the fact that human connections and bonds between individuals are only formed when we are often seen and valued.

During an authentic human interaction, people often are seen getting involved with each other, exchanging positive energy and building mutual trust. By connecting to others on a deeper level will make you feel heard and understood which also gives you a sense of belonging and identity.

Try engaging in your favourite activities that will give you joy and immense satisfaction. The activities can include cooking, gardening, painting, writing, or even reading. Being creative can help you know yourself and what you are capable of. Creativity is such a powerful and strong bridge that connects us to ourselves and others. Another way to come out of loneliness is to practice self-compassion and self-care. Accept yourself as you are: own the personality, uniqueness, beauty and worthiness you possess and be proud of it! Loneliness can happen in different ways: sense of being physically alone, being emotionally or physically hurt by someone whom you trusted, being isolated as a minority in communities, changes to certain life conditions and circumstances, not getting enough sense of inclusion, being in a long distance relationship, and certain changes to personal relationships or family life in general.

Living alone and not having contact with your community or any neighbours will make you feel more lonelier. But that doesn't mean that having a lot of friends and people to talk with will make you feel understood and happier. You can still feel miserable and lonely in a crowd and with the company of your friends. So remember that loneliness is not something related to the quantity of people you have in your lives, but rather the quality of people you interact and have relationships with. So choose your people wisely! A famous quote by Arthur C. Clarke:

"Two possibilities exist: either we are alone in the Universe or we are not. Both are equally terrifying."

Conclusion

Remember, loneliness isn't a reflection of your worth and it won't help increase your happiness either. Longing to break free from loneliness is a reminder that you're ready to expand your circle, to embrace new experiences, and to connect with the world around you. Know the worth of your life and your ability to offer goodness to this world. Believe in yourself and the people around you. Believe that you can overcome any challenges not just by yourself but sometimes with the help of others who have walked the same path as you are now. So take time to connect to the outer world, embrace the beauty of connection, know the power and possibilities life brings to you by being in a community, and look out for the love and support that awaits you!

"We are not alone, we are all one!"

6.9. "AVOID COMPARISON"

Starting from an earlier age, human nature tends to compare with others. A deadliest poison to our happiness is comparison. When we constantly measure ourselves against others, we open the door of inadequacy, jealousy, low self-esteem, and dissatisfaction.

We forget that each person's journey is unique, with its own set of challenges, opportunities, and experiences. By comparing ourselves to others, we not only undermine our own strengths, abilities and accomplishments but also overlook the beauty of our individuality.

Children discover very quickly that not everyone leads an equal life, and not everyone gets similar opportunities in their life. As a child, they discover that some friends have wide collections of toys, and some have a better environment in their home as some lead a better lifestyle. They start comparing what others have and what they themselves don't have.

After reaching their teenage years, this phase of comparisons doesn't stop but rather intensifies with peers' bullying which impacts them very badly. Unintentional and unwanted sibling comparisons and the desire to prove yourself in front of parents can impact adversely during adulthood.

You can find it affecting the relationships both inside and outside the family dynamic. Negative thoughts and negative self-talks further ruin your life.

Are you holding yourself back by comparing your limitations to someone else's strengths? Remember, you possess unique gifts and talents that others may not. Do not let society's expectations or past hurts define your worth.

Take inspiration from Aman's story in the movie "Saajan", who despite being an orphan and physically challenged, found love and acceptance through his poetry. His journey shows us that our perceived weaknesses can become our greatest strengths.

Let go of the need to compare and focus on cultivating your own uniqueness, beauty of character and purpose. Embrace your individuality and start living the life that truly belongs to you.

To compare you with others is a big mistake you can commit in your life. Every individual is a unique creation of God with their naturally gifted inherent talents. You can use those talents with your acquired skills, qualifications or talents if any like apostleship, administration, craftsmanship, discernment, encouragement, charity, faith, giving, helping, hospitality; intercession, knowledge, leadership, mercy, prophecy, philosophy, shepherding, teaching, interpretation, etc. to create a more contented and happy future for yourself.

We might not have any control over the physical or mental disabilities or weaknesses, but we definitely have control over the variety of disabilities and weaknesses like procrastination, greediness, aggressiveness, laziness, lack of confidence, fear, being judgemental, disorganized, communication problem, imitation, jealousy, being monotonous, overconfidence, arrogance, people pleasing behaviour, degradation, etc.

We need to get rid of these negative traits and disabilities first before working on our inherited talents. There is no point in comparing ourselves with others as every person is unique with his own passions or aspirations and might have walked a different journey than yours.

If you are a proven singer, the other person might have passion in dancing or any other activities. If you go to any park, you can find various trees planted there; and that is what makes the park attractive as a whole.

Here are some practical ways to stop yourselves being envious and to regain your power.

- Distinguish what triggers you.
- Practice gratitude and gratefulness.

- Recognise your strengths and accomplishments.
- Put efforts to build upon your inherited talent or passion.
- Have a habit of honest but positive self-talk
- Reward yourself for your efforts and accomplishments.
- Always have strong belief and willpower to change your situation.

Conclusion

As we journey through life, it's essential to recognise that our worth and value aren't defined by how we stack up against others. By letting go of the need to compare, we can break free from the shackles of self-doubt and inadequacy.

Instead, we can focus on cultivating our own unique strengths, passions, and talents, and celebrate the successes of those around us. By embracing our individuality and rejecting the comparison trap, we can unlock a more authentic, fulfilling, and joyful life. I want to suggest you to stay away from three types of people:

- People who believe in unhealthy competition
- People who appreciate less and complain more
- People who compare you with others.

"Your path is unique, don't measure it with someone else's ruler"

6.10. "DEFEATS - STEPPING STONES TO SUCCESS"

Failures in life are more important and much needed than we think. Its importance lies in the fact that it has the power to reveal the potential strength in a person. It somewhat resembles the process of extracting pure metal out of its ore by subjecting it to the high temperature. Wonderful outcomes in our life are the result of many struggles that we face in our lives and what measures or efforts we take to overcome it.

We all as humans never want to fail. Yet, in the path of life come unforeseen obstacles and circumstances that if not approached cautiously, can lead to failure. These obstacles and hurdles that get placed in our path to hinder our progress, are what we wrongly interpret as failures.

We have been conditioned to treat these hurdles disguised as failures, to be a complete waste of time. But knowing how to stand up again and keep going without succumbing to those hurdles is the best way to progress and succeed. Each setback is one step closer to attaining your desired goal and success.

When failure happens, it shows us what we shouldn't be doing and what we need to be doing. If we ignore those signs and hesitate learning from it, then it will continue to happen again. When you are sure that you're on the right path, consider learning from your mistakes that led you to failure in the past, and rectify them before trying again.

You might have heard many success stories of personalities of the past and present, who have tasted failures several times before getting fame and fortune. Their paths were filled with obstacles and challenges. The one thing that kept them going towards success was their desire and passion for their work. Great accomplishments come with defeat knocking the door several times.

The former American president Mr. Abraham Lincoln, one of the greatest men of all time, endured a steady stream of failure and defeat before becoming president of the United States. They were born in poverty and struggled a lot in their life. After tasting several defeats they were finally elected as the President of the US in the year 1860. Their resilience, determination and persistence even after being continuously and miserably failing for thirty years, is something that we all need to inspire from. They used vanquish as a milestone to success.

Failure doesn't mean that you are incapable of doing anything or you don't deserve the things you aspire for. You have to set living examples for others with a positive mindset to accept your weakness. It requires a lot of courage to accept weakness and failure, to restart the process on the way to success without losing hope and enthusiasm. Thinking and fearing constantly about failure, will hinder your ability to progress and will not let you push forward.

> *"Failure is another stepping stone to greatness"*
>
> \- Oprah Winfrey

Imagine a student didn't get selected through an entrance examination or a job seeker couldn't find a suitable job that matches their profile. In the above set of circumstances, losing self confidence and motivation is normal. It's a universal truth that all people in this world have to go through the phase of failure at some point of their lives. You may also have faced the same situation in your life at least for once. It always provides valuable lessons for your personal growth as well as your future aspects. Learning, recognising and changing the things that lead you to failure in the first place, is the foundation of a successful life.

Conclusion

Keep a positive attitude and ignite your enthusiasm with new skills needed for a better future. Update yourself with the latest information related to your subject interest. Avoid being distracted and panicking about your work. Plan ahead and change the approach with all the past failures in mind. Have a positive mindset to chase your dreams with full confidence. With no effort to change or with a lack of motivation, you might experience failure repeatedly without any room for a progressive future.

You will get success in your future endeavors by learning from your past mistakes and making changes to your approach that resulted in your failure. Some experience success earlier and some get a taste of success later in their life. Remember the above mentioned example of the former President of the US who fought all those odds with much resilience and patience to get to the place he dreamt of. So never fear failure, as it's an important and essential part of your journey to success.

It has the ability to teach us the lessons of life through experiences, thus forcing us to reassess our past decisions and approaches that went wrong. The important thing is to understand your mistakes and learn from them, and to find the most effective way forward which can lead you to victory. That's when you can really appreciate your efforts and victories.

"Rise from the ashes, stronger than before."

PART 7:

Character Development

7.1. "BUILD YOUR MORAL CONSCIENCE"

Every individual lives within a society governed by rules and norms, some dictated by law and others by personal and public morality. Our moral principles are shaped by various factors, including education, family, religion, culture and surroundings. As we go through life's challenges, our moral compass evolves, influenced by external factors and guided by our conscience.

However, the concept of conscience can be interpreted differently by each person. Unfortunately, I've witnessed firsthand how the lack of moral understanding and empathy can lead to harmful behaviours, such as bullying, degrading, slandering and rumour-spreading. It's disheartening to see how people can harbor hatred and hostility towards one another and go to any extent to damage one's reputation. Ultimately, our intentions and actions are a reflection of our moral values and the society we live in.

Moral conscience is a logical process that takes place in an individual's mind about his action being right or wrong. A bold and honest person, if he upholds his moral conscience even in adversities, will be able to achieve greater things in his life. Those who are brave, have immense abilities and inner strength to transform any worst situation into a winning one. A courageous person approaches life's challenges as tasks that test their inner strength.

He will have a different concept about life and its struggles. His positive attitude will make him feel more stronger than his challenges. This makes him more determined to achieve his goal within a set time. For an ordinary fearful person, even the smallest struggle will be too much to handle. The constant troubles in his life might have made him stay in despair.

Every day of his life will be felt as a burden, making him more depressed and not capable of recognising his purpose in life. No matter how much we emphasize adhering to moral conscience and high values, people still take it as merely personal choices depending on how much benefit that can bring to them. Despite having strict measures in place, there are institutions, political bodies and organizations where people often compromise their moral values for better prospects, monetary gains or to secure their jobs.

There are many contributions made by moral thinkers and philosophers, and for reference you can read biographies and books about Swami Vivekananda, Mahatma Gandhi, Adi Shankaracharya, Lord Buddha, etc. The Father of our Nation, Mahatma Gandhi, was a strong believer of God, and having a deep faith in God gave him immense courage and determination to achieve greatness through morality, peace and non-violence in his life. According to him, truth is nothing but the reflection of God. In his autobiography, "My Experiment with Truth" he mentioned that truth can be achieved in a wider sense, where truth doesn't mean only being truthful in speech, but should also be reflected in action and should be applied in all fields of life. Similarly, Swami Vivekananda worked on a wide range of subjects - Vedanta Philosophy, Karma Yoga, Raja Yoga, etc. and was one the earliest philosophers to be identified as a socialist. According to him:

"If you want to speak about the politics of India, you must explain it through the language of religion."

He emphasized the need to instill in the people, a sense of patriotism, human dignity and national pride. His thoughts as a progressive and empathetic thinker, helped the people of India to develop their patriotic, moral and national consciousness.

Conclusion

Don't let the darkness in others kill the light in you - in other words, you don't need to engage in their counter-productive thinking and negative judgements. By disengaging from those activities, you can spare yourself from mental turmoil and distress in the future. You have to gauge the worth and conduct of the individual you pay your attention and time to. Pay attention to how they treat others and if their words and actions match. You should take into consideration certain principles or moral values that will form your behaviour and guide you in your decision-making. The way you think should place heavy importance on respect and fairness to all, whilst being socially responsible. It pertains to considering the outcome that may occur as a direct or indirect effect of any of those actions or decisions. Remember that your choices may have an impact not only on you but on others around you too; make decisions that benefit everyone, not just yourself.

"Be true to your conscience,
you will never go through the wrong path"

7.2. "SELF RELIANCE LEADS TO SUCCESS!"

In today's uncertain times, individuals often find themselves lost and disconnected from their environment. Many lack the refined skills that are needed to handle life's complexities. Some passively observe as events unfold, whilst others take a more proactive approach. However, some are completely unaware of what's happening around them!

True strength lies in individuals who won't hesitate to take charge and make things happen. Aspire to have that driving force within you which will empower you to transform your life. Remember that your choices and decisions will not only shape your own life but also impact the lives of others.

A local farmer near my native place in Kerala, despite facing challenges, with limited resources and in heavy rainfall and other harsh weather conditions, was so determined that he found a new farming method to maximise his yearly production and thereby overcoming the challenges.

He tactfully decided to farm rice and other grains for 6 months, and the other half year he used to cultivate long beans, red amaranth and bitter gourd in the same paddy field.

By cultivating long beans, he could bring the essential nutrients back into the field which helped him grow and get great yields from the next batch of rice and grains cultivation. Instead of relying on others or the Government for any help, he along with his wife took charge of the farming experience and experimented with new techniques that turned profitable.

After facing too many challenges and failures, they thought of trying various options to help themselves out. Finally, he could taste success after constant hard work, determination, and experimenting with new techniques by avoiding past mistakes.

Through his hard work, self-reliance and his wife's support, they were able to increase their crop yield, improve their family's livelihood, and become a role model for their community. Their success teaches us that with self-reliance and perseverance, anyone can overcome obstacles and achieve their goals.

Jyoti, a young entrepreneur who dreamt of starting her bakery, with limited financial resources, wasn't able to afford to rent a commercial kitchen or hire the staff needed. Undaunted and determined, Jyoti thought of starting it small at first for her survival. She converted a small room in her home into a makeshift bakery, taught herself new recipes, and invested in affordable yet reliable basic equipment.

Through social media and word-of-mouth, she built a loyal customer base. As her business grew, she continued to adapt and innovate, saved money wisely and eventually expanded a small storefront. Jyoti's self-reliance and resourcefulness had turned her passion into a thriving business, inspiring other men and women in her community to pursue their entrepreneurial dreams.

"When you're lost, search for and find yourself!

Try new things and take risks. This will help you overcome the initial hesitation you feel when making decisions.

A Simple Experiment:

Sit outside without your phone or any other technology for an hour. Let yourself feel bored. See where your thoughts take you. This will help you understand if you're truly focused on your goals or if you need to make any changes.

Inspiring Words:

The American poet Edgar Albert Guest wrote a poem called "It Couldn't Be Done." Here's an excerpt:

Many people will tell you that something can't be done.
They'll warn you of dangers and predict failure.
But don't listen!
Just get started with confidence and a positive attitude.
You'll be surprised at what you can achieve!

These words encourage us to take action and believe in ourselves.

Conclusion

Sometimes the small decisions that we choose or do not choose to make can make or break big things in our lives! If things go wrong, then calm your mind and avoid taking things too personally to avoid slipping into depression and inactivity. When you are at peace, you think more logically which will open doors to new possibilities and self-reflection.

Every small choice that you make will help you learn and grow. Through this self-discovery path, you will recognise your strengths, passions, and what all possibilities can be there for you. By evaluating your decisions, you can help yourself make better choices and decisions in the future.

This will help you make informed choices, and in avoiding mistakes that might otherwise happen again. With each step of faith in ourselves, we can turn our dreams into achievements. And when we look back, we realize that our greatest accomplishment is not what we've done, but the incredible potential that's still within us, ready to be tapped.

"Empowered by self-belief,
you can turn the ordinary into extraordinary."

7.3. "BACK UP YOUR WORDS WITH ACTIONS"

The Power of Action: Why Speaking Less and Doing More Matters?

In today's world, it's easy to get caught up in talking about our plans and goals. However, intelligent and successful individuals know that actions speak louder than words. Here, we'll discuss why taking action is crucial for achieving greater success. By adopting a positive mindset that values action over words, you'll be able to turn your ideas into actual results that will earn you respect and add value to your words.

The Problem with Empty Words

How many times have you heard someone make big promises or boast about their accomplishments, only to fail to deliver? Words are easy to say, but actions require constant effort and dedication. When we speak without thinking, we can come across as insincere or as an unreliable person. On the other hand, when we focus on taking action, we build trust and credibility with others.

The Benefits of Action

So, what happens when we focus on action rather than words? Here are just a few benefits:

- **Builds Trust:** When we follow through on our commitments, we build trust with others. This is essential in both personal and professional relationships. Consistently, delivering on our promises and maintaining transparency helps to strengthen relationships, build trust, and prove yourself as a reliable person.
- **Open doors to great opportunities:** By taking action, people can see our strengths, skills, and trustworthiness

which will open new opportunities. This will ultimately help us to have more experience and in achieving goals with greater ease and confidence.

- **Earns Respect:** When we focus on taking action, we demonstrate our capabilities and earn respect from others. When we deliver results to the highest standards, we show others that we are capable, skilled, hardworking, and committed. This earns us respect and admiration from those around us.
- **Leads to Success:** Taking action is essential to achieving our goals. When we focus on doing rather than talking, we're more likely to succeed. By putting our words and plans into action, we overcome obstacles, learn to observe our past mistakes, and stay motivated to reach our objectives, ultimately achieving the success we strive for.

Wisdom from the notables

The importance of action over words is not a new concept. Here are some wise words by some notable individuals from our history:

"Action speaks louder than words."

- English Proverb

"Try not to become a man of success, but rather a man of value."

- Albert Einstein

Conclusion

In conclusion, speaking less and doing more is essential to achieving success and earning the respect of others. By focusing on action rather than words, we build trust, demonstrate our capabilities, and achieve our goals. Remember, it's not what you say that matters, but what you do that counts.

"Actions build trust, words without action break it"

7.4. "TURN MISTAKES INTO LESSONS"

Have you ever made mistakes that resulted in loss or failure and felt like giving up? We've all been there at some point in our lives. But what if you could use those mistakes to learn from and take the precautionary steps needed to avoid the pitfalls in future?

The Power of Learning from Mistakes

As Napoleon Hill said, "When defeat comes, accept it as a signal that your plans are not sound; rebuild those plans and start once more towards the coveted goal." Mistakes are inevitable in our lives, but it's how we respond to them and learn from them that matters.

Real-Life Example: Thomas Edison's Journey to Success

Thomas Edison, known as the inventor of the light bulb, also made several mistakes before the invention. Edison experimented with over 1,000 filaments before finding the right one. When asked about his failures, Edison said, "I have not failed. I've just found 10,000 ways that won't work." Edison's persistence and ability to learn from his mistakes ultimately led to the groundbreaking invention.

How to Learn from Past Mistakes

Here are some simple yet powerful steps to help you learn from your past mistakes:

- **Acknowledge and accept your mistakes**: Firstly, recognise your errors and take responsibility for them. Don't avoid them by blaming others or making excuses.
- **Analyze and identify lessons**: Reflect on what went wrong and what you could have done differently. Identify the areas you need to improvise.

- **Extract valuable insights:** Turn lessons into actionable advice for future situations.
- **Adjust your approach:** Apply the learned insights to modify your behaviour, decision-making, and problem-solving strategies.
- **Practice self-compassion:** Treat yourself with kindness and understanding when you make mistakes, just as you would a friend.
- **Embrace a growth mindset:** View mistakes as opportunities to grow, learn, and improve without worrying about the past.
- **Develop resilience:** Learn to bounce back from setbacks and use them as motivation to keep moving forward.
- **Cultivate a Culture of Learning:** Encourage others to share their mistakes and learn from them, developing a culture of openness and growth.

Benefits of Learning from Past Mistakes

By learning from your past mistakes, you can:
- Improve your problem-solving skills
- Enhance your decision-making abilities
- Develop your emotional intelligence
- Boost your self-awareness
- Can have Increased resilience
- Encourage personal growth and wisdom
- Foster a culture of learning and innovation

Conclusion

Mistakes are not failures, but valuable learning experiences that can shape your future successes. Remember, "Don't let your past dictate who you are, but let it become a lesson that strengthens the person you will become." So, don't be afraid to make mistakes. Instead, learn from them, and use them as stepping stones to success.

Key Takeaways
- Acknowledge and accept mistakes
- Analyze and identify lessons
- Extract valuable insights
- Adjust behaviour and approach
- Practice self-compassion
- Embrace a growth mindset
- Develop resilience
- Cultivate a culture of learning

"A failure fails once. A success fails multiple times"

7.5. "TRUST IN THE PROVIDENCE OF GOD"

This phrase is a powerful expression of faith and surrender. It implies having confidence in the creator's guidance, care, and sovereignty over all aspects of life. It's also a reminder to trust that when he puts us through challenges, he has the power to reward us for the effort that we take to overcome those challenges too. While we put in our efforts, he will guide us through our confusion and protect us from any potential danger. In essence, it's a declaration of dependence on the almighty's wisdom, love, and provision. It's a phrase that can bring you comfort, peace, and hope in times of uncertainty or challenge.

There are several religions in this world. Religion comprises certain beliefs and practices based on people's upbringing or their faith in a particular form of divine energy. You can observe that man cannot logically answer all those questions due to their limitations of knowledge and understanding about the universe as a whole. I belong to a religious family where I grew up seeing several rites and rituals; therefore it played an important role in my life. On a global scale, almost everyone practices a particular form of religion.

Whether it is Islam, Christianity, Judaism, or any other religion, they all collectively believe in the mightier powers of our creator. Many of these religions are either monotheistic or polytheistic. Religions like Islam, Judaism and Christianity are monotheistic that is, believing in one God, whereas faiths like Hinduism are polytheistic and worship several deities according to personal preferences or likeness.

Being polytheistic, Hindus all over the world claim not to be a religion but a way to attain 'moksha' or liberation from worldly materials or sufferings. They also consider worshipping as an individual choice, where one can pick their own choices of deities or deities to seek enlightenment and to get closer to the supreme energy. 'Moksha' is widely used as a term in Sanatan religions like Hinduism, Sikhism, Buddhism and Jainism to refer to liberation or freedom that releases a person from the cycle of death and rebirth, which is part of 'samsara' or worldly pleasures and sufferings.

It also means to free oneself finally from ignorance, greed, worldly pleasures, attachments, sadness and suffering to attain enlightenment, knowledge of oneself, self-actualization and the realization that we all are part of that supreme energy and we all will finally be absorbed into it.

The religions like Hinduism and Buddhism, take unique methods in demystifying ideas of birth and death and explain how and why these events occur through their teachings, traditions, cultures, and beliefs. Thus religion is a social institution that attempts to explain what is thought to be inexplicable.

It also plays a significant role in shaping behaviours, thoughts, principles, morals, rules, values, and practices and in influencing art and culture, thus providing a sense of community and spiritual guidance for people across the globe. Let me tell you a story of a hardcore devotee and his conversations with God. The devotee once had a wonderful dream in which he saw himself walking with God on a seashore. God said,

> **"Look here on the sand. You will find different happenings of your life marked on it"**

Upon watching it carefully, he notices two pairs of footprints on the sand and asks God the reason behind it. God replied:

> **"One pair is yours and another pair is mine. I was with you from the very moment of your birth"**

After listening to this, the man felt more confident than before. As he hails God for his love, care, and concern, he notices something very strange and surprising! In the most difficult situation of his life, he could find only one pair of footprints. The thought that God had left him to be alone when in trouble left him hurt and very sad.

Suddenly his beautiful smile disappeared and after a few moments of thought, and then in despair and with a trembling voice he asked:

'O Lord, you said that you would always be beside me. Then why did you choose to leave me alone when I need you the most?'

God with much affection replied:

"My dear son, do you believe that I will leave you in your suffering and pain? Don't you know that you won't be able to see two pairs of footprints in certain situations? On those occasions, I will be carrying you on my shoulder to protect you, and the footprints you may find on the sand will be not yours, but mine!"

To believe in the providence of God means to have undoubted faith and trust in his mercy and goodness. It is based on the conviction that God has created all and he will continue to stay with you all through your life. The challenges and sufferings in this world can rightly be compared to the waves and tides of an ocean.

In all your lives, you have to face rough tides with occasional breaks of calmness and smooth water layers. At times you will feel as if all the powers of the universe are conspiring against you, but in those times remember that these tides are necessary too to remind you of your irrelevant ego and attitudes, which can both be humbling and exalting.

But sailing through those rough tides without losing faith, hope and courage is what will help you reach the shore safely. Remember that "a calm sea never creates a good sailor."

*"Be spiritually humble to experience
your inner peace and faith!"*

7.6. "PERSEVERANCE ALWAYS PAYS OFF"

Have you ever felt like giving up on your dreams, thinking the journey ahead is too long, hard and uncertain? You're not alone. But what if you could tap into a powerful mindset that would help you overcome the obstacles and achieve your goals?

Understanding the Power of Perseverance

Perseverance is more than just persistence; it's a mindset that helps you navigate challenges with resilience and determination. You can face your insecurities, and fears while learning from mistakes and moving forward; no matter what!

Examples of Perseverance

Consider a sailor who bravely navigates through stormy seas without losing hope or the story of two frogs falling into a cream bucket. One frog eventually gave up, while the other kept struggling, thus escaping to safety. These stories illustrate the power of perseverance in the face of adversity.

Developing Perseverance in Daily Life

So, how can you cultivate perseverance in your daily life? Here are a few strategies:

- **Set clear goals**: Identify what you want to achieve and create a plan to get there.
- **Develop emotional resilience**: Learn to bounce back from setbacks.
- **Cultivate a growth mindset:** Believe that your abilities can be developed through hard work and dedication.

- **Surround yourself with positive influences:** Seek out supportive people who encourage and motivate you.
- **Practice self-care:** Take care of your physical, mental, and emotional well-being.

The Importance of Mental Strength

Mental strength is much needed when it comes to perseverance. It's the ability to stay focused, motivated, and composed in adverse situations. By developing mental toughness, you'll be better equipped to handle challenges and setbacks in your life.

Inspiring quote from Vivekananda

"It is not that we are weak, but that we are not enough in earnest; that's our real weakness."

These words remind us that perseverance is not just about external circumstances, but also about our internal mindset and commitment.

Conclusion

Perseverance is a powerful mindset that can help you overcome any obstacle and in achieving your goals. By developing emotional resilience, cultivating a growth mindset, and surrounding yourself with positive influences, you'll be better equipped to handle challenges and setbacks. Remember, perseverance always pays off, so keep pushing forward without losing hope, even when the journey gets tough.

Key Takeaways:

- Perseverance is a mindset that helps you navigate challenges with resilience and determination.

- Developing emotional resilience is critical for perseverance.
- Cultivate a growth mindset to believe in your abilities.
- Surround yourself with positive influences.
- Practice self-care to maintain your physical, mental, and emotional well-being.

"Everyone wants success;
many have no perseverance and patience"

7.7. "ATTAIN PERFECTION THROUGH PRACTICE"

Most of us strangely attribute the success of great men to mere luck, opportunities and inborn talents. But we never try to notice and understand the challenges they overcame and the consistent hard work they put themselves through their journey to success. They toiled day and night working round the clock to reach the peak of glory and perfection. Have you ever thought of what exactly 'perfection' means and how to achieve it? Perfection is something that can be attained through a strong desire to reach excellence and constantly working towards achieving it.

Diego Armando Maradona, a footballer of all time, was once asked by a reporter what made him such a great player for which he confidently said, "Practice, practice and only practice." Similarly, I heard a famous Paralympic medal winner who is also an Indian motivational speaker saying-

"There is ability beyond disability.
It's all about mind over body."

When Deepa Malik was just six, she was diagnosed with a spinal tumour, but instead of succumbing to the negative feelings and sickness, she went on to build a strong spirit. She left the comfort of her bed and chose to play an outdoor sport which was a challenge that even the healthy would have been wary of. She began a long and tough journey, stayed determined and made consistent efforts that culminated in a silver medal at the 2016 Paralympics in Rio.

Every person is assigned certain responsibilities in his life whether it be naturally inherited or self-taken. He must deliver the best by being truly dedicated and by working sincerely towards fulfilling it. Mostly the young generation these days take responsibilities as mere tasks and are least worried about completing these responsibilities with perfection.

They simply do it to avoid getting scolded by their elders or just for the sake of being obedient. Many of them will be more focused on finishing off those heaps of assignments, often compromising the quality of work and the amount of knowledge through research they were supposed to do.

My sincere suggestion to all the students and youngsters with this mentality is to not compromise on these essential skills as they are in place to prepare you for more difficult challenges ahead and to improve your efficiency.

Do it with utmost dedication as these are the essential skills that will empower you, making you stronger to face any challenges later in life. Always adapt to changes or else you will drown in your complacencies, making you weaker day by day.

Do not consider perfection as something impossible to attain, instead take that up as a life challenge and as an achievement to accomplish. Some activities that we normally have in our daily routine are quite repetitive, continuous and monotonous and somehow we just carry on doing things like pre-programmed robots!

What made Michael Jackson's moves so perfect? It was his spontaneity and timing that made his move look so magical and perfect. He was so spontaneous and knew which move would look great to follow after what. Michael himself said that we shouldn't think, but feel when dancing! With this unique approach since childhood and with his unique singing and dancing style, he conquered the world that everyone remembers him whenever we mention pop-singing or 'moon-walking'. Taking the amount of time he spent in the music industry into consideration, which counted as almost his entire life is what made those moves so perfect. His dedication to practice towards perfection gave him his perfect moves and vocal abilities.

We can say that perfection is almost asymptotic as the amount of time required for improvement may seem to continually increase as one nears perfection. It is perceived to be unattainable in many cases and sometimes might seem to require never-ending efforts. So it's the time to wake up and break the stereotypical thoughts, think outside your boundaries, practice towards perfection and aim towards your goals.

*"**Strive for excellence, practice with passion, and achieve great success always**"*

7.8. "BE A GOOD ORGANISER"

In today's fast-paced world, being organised is crucial for achieving success in both personal and professional life. A good organiser or leader is someone who can give clear directions, manage their team effectively, and make informed decisions. They possess a unique combination of skills, including clear vision, excellent interpersonal relationships, creativity, and problem-solving abilities. So you have to possess these qualities of a leader to lead your life to success.

Characteristics of a Good Organiser

A good organiser should have the following qualities:

- **Clear vision:** A clear understanding of what needs to be achieved and an effective plan for achieving it.
- **Good interpersonal relationships:** The ability to build strong relationships with peers, teammates, stakeholders, and clients.
- **Creativity:** The ability to think outside the box and come up with innovative ideas and effective solutions to problems or prospective challenges.
- **Problem-solving abilities:** The ability to analyse problems, identify efficient solutions, and implement them effectively.
- **Time management skills:** The ability to recognise and prioritise tasks, manage time effectively, set time for each task and meet those deadlines.

Examples of Effective Organisers in Indian History

India has been fortunate to have had many great leaders who were excellent organizers. Sardar Vallabh Bhai Patel, India's Iron Man, played a crucial role in integrating back the country's princely states after independence. His exceptional organisational skills helped him to bring back together over 560 princely states into a unified India.

Another notable example is Netaji Subhash Chandra Bose, a prominent freedom fighter who demonstrated exceptional leadership and organisational skills. He founded the highly organised Indian National Army (INA) and led it against the British Empire during World War II.

Rani Lakshmibai, the Queen of Jhansi, is another example of a great organizer. She played a key role in the Indian Rebellion of 1857 against the British East India Company. Her bravery, determination, leadership, and organisational skills inspired many Indians to fight for their freedom.

Takeaways for Effective Organisation

- **Plan and prioritise:** Keep journals. Create daily, weekly, and monthly plans to stay organized and focused.
- **Stay focused:** Avoid multitasking and concentrate on completing one task at a time. If you need to finish multiple tasks a day, try setting time for each task and focus on one particular task before moving on to the next.
- **Develop leadership skills:** Work on your analysing, decision-making, communication, and problem-solving abilities.
- **Foster a collaborative work environment:** Encourage open communication, motivate your team members to do better, and recognise their contributions.
- **Use technology to your advantage:** Utilize digital tools such as calendars, planners, and project management software to stay organised and on track.

Best Practices for Effective Organization

- **Set clear goals and objectives:** Establish clear goals for yourself and your team.

- **Create a schedule:** Plan out your day/week/month, and stick to your schedule.
- **Use a task list or to-do list:** Write down all the tasks you need to complete and check them off as you finish them.
- **Avoid procrastination:** Break down large tasks into smaller, manageable chunks, and focus on completing one task at a time.
- **Take breaks and practice self-care:** Take regular breaks to recharge and refocus, and prioritise self-care i.e. exercise, meditation, and time with loved ones.

Conclusion

Effective organisation has always been a crucial skill for achieving success in all areas of life. By developing leadership skills, fostering a collaborative work environment, and using technology to your advantage, you can certainly become a more effective organiser and play a vital role in the development of your business or career. Remember to set clear goals and objectives, create a schedule and stick to it, use a task list or to-do list, avoid procrastination, take breaks between tasks and practice self-care. With much practice and dedication, you can be a master organiser and attain success in your life.

"Staying organised is the way to stay successful"

7.9. "TRUTH ALWAYS TRIUMPHS"

Swami Vivekananda, one of India's most revered philosophers, once said:

"Truth alone triumphs"

These three words encapsulate the importance of honesty and integrity in our personal and professional lives. Truth is the foundation upon which we build our relationships, our careers, and our reputation.

The Importance of Honesty

Honesty is a vital virtue that plays a crucial role in our lives. It refers to the quality of being truthful and transparent in our words and actions. When we are honest, we build trust with others, and our relationships become stronger and more meaningful. Honesty also helps us to develop a clear conscience, which is essential for our mental and emotional well-being.

Examples of Truthfulness in Indian History

Indian history is replete with examples of truthfulness and honesty. One of the most famous examples is that of Harishchandra, a king who was known for their honesty and integrity. Harishchandra was tested by the sage Vishwamitra, who asked him to give up his kingdom and family in exchange for a life of poverty and hardship. Harishchandra agreed, and his honesty and integrity were ultimately rewarded.

Another example of truthfulness is Mahatma Gandhi, who strongly advocated nonviolent resistance and honesty. Gandhi's commitment to truth and nonviolence inspired a nation and helped bring India independence from British rule.

The Story of Birbal and the Stick

A famous folktale from Indian history illustrates the importance of truthfulness. The story goes like this: Akbar, the Mughal emperor, asked his trusted courtier, Birbal, to solve a case involving a wealthy man and his servant. Birbal, known for his clever methods and tricks, asked the wealthy man to bring the servant and a stick.

Birbal then told the servant that the stick would grow longer if the person holding it was telling the truth, but shrink if he was lying. The servant, believing this, was asked if he had stolen the item. The servant denied it, but Birbal noticed that the stick 'shrunk' in his hands.

Birbal then asked the wealthy man to hold the stick and asked the servant if he had stolen the item. When the servant again denied it, the stick 'grew longer' in the wealthy man's hands. Birbal declared that the servant was indeed the thief, as the stick had 'shrunk' when he held it, indicating his guilt.

The Importance of Integrity in Professional Life

In professional life, integrity is essential for success. When we act with honesty and integrity, we build trust with our colleagues, clients, and customers. We also develop a strong reputation, which can help us to advance in our careers and in achieving our goals.

The Benefits of Truthfulness

Truthfulness has numerous benefits in our personal and professional lives. When we are truthful, we:

- Build trust with others
- Develop a clear conscience
- Establish a strong reputation and goodwill
- Achieve success and advancement in our careers
- Cultivate a positive and respectful work culture

Conclusion

In conclusion, truth alone triumphs. Honesty and integrity are essential virtues that play a crucial role in our personal and professional lives. By acting with truthfulness and integrity, we build trust, develop strong relationships, and achieve success. As Swami Vivekananda so eloquently put it, "Truth alone triumphs." It's a habit that, when practised every day, will take care of our mental and emotional well-being.

"Honesty is the best policy; practice it daily"

7.10. "COMMITMENT FACILITATES SUCCESS"

Success is a lifelong journey of learning, growing, and self-improvement, where every step forward is a step closer to achieving our dreams. In this journey, we must stay focused, work hard, and persevere through challenges, just like the great entrepreneurs and leaders who have inspired us. By embracing this journey, we can unlock our full potential, achieve greatness, and make a positive impact on the world around us.

The Importance of Consistent Efforts

The first step in preparing the secret recipe to success is to add a small quantity of consistent effort. These efforts should be made with utmost dedication and a commitment to following the rules of success. When you make small efforts with consistency, you build momentum. Without being able to see huge results in the beginning, you are now moving closer to your goal.

The Power of Commitment

With unwavering commitment, the impossible becomes possible. By embracing a daily rhythm of purposeful actions, you'll cultivate a landscape of positive habits and empowering beliefs. Trust in your potential and your transformative journey, and you'll unlock the doors to remarkable achievements.

The Difference Between Agreement and Commitment

What is the difference between agreeing to do something and committing to do something? An agreement is a legal contract between two or multiple parties, but commitment makes a person emotionally bound to initiate a course of steps regardless of how difficult it is.

The Importance of Emotional Involvement

If you are merely involved in something, there remains an option to skip it at any moment you want to do so. But if you are committed, it means you are supposed to do it at any cost, no matter how much and for what it is.

Examples of Commitment in Indian Culture

As discussed in our previous chapters, Indian culture has several mentions of commitment too as dharma. The concept of "dharma" emphasises the importance of righteousness, living an orderly virtuous life, and staying committed to one's values and principles.

The Gita also teaches us about the importance of detaching oneself from excessive worldly pleasures and living a simple contented life, which can help us avoid the pitfalls of materialism and greediness that result from it.

The Benefits of Commitment

Commitment has numerous benefits in our personal and professional lives. When we are committed to our goals and values, we:

- Build trust with others
- Develop a strong reputation
- Achieve success and advancement in our careers
- Cultivate a positive and respectful work culture
- Experience personal growth and fulfilment

Conclusion

In conclusion, commitment is the secret ingredient to success. By making consistent efforts, embracing a daily rhythm of purposeful actions, and being emotionally involved, you can unlock the doors to remarkable achievements.

Staying true to your word and your values will lead you to a better future. Staying true to your word and your values will lead you to a future filled with integrity and promise.Remember, success is a journey, not a destination. It is a culmination of efforts, strategies, and resilience. So, start your journey today, and let the rhythm of consistent efforts and commitment harmonise your path to greatness.

> *"Commitment is the key that brings you success by connecting all elements to boost inner goals"*

PART 8:

Self-Awareness, Resilience and Courage

8.1. "FACE CHALLENGES HEAD-ON"

Wise men have always said that challenges are growth opportunities. Swami Vivekananda aptly stated:

"We are what our thoughts have made us; so change your thoughts and you change your life."

This profound thought can inspire students, youth and adults alike to develop a positive mindset that can help them to overcome hurdles in their lives. Everyone on the face of this planet has at some point experienced unnecessary stress, nervousness and panic due to events or thoughts that might have triggered those feelings. Understand that these are perfectly normal and when confronted with challenges, we all have two choices: either to stay away or to courageously face them head-on. A person who dares to face and overcome challenges rather than dodging them is the one who steadily moves forward in life.

It's not an easy task to live in this practical world as nobody is free from troubles and stress. Always try to take a clever step in your life. Most of us consider life as easy as it's shown in series and movies. Real life is completely different to the fantasy reel life where the actors get plenty of chances to retake the scenes to perfection. We shouldn't succumb to the stress and fear that comes with challenges, but we should use those situations to reflect upon ourselves and to empower ourselves by bringing in the necessary changes that are needed!

Challenges in life are a gift of our creator; accept it as a blessing and with much gratitude. Let these challenges make you leave your comfort zone. No matter how big or small the challenge is, you should never slip off the path of self-improvement. Each morning gives you a new hope of continuing with your life and a chance to do something better. The only thing you have to do is to grab that opportunity with both your hands and work towards betterment. Let me refer to a quote by Joshua Marine, an American educator, writer and philosopher at this point:

> *"Challenges are what make life interesting.*
> *Overcoming them is what makes them meaningful."*

He emphasises the importance of challenges in giving life significance and purpose.

You can try overcoming small challenges like waking up early in the morning for a regular walk or exercise, or shaking off your bad habits like smoking, consuming unhealthy beverages like alcohol etc. For each individual, challenges and experiences might be different. Imagine your life, without any challenges or a set task of self-improvement at all.

You would wake up late every morning, just to waste your time playing games on your mobile or binge-watching movies. You will not feel any motivation and will try ignoring new opportunities that will come your way. You wouldn't seize any chance of improving your skills, or will never try to know your unique talent that might make you feel more content and happier, or take up new hobbies to enhance the quality of your life.

As we sail through the challenges of life, it's important to remember that *"the only way to do great work is to love what you do"* (Steve Jobs). Cultivating this mindset will help you approach greater difficulties with a positive attitude and find effective solutions to those problems.

Conclusion

As you stand tall in adversity, remember that every obstacle you face is an opportunity to forge your inner strength, build your resilience, and unleash your untapped potential. Grapple with the issue, learn through the experience, and emerge victorious. For it's in the darkest phases of life that we rediscover ourselves and our innermost courage. It is in these adversities that we find our strength to endure, our strong willpower to rise, to prevail over, and to succeed.

So, never run away from these challenges, but confront them with courage and determination, and transform those obstacles into opportunities for our growth and success. This right mindset encourages individuals to view obstacles as opportunities for growth and self-improvement. Ultimately, this approach allows us to find meaning amid struggle, and to emerge stronger, wiser, and more compassionate individuals.

"Courage grows when we confront our fears"

8.2. "DEFEAT *FEAR* - YOUR WORST ENEMY"

A person who has fear instilled deep in them will always be anxious and will continuously overthink any situation he might face. This fear forms as a habit just like how a smoker turns into a chain-smoker. Irrespective of the background, if a person feeds the habit of overthinking, unknowingly his worry will reach the next level of anxiety leading to stress, tension and panic attacks. The most surprising thing is that this situation is created by people themselves out of their negative thoughts about the outcome and the people around them. Being sceptical, they tend to lie unnecessarily which is mostly quite evident, out of their fear of being used or abused.

Fear is like an uninvited guest which sits in our brain making sceptical decisions for us and making us incapable of thinking logically and straight. This can transform a person who is capable of thinking wisely, to get annoyed most of the time and will even respond to people in a way which won't make sense. This is because their fearful mind will always give them advice based on their sceptical views about others. Even if they want to get rid of the fear, it will follow them anywhere and everywhere to show their superiority over them. Now these people will have to follow its instructions in such a way that they become its 'permanent slave' and the fear becomes their ' master.'

Now this fear is very different from the fear and respect we have towards our creator. The fear of God is our adherence to the standards that God is believed to have set for us so that we can live in peace and with mutual respect. Some people do not naturally seek to honour God, as it's their sins, greed and insecurity that lead them to fear God. They never truly love or respect him.

Do you know that some techniques can help us get rid of anxiety and fear? The first thing is to accept the fact that nobody is perfect in this world, so chill and take people as they are. Change the way you think about life too as it's full of challenges and possibilities too. Think about your worst fear and what steps you will consider initiating to resolve it.

Take some time every day to practice meditation as it will bring peace and happiness in your mind. Do the activities that excite you and step out for a walk or jog every day. Sometimes you need to master yourself to overcome the thoughts that make you feel fear and anxiety.

Keeping yourself busy but calm will transform you into a much more positive and practical person. It will keep you away from the stage of unwanted thoughts of why you are on this earth and so on.

The most extreme degree of fear is what we call to be terrified. In many cases, being terrified, afraid, frightened, alarmed, scared etc. shows the different degrees of fear based on the situation that you might face. When a child is born, he starts his journey of life with the very first cry and the discomfort of being pulled out into this world. From the moment he is born, he gets bonded to the cycle of pain, discomfort, fear and anxiety.

Conclusion

Every person who has to live in this world of responsibilities will surely experience anxiety and fear. One should cultivate in oneself the power of improvising the worst habits and building the best positive qualities at the same time. It should be the responsibility and commitment of every person to utilize this positive energy.

Remember that a pleasant and happy life always has a dark shade on the other end. It's just like two faces of a coin, different yet important to add value. The one who is supposed to be happy might have another sort of fear and worry that will snatch away the beauty of their present happiness. It's this state of inaction and not willingness to change that creates many more problems in one's life. So stay clear of fear and anxiety as it has the power to control and drag your mind to an insane

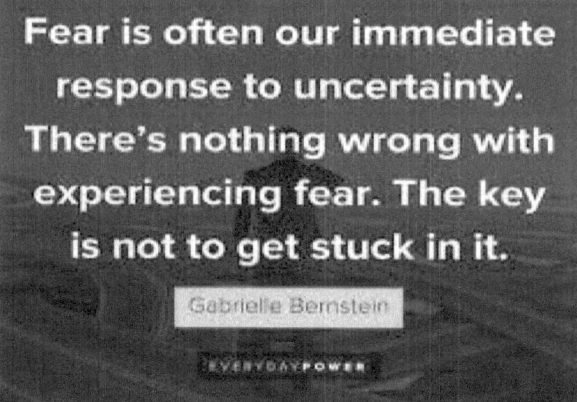

state!

> *"People want everything they like;*
> *fear snatches everything they need"*

8.3. "ELIMINATE SELF-DOUBT"

Self-doubt is a harmful thought pattern that makes us question our abilities, doubt our decisions, and lose confidence in ourselves.

In many situations, we confuse ourselves about whether an assigned task will be completed or not. Have you ever thought about why self-doubt arises? The seeds for these problems can be planted in our early life.

Some examples of these include:

- **Lack of emotional support**: Inadequate emotional support from guardians can lead to mental trauma where the children feel uncertain or insecure about themselves.
- **Parental rejection**: Constant criticism or negative feedback can lead to feeling uncertain and insecure about the present and future.
- **Comparison with others**: Comparing children with their siblings can weaken their confidence and self-worth.
- **Bad experiences**: Bad events such as bullying, abuse or neglect can notably impact a child's identity and lead to self-doubt.
- **Negative self-talk**: Children may adopt negative self-talk patterns from the environment they live in, leading to a lack of confidence.
- **Unhealthy attachment patterns**: An anxious or avoidant attachment can lead to uncertainty about oneself.

The Causes of Self-Doubt

So, what causes self-doubt? Is it a lack of confidence, a fear of failure, or something deeper?

The truth is that self-doubt can arise from a multitude of factors, including:
- A lack of clear goals and direction
- Poor time management and prioritisation
- Negative self-talk and self-criticism
- Fear of failure and fear of success
- Lack of self-awareness and self-acceptance

The Consequences of Self-Doubt

Self-doubt can have far-reaching consequences on our lives. It can:
- Prevent us from achieving our dreams and goals
- Hold us back from taking risks and stepping out of our comfort zones
- Lead to anxiety, depression, and other mental health issues
- Damage our relationships and reputation
- Limit our imagination and originality

Eliminating Self-Doubt

So, how can we eliminate self-doubt and unlock our full potential? Here are a few strategies:
- Practice self-awareness and self-acceptance
- Set clear goals and priorities
- Develop a growth mindset and embrace challenges
- Surround yourself with positive and supportive people
- Practice mindfulness and self-compassion

Conclusion

In conclusion, self-doubt is a common obstacle that can hold us back from achieving our goals and realising our potential. However, by understanding the causes of self-doubt, recognising its consequences, and implementing strategies to eliminate it, we can break free from self-doubt and step into a brighter tomorrow.

"Believe in yourself, eliminate self-doubt, and achieve greatness"

8.4. "SHAPE YOUR FORTUNE"

Shaping your fortune means taking control of your life and destiny, and actively working to create the future you always desired for. It implies that your fate is not simply predetermined, but rather it's something that is completely in your control and you can mould and shape it whichever way you want it through your choices, actions, and decisions. Our creator will always support you if you are willing to support yourself and walk the path of hard work and righteousness.

Most people forget their role towards uplifting themselves during tough times. You don't need to always have control over the issues that befall you, but you have the power to fight it off and deliver your best. Don't ever get disappointed if you are unsuccessful despite your continuous efforts. Remember that every failure brings you closer to success, and every setback is an opportunity for us to learn and come back even stronger, more robust and wiser. So never fear failure.

Whenever something wrong happens in your life, you might feel that it's your fate or destiny which is beyond your power and control. Most people of all races think that we as humans are essentially powerless and helpless before our fate or fortune and leave the matter as if it is irreversible. From a practical and much more realistic angle, this concept has been proven to be a great mistake one can make. The actions and inactions that a person takes or refuses to take will rather decide his fate. With repeated efforts and determination, you can turn a failing venture into a successful one or a losing game into a winning one.

Failure is life's greatest teacher, and it's your decision if you want to learn and pay attention to it or not. If you have a close study of most of the famous thinkers from the past, you'll realize that being exposed to failure was not an unusual idea. So come out of your comfort zone, evaluate your strengths and weaknesses, and never stop believing in yourself.

Various people have shaped their fortunes through hard work, determination, and a willingness to take risks. Oprah Winfrey is one such person who tops my list when it comes to the power of building oneself up after countless struggles. She is a self-made media mogul, who inspired many with her story of overcoming adversity and has built a brand around empowerment and personal growth.

Conclusion

Maintaining a positive attitude and a fearless mindset are considered the most important pillars of success. The first step is to develop a positive mindset, which allows you to gain valuable insights from any situation and the courage to stay determined. Always try to find ways to work on your abilities and your weaknesses too. For this, you don't have to visit an astrologer or a tarot card reader to know your future as you are the creator of your destiny.

It depends upon you whether you want to construct it or destroy it! It's very easy and takes no effort to jeopardize your future. You can choose to be your saviour or destroyer! So it's important to recognize the signs of self-destruction and take corrective action before it's too late. In the end, only you can save yourself from the darkness of regret, transforming your struggles into stepping stones for success while setting examples for others too.

As you are on the journey to shape your destiny, remember that the power to create the life you desire lies within you. With determination, resilience, and a willingness to learn from your mistakes, you can transform your dreams into reality. Don't let fear or doubt hold you back, for every obstacle is an opportunity to grow stronger and wiser. Believe in yourself, stay focused, and keep moving forward- your fortune awaits, and the world is ready to witness your triumph.

"Believe In Yourself To Shape Your Fortune."

8.5. "HAVE COURAGE TO TAKE ACTION"

This chapter mainly focuses on the importance of being positive and hopeful in every aspect of life. Having a positive attitude towards life and being hopeful helps in our overall well-being. It encourages us to be persistent and to keep trying, even during major setbacks in life.

What does being hopeful mean and how do we overcome the fear of failure?

Hope is the light that guides us through life's difficulties and challenges. It's the spark that ignites our strength, helping us overcome hurdles to achieve our dreams. Hope is not just a feeling or a thought; it's a choice that we make - a mindset that we cultivate to be focused, through being at peace.

By choosing hope, we open ourselves up to a world of chances and possibilities, which can empower us to transform obstacles into opportunities, and challenges into catalysts for growth and progress.

In short, it's a positive state of mind that guides us forward every day and teaches us to keep moving no matter what the circumstances are at present. Practice this state of mind and you'll see that every day will bring you new opportunities with great ideas to keep you moving forward.

Imagine you are on a hike, and the trail ahead seems uncertain. You can choose to focus on the darkness and fear the unknown, or you can look for the glimmer of light in the distance, guiding you forward. That glimmer is hope. When we choose hope, we open ourselves up to possibilities and opportunities.

We begin to see challenges as stepping stones to success, rather than roadblocks. With hope, we're more resilient, more determined, and more likely to achieve our goals.

Let's say you are facing a difficult exam, be it a competitive exam like NEET. Instead of feeling overwhelmed, you should enjoy the process of preparing yourself and experience the work and effort you need to put in. You should believe in your ability to learn and grow and trust that you'll do your best. With this hopeful mindset, you can approach the exam with courage and purpose.

Simple Words to Live By:
- Believe in your capabilities and abilities.
- Practice self-care.
- Learn from past mistakes of yours and others.
- Focus on the positive aspects of a situation.
- Dream big but achievable tasks and work towards them.
- Share your vision with other prospective people.
- Grow your skills and knowledge.
- Forgive yourself first for your past mistakes.
- Trust that everything will work out well in the end.
- Take small and calculated steps persistently to reach your goals.
- Surround yourself with uplifting, encouraging and positive people.

Conclusion

Being hopeful helps us to see challenges and difficulties as opportunities to learn rather than treating them as mere failures or setbacks. The right mindset of hope can help one to relieve stress and depression in adverse situations. In conclusion, hope is a powerful tool that can transform our lives. By choosing hope, we can overcome fear, doubt, and uncertainty that live deep inside our minds.

We can achieve our dreams, grow as individuals, and live a positive life filled with purpose and meaning. So, let's choose hope today, practice it every day, and watch our lives get transformed in amazing ways. Let's hold faith, nurture a positive attitude, and trust that nature will conspire to make our dreams a reality, leading us down a path of purpose, fulfillment and endless joy.

"Hope, a powerful tool to overcome challenges"

8.6. "DESTROY YOUR INFLATED EGO"

This chapter would likely encourage readers to challenge their self-perceptions, overcome self-doubt, and develop a more growth-oriented mindset to achieve their goals. Remember the quote by Albert Einstein:

"The greatest illusion in this world is the illusion of separation."

Do you often compare yourself to others, feel jealous, or criticise others to feel superior? If so, you're not alone. Our ego can be a major obstacle to achieving our goals and fulfilling lives. In this chapter, we'll explore the reasons that lead to ego and how letting go of it can be liberating.

What is Ego?

Our ego is our perceived sense of self. It's the story we tell ourselves about who we are, what we're capable of, and how we fit into this world. However, this story can be limiting and often inaccurate.

The Dangers of an Inflated Ego

When our ego becomes inflated, we start to believe our hype. We become critical of others, compare ourselves to those around us, and feel superior. This can lead to:

- Jealousy and resentment towards others
- A constant need for validation and recognition
- Difficulty in forming meaningful relationships
- A lack of self-awareness and personal growth

Letting Go of Ego

So, how do we let go of our ego and start living a more authentic life?

- Practice self-awareness: Take time to reflect on your thoughts, feelings, and actions. Recognize when your ego is taking over you and try to let it go.
- Understand others with compassion: Instead of comparing yourself to others, try to focus on their strengths and weaknesses. Practice empathy and compassion.
- Practice gratitude: Focus on the things you're grateful for, rather than dwelling on your accomplishments.
- Embrace your uniqueness: Recognize that you're unique and special and that your worth isn't defined by any external validation.

Conclusion

Letting go of our ego can often be challenging, but it's altogether a rewarding experience. By practising self-awareness, empathy, gratitude, and embracing our uniqueness, we can start to live a more authentic and fulfilling life. Remember, your worth isn't defined by your inflated ego – it's defined by who you are as a person.

Key Takeaways:

- Recognise the dangers of an inflated ego
- Practice self-awareness and let go of ego-driven thoughts and behaviours.
- Focus on others and cultivate empathy and compassion.
- Embrace your uniqueness; your worth isn't defined by external validation.

"Free yourself from ego's grip"

8.7. "ELIMINATE NEGATIVE COMPLEXES"

Through this chapter, let's understand what complexes are, how they can affect our minds and behaviour, and know certain ways we can eliminate them. Complex in the psychological term, means a group of feelings, thoughts and experiences that pre-exist in a person's mind which subconsciously influence the way he behaves. Complexes are the hurdles that can easily stop you from enjoying your real life.

Complexes can be categorized into two main types: Inferiority Complex and Superiority Complex. Both can be damaging to our mental health and well-being.

Inferiority Complex

An inferiority complex is a feeling of inadequacy in oneself or having low self-esteem. It can cause us to feel hopeless, frustrated, and socially distant from others. This complex can be particularly damaging as it can obstruct our ability to achieve our goals and reach our full potential.

Superiority Complex

A superiority complex, on the other hand, is a belief that we are better than others. This complex can cause us to feel arrogant and disconnected from others. In the society we live in, most people who lead a luxurious life are filled with such kinds of thoughts. They feel themselves as the most blessed and accomplished ones.

Sometimes such people compare themselves with the less privileged class and feel overly proud of their achievements. If someone achieves success in a comparatively short time in their career, they may feel superior and more talented. They will find ways to be rude or disrespectful to those who disagree with them.

The Impact of Complexes

Complexes can have a significant impact on our mental health and well-being:

- Depression and Anxiety or acting weird.
- Low self-esteem or over-confidence
- Social isolation or disconnection from people they consider as less accomplished.
- Negative thoughts and self-doubt or perceived self-importance.

Breaking Free from Complexes

So, how can we break free from these limiting complexes? Here are a few strategies:

- **Practice self-awareness**: Recognise when you're feeling inadequate or superior.
- **Challenge negative thoughts**: Replace negative self-talk with positive affirmations.
- **Focus on your strengths**: Celebrate your achievements and strengths.
- **Seek support**: Surround yourself with positive and supportive people.

Conclusion

Breaking free from complexes requires constant effort and dedication, but believe me, it's worth it. By practising self-awareness, blocking negative thoughts, focusing on our strengths, working on our skills and seeking support, we can overcome these limiting complexes and reach our highest potential.

Key Takeaways:

- Recognise the impact of complexes on our mental health and well-being.
- Practice self-awareness and challenge negative thoughts.

- Focus on your strengths and celebrate your achievements.
- Seek support from positive and supportive people.
- Break free from complexes and reach your true potential.

"Break free, be great, and achieve your dreams"

8.8. "BE PASSIONATE WITHOUT GREED"

In this chapter, we will see why working with passion without any greed brings joy and satisfaction in life. Being passionate about something is the positive desire you possess which can help you achieve higher positions and achievements in that particular area of your interest. A man of desire will always enjoy doing things with unparalleled integrity and passion. He will be happy with what he has at that moment and will be very much satisfied with his achievements. He will always look for ways to search for a chance for the construction of a better tomorrow without hampering his present.

Do passion and greed give us the same amount of satisfaction and results?

There have always been confusions between passion and greed especially when in some situations where people find it extremely difficult to differentiate between the two. So what exactly is greed? It's an extreme expression of ambitions and desires as it takes away the happiness of the present. It is because of myths and beliefs that people started thinking that for them to be happy, they need to gain everything in their lives. It makes a person compare himself with others without knowing his worth and merit.

One negative trait that greed brings is that it compels man to take even wrong and unfair steps to gain something that he desires. Such planning and shortcut wrong methods will make him violate honesty, sincerity and integrity in his life. He may not be bothered or worried about the negative impacts or consequences that it might bring to him and his family.

At this stage of greediness, he will start being imprudent and irrational to others. All these will create a situation where he will prove to be a man of selfishness, a disastrous monster with no soul and a man of no honour or character. His inflated ego and pride won't let him accept the fact and he becomes scared to face any criticism or failures.

You can enjoy success, money and fame without compromising your standards and morals. There's nothing wrong with getting rich or famous, but you should be careful not to lose your goodness and without selling your soul. Let's look at a writer's career as an example! Let's say a passionate writer makes his income primarily from writing articles on a website where the readers are charged 100 rupees a month to read any article or news feed on that website.

This writer might have to spend 6-7 years working on his writing skills on that particular platform to earn a good decent amount. But as he enjoys his work as a writer, he doesn't feel guilty of getting advantage and making money out of it.

As he spent so much time and effort cultivating his writing skills, he doesn't feel bad about charging his readers. On the contrary, he will feel more satisfied about sharing his knowledge and experiences with his readers and getting benefited too at the same time.

There are a few things to keep in mind to be successful without having to compromise on your morality.

- **Enjoy the things you do and do the things you enjoy:**
  - When someone hates the thing they do for a living, that's when we say that they've sold their soul.
  - Try finding the right things that you enjoy doing the most. Soon you will see yourself getting good at it and mastering it for a living.
- **Live an honest life:**
  - Never cheat, lie, swindle and boast to earn a living.
  - You will never feel good about it yourself and will lose credibility and create trust issues with people.
  - Take the right and honest path and you will never feel guilty of your actions.

- **Understand right from wrong:**
    - Some people say that being wealthy and successful means being greedy. Never fall for this myth. Those people are hypocrites who wear modesty masks over their greediness and fool the public. Wealth can be acquired through hard work and honesty.
    - Always know right from wrong and take steps after analysing carefully so that the step you are about to take makes sense and doesn't cause trouble to yourself or others.

Greed is an offspring of the illusion of control and resistance to many things. One cannot give up this negativity until one stops lingering on the materialistic side of things and sees that life can be out of their control. In other words, they need to realise that they can't always acquire and keep things their way, no matter what strategy they come up with.

What can a person be greedy about? He can be greedy about his wealth and possessions, his power, looks, interests, or any other things that satisfy or stroke his egoistic mind. One, who leaves greed and ego and keeps the desire for his self-survival, will eventually become a better and reformed person.

When someone does not have greed, he begins to see opportunities in abundance rather than scarcity, which leads him to less competition and stress on himself. That's when he experiences the process to be more satisfying and enjoyable. He begins to create a win-win situation by competing with himself. The universe supports those people who can discard their ego and greed to help themselves and others.

> *"You have succeeded in life when all you really want is only what you really need"*
>
> **Vernon Howard**

Conclusion

It's mostly the greed that crushes a man's happiness and his ego that results in him losing everything. Never come into any influence of people who force you to do so. You can prove yourself to be a better person if you give up your unwanted greed and negativity. Give up these negative traits and you will see yourself again as the happiest person on this planet. In the end, it is not the intensity of our desires that defines us, but the intensity of our pursuits. To be passionate without greed is to embrace our ambitions with a sense of purpose, not possession.

It is to drive forward with dedication, yet stay unbound by the limits of aspiration. By cultivating this balance, we can transform our passions into a powerful force that inspires, influences and uplift others, rather than merely serving our interests. In this way, we can truly make a meaningful impact, leaving behind a trail of positivity that echoes far beyond our accomplishments.

"Pursue excellence with dedication, not domination"

8.9. "VALUE GENUINE ADVICE"

Honest people don't care much about pleasing people or being popular. They are mostly straight-forwards who do not believe in speaking what's just desirable. They will stand up for what they believe in, even if others don't tolerate to hear it. They know that telling the truth and being genuine is the right thing to do, regardless of the implications it might bring upon them or their image. Honesty is considered an important element in developing trust and strong relationships.

Honesty means being transparent and real in your words and actions and expressing truthfully without deceit or pretence. It also involves expressing and conveying your thoughts and feelings sincerely. If you uphold honesty and integrity, you can create the foundation of trust and mutual respect. Everyone likes to give advice, but few manage to give the honest one.

Just try asking one and there will be thousands ready to offer! The easiest and cheapest thing to offer someone in this world is advice, so why those can't be offered genuinely? There is nothing more precious than the sincere advice of a well-wisher, who honestly cares and thinks of uplifting you. If you receive new ideas from these people, analyse if they fit right for your circumstances and execute them well into your life. Someone's insightful and impartial advice based on their own experience is something to be highly valued.

There was some advice we always used to hear from the elders in our family. They used to say that the advice of elders and experienced people is like biting a gooseberry! It will taste bitter at first, but will turn sweeter later! Those elders achieved their ability to advice through their own good and bad life experiences. You should always be careful when passing on any advice to others and make sure that they are receiving the best and most impartial advice they will ever get. It is advisable not to pass any unnecessary judgement and unwarranted advice, unless and until they seek you out for an honest opinion. This can avoid unnecessary heartaches, fights or the risk of being misunderstood later on.

Nothing in this world is harder than speaking the truth, nothing is easier than flattery. Sometimes it's very difficult to speak the truth while being trapped in a most unfavorable situation. It's very difficult for any person not to favour lying if it poses a considerable threat to his own life! But some people stay honest during those situations too.

We should have that sensitivity to know how and when to speak our minds while giving valuable advice. If you hold emotional honesty with yourself, you will always try to be honest in your opinion and advice to others too. Also, try to be honest with yourself by accepting constructive criticism from others when needed. 'Honesty is the best policy' is a popular term that was taught to us during our childhood days.

You should discuss and reinforce these qualities to the coming generations too by demonstrating them throughout your life and by setting good examples. They should be taught about the benefits of staying sincere and truthful, irrespective of how bad the situation may appear to be. This is my personal opinion that the world's biggest sinners are those people who speak words that will calm your heart, and then discreetly talk behind your back! Everyone wants to know the truth, but few manage to say it. So, honesty is an expensive gift. Don't expect it from malignant people!

Honesty is considered as highest of all human values as it brings respect for the person who holds it. Self-discipline is among the factors which describe a person who lives with high morals and compassion. Sometimes you lose your morals and wrong things seep into your mind. In this condition, you need to bring back the past lost values such as honesty, integrity, faithfulness, loyalty, manners, responsibility, commitment, reliability, etc.

By embracing all elements, you can lead a meaningful life. Success is the outcome of all aforementioned elements. Let us all strive to be more honest in our thoughts, words, and actions because truly honest people are incredibly strong and courageous! The moral ethics of a person is known through honesty.

> *"Where there's a value for honest advice,*
> *there is a reliable way to solutions"*

8.10. "MASTER THE ART OF SELF-REFLECTION"

There are different perceptions of looking at your life. Some people look at it as a battlefield while for others it's merely a playground. For some, it's a garden of thorns, whereas for others it's a mixture of thorns and flowers. Some consider life as a long series of problems; some take it as a challenge. It varies from person to person by judging it from their experience. Thus we cannot say that one's understanding of life is common or silly, but it's very meaningful.

The lives of great men and women who have tasted success after facing life's difficulties with much courage, demonstrate that the most effective way to approach life is by viewing it as a mental barrier that can easily be overcome.

In other words, self-reflection is the process of looking within yourself to understand your thoughts, feelings, and actions. It's like taking a step back to examine your life, values, and goals.

The Importance of Self-Reflection

Have you ever thought of the importance of self-reflection and introspection? How insight into life can lead to personal growth and transformation. For this, you have to understand your values and beliefs.

Understanding Your Values and Beliefs

You can explore your core values and beliefs through:

- Identifying what matters most to you in life.
- Examining your assumptions and beliefs.
- Aligning your actions with your values and beliefs.

Let's consider Pooja, a marketing research analyst who is highly creative and likes to have a work-life balance.

Through much introspection and self-reflection, she soon realizes that her current job role is not giving her any opportunity to use her creative side and is demanding long hours. She decides to move into a job role that well aligns with her values, giving her much work satisfaction and quality time for herself and her family.

Recognizing Your Strengths and Weaknesses

To acknowledge your strengths and weaknesses:

- Celebrate your positive qualities and skills.
- Face your weaknesses and work on areas for improvement.
- Use self-awareness to make positive changes.

A young entrepreneur Kiran, recognises his strengths in innovation and leadership. However, he also acknowledges his weakness in time management. Through much self-reflection, he develops strategies to improve his time management skills, leading to increased productivity and efficiency at work.

Exploring Your Passions and Purpose

Discover what brings you joy and fulfillment:

- Examine your sense of purpose and meaning.
- Align your passions and purpose with your goals and actions.

Kripa, a software engineer, through self-reflection, realises she is more passionate about environmental conservation. She begins to volunteer for environmental organizations and eventually transitions to a role that combines her technical skills with her passion for conservation.

Understanding Your Relationships

Furthermore, examine your relationships with others:

- Identify positive and negative patterns.
- Nurture healthy relationships and set boundaries.

Through introspection, Mahesh the manager, recognizes that his micromanaging style is damaging his reputation and relationships with his team members. So he makes a conscious effort to delegate the tasks and put trust in the team, leading to improved collaboration and productivity.

Embracing Your Emotions and Vulnerability

Finally, acknowledge and accept your emotions:
- Practice vulnerability and openness.
- Use emotional intelligence to improve relationships and decision-making.

Let's look at the case of Disha, a leader, who learns to recognize and express her emotions healthily. After working on those weaknesses, she becomes more approachable and empathetic, fostering stronger relationships with her colleagues and stakeholders.

Conclusion

Mastering the art of self-reflection is a powerful tool for personal growth and transformation. By exploring your values, strengths, passions, relationships, and emotions, you can unlock the power of insight and self-awareness. Remember, self-reflection is not a one-time event, but a continuous process that requires patience, courage, and commitment.

Key Takeaways:
- Self-reflection is essential for personal growth and transformation.
- Explore your values, strengths, passions, relationships, and emotions.
- Use self-awareness to make positive changes in your life.
- Practice vulnerability, openness, and emotional intelligence.

- Mastering the art of self-reflection is a continuous process that requires patience, courage, and commitment.

"A mirror's reflection is a call to action"

uplift others, rather than merely serving our own interests. In this way, we can truly make a meaningful impact, leaving behind a trail of positivity that echoes far beyond our own accomplishments.

"Pursue excellence with dedication, not domination"

PART 9:

Leadership, Teamwork and Empowerment

9.1. "BE PRUDENT BUT DIPLOMATIC"

Here in this chapter, we'll explore the importance of being prudent and diplomatic in our interactions with others. We'll discuss how to navigate complex situations tactfully and with grace, and how to build strong relationships through effective communication.

> *"Diplomacy is the art of telling people to go to hell in such a way that they ask for directions."*
>
> **Winston Churchill**

Prudence is your ability to know what is to be done and what is to be avoided in a particular situation. It can be described as your qualities that enable you to make certain judgements and decisions so that you can take fair steps to avoid unnecessary risks. People who are imprudent and indiscreet definitely will fall from one mistake to another without gaining much from their lives.

So it's the way of thinking before taking any action that makes you prudent. You should be very careful what you speak, how you say it, the moment you speak and to whom you are communicating with. Being very careful means to think or pay attention to your thoughts before you speak out.

Many times, people prove themselves imprudent by saying something that is not sensible or carefully thought out. Similarly, you should think about the consequences before taking any action. The difference between those who win and those who lose is in the application of prudence and wisdom.

You should have a practical approach to life and its problems. A wrong step taken without much care and thought can be a threatening one. You should have a deep analysis of the situation; try to understand the consequences thereafter. Sometimes an easy solution is the best option for all.

Let's look at what diplomacy is. Diplomacy is the skill of dealing with any situation without upsetting or offending someone. When you are diplomatic and tactful, you can be a lot more honest with direct feedback, expressing your opinions and views without annoying others. The diplomacy in your life depends upon your ability to find an easy but most powerful way to sort out the problems.

Sometimes you have to amend your approach wisely. In workplaces, being able to get on with anyone and be able to manage and maintain good working relationships, yet putting out your concerns in a tactical way is a much desirable trait to possess. You can express your opinion without offending anyone by being diplomatic.

You can make good relationships with a wider range of colleagues and can make your time a lot more enjoyable there. Thus, you have to practice diplomacy at work so that you can advance your career, be desirable and appreciated by more people, build better relationships and be more professional. Diplomacy at work is not like manipulating people but it's like packaging your message in a more palatable form.

Conclusion

Most of the youngsters these days don't keep a practical approach towards life. They think that the problems that they face will remain forever and refrain from doing anything about it. Some are very impulsive that they say and do things without considering the consequences it can bring along. Remember, a wrong step taken without much care and thought can be very threatening.

You should understand your problems on time and should discuss them with your elders for a better solution. You should try to understand how the diplomats play a key role in improving the relations of our country with other foreign countries.

In the same way, you should be diplomatic in your daily interactions with people and your activities. The diplomacy in your life depends on your ability to find a genuine but easy and the most powerful way to sort out the problems. Sometimes, you have to amend it wisely according to the situation you are in.

"A prudent word, diplomatic actions lead you to a brighter future"

9.2. "JOURNEY TOWARDS PERFECTION"

As the age-old adage goes, "Practice makes perfect." But have we ever stopped to ponder what perfection truly means? Is it an attainable goal, or is it merely a fantasy? In today's fast-paced world, it's easy to get caught up in the hustle and bustle of daily life and lose sight of what's truly important. As Indians, we're often encouraged to strive for excellence, but what does that mean?

The Pursuit of Excellence vs. Perfection

Excellence is the attempt to do something to the best of one's ability. It's a noble pursuit that encourages us to strive for greatness. On the other hand, perfection is the definitive 100% right way of performing a task. While excellence is achievable, perfection is often an unattainable goal. However, it's the pursuit of perfection that drives us to be better, to innovate, and to push beyond our limitations.

The Modern Generation's Approach to Perfection

In today's world, it's easy to get caught up in the idea of "good enough." We're often more focused on completing tasks quickly rather than doing them perfectly. This approach can lead to a lack of dedication, sincerity, and quality in our work. As a result, we miss out on the opportunity to truly excel and make a meaningful impact.

The Importance of Striving for Perfection

Aspire yourself for perfection means:
- Setting a high standard goal
- Feeling better than yesterday
- Setting a positive example for others
- Improving yourself is a steady process

- Striving for excellence in all aspects of life
- Pursuing precision, accuracy, and perfectionism
- Embodying excellence in character, virtue, and morals

So, why is it important to strive for perfection? As Vernor Steffan Vinge so eloquently put it:

> *"Embrace the pursuit of perfection, where the journey itself is a destination"*

When we strive for perfection, we're not just improving ourselves, we're also inspiring others to do the same. This pursuit ignites a spark that sets off a chain reaction of growth, innovation, and progress.

Key Takeaways
- Striving for perfection means setting high standards and continuously improving ourselves.
- It's a journey, not a destination, and it's the pursuit itself that's truly valuable.
- When we strive for perfection, we inspire others to do the same, leading to a ripple effect of growth and innovation.
- Embodying excellence in character, virtue, and morals is just as important as striving for perfection in our actions.

In conclusion, the pursuit of perfection is a noble and worthwhile goal. While it may be unattainable, it's the journey itself that's truly valuable. By striving for perfection, we can unlock our full potential, inspire others, and make a meaningful impact on the world.

> *"Perfection is the pursuit of excellence, not the attainment of it"*

9.3. "TAKE A HELL-BENT RESOLUTION"

We're no strangers to the concept of resolutions. Whether it's a New Year's resolution or a promise to ourselves to make a change, we've all been there. But have you ever stopped to think about what it truly means to take a resolution? Is it just a casual promise to ourselves, or is it something more?

In today's fast-paced world, it's easy to get caught up in the hustle and bustle of daily life and lose sight of what's truly important. But when we take a hell-bent resolution, we're making a powerful commitment to ourselves to achieve our goals. It's a declaration of unwavering determination, uncompromising passion, and unrelenting dedication.

The Power of Hell-Bent Resolution

So, what does it mean to take a hell-bent resolution? It means being willing to put in the hard work and effort required to achieve our goals. It means being unwavering in the face of obstacles and challenges, and staying committed even when faced with setbacks.

When we make a hell-bent resolution, we're not just making a promise to ourselves – we're committing to our future. We're declaring that we're willing to do whatever it takes to achieve our goals and that we won't let anything stand in our way.

The Key to Achieving Success

So, how can we take a hell-bent resolution and make it a reality? The key is to choose our goals wisely and go after them with unrelenting determination. It means being clear about what we want to achieve and making a plan to get there. It means being willing to put in the hard work and effort required to achieve our goals, and staying committed even when faced with setbacks.

In conclusion, taking a hell-bent resolution is a powerful way to unlock our full potential and achieve our goals. By choosing our goals wisely and going after them with unrelenting determination, we can achieve remarkable things and create our own success stories.

"Continuous effort makes the impossible possible"

9.4. "MAKE HARD WORK YOUR MOTTO"

In the journey of life, success is the ultimate destination that we all strive for. But have you ever wondered what sets apart those who achieve greatness from those who don't? The answer lies in the power of hard work. As the saying goes:

> *"Success comes to those who are willing to sacrifice to reach worthwhile goals."*

In India, we have many examples of individuals who have achieved greatness through sheer hard work and determination. From the likes of Mahatma Gandhi to Sachin Tendulkar, each of these individuals has demonstrated that success is not just a matter of luck, but rather a result of consistent effort and perseverance.

The Importance of Self-Esteem

Self-esteem is a critical factor in achieving success. Believing in oneself, one's abilities and one's worth is essential to overcoming obstacles and staying motivated. As the saying goes, "Believe you can do it, believe you will get it, believe you deserve it, and believe in yourself." When we have faith in ourselves, we're more likely to take risks, push beyond our comfort zones, and strive for excellence.

The Spider's Web: A Lesson in Strategic Hard Work

The story of the spider's web is a powerful metaphor that highlights the importance of strategic hard work. While some people chase after fleeting opportunities, others build a foundation that will attract success to them. The rich and successful often have the qualities of spiders, working hard to build assets that will generate wealth and prosperity.

Breaking Down Barriers to Success

While hard work is essential to achieving success, it's not the only factor. Access to education, opportunities, resources, and support systems can also play a critical role in determining one's success ratio.

Unfortunately, systemic barriers can prevent individuals from achieving their full potential.

However, by acknowledging these barriers and seeking out support, we can overcome them and achieve our goals.

Conclusion

In conclusion, setting hard work as your motto is the key to unlocking success. By combining consistent effort with strategic planning, self-esteem, and a willingness to overcome obstacles, we can achieve greatness and realize our dreams. So, let us adopt the motto of hard work and make it our guiding principle in the pursuit of success.

"Walk the path of hard work, success will surely follow"

9.5. "STICK TO YOUR WORK ETHIC"

Success is not a destination, but a journey that requires hard work, dedication, and perseverance. It is a culmination of efforts, sacrifices, and a strong work ethic. In this chapter, we will explore the importance of sticking to your work ethic and how it can lead to achieving your goals and realising your dreams.

Hard Work and Determination

Success stories of great men and women are a testament to the power of hard work and determination. They did not achieve greatness by being idle or waiting for opportunities to come their way. Instead, they worked tirelessly, day and night, with a laser-sharp focus on their goals. Hard work with purpose and determination can bring about significant changes in one's life.

Self-Esteem: The Strongest Factor of Success

Self-esteem is the strongest factor that predicts success. If one has belief in oneself, one's abilities, and one's worth, he will be destined to achieve great things. It is this confidence that allows one to achieve his goals and overcome obstacles. Self-esteem is not just about feeling good about oneself, but also about being willing to take risks, face challenges, and learn from failures.

The Power of Obedience

Obedience is a vital aspect of maintaining a strong work ethic. It is about adhering to established protocols, respecting authority, and prioritising collective success. Obedience is not just about following rules but also about being accountable, responsible, and committed to one's work. It is about being obedient to oneself, one's values, and one's principles.

Lessons from the Past

The story of Ekalavya, a character from the epic Mahabharata, is a great example of obedience and dedication. Ekalavya was a student who learned archery by himself, but he was also obedient to his virtual teacher, Dronacharya. He practised archery with consistency and dedication, and his obedience and hard work made him a great archer.

The Importance of Punctuality and Obedience

Punctuality and obedience are essential qualities that can unlock blessings and success in one's life. It's about being on time, meeting deadlines, and being accountable for one's actions. It also involves being obedient to oneself, one's values, and one's principles.

Conclusion

In conclusion, sticking to your work ethic is crucial for achieving success and realizing your dreams. It is about hard work, determination, self-esteem, obedience, and punctuality. It is about being committed to one's goals, values, and principles. By incorporating these qualities into one's life, one can unlock their full potential and achieve greatness.

Key Takeaways

- Hard work and determination are essential for achieving success.
- Self-esteem is the strongest factor of success.
- Obedience is vital for maintaining a strong work ethic.
- Punctuality and obedience can unlock blessings and success in one's life.
- Sticking to your work ethic requires commitment, accountability, and responsibility.

"Be obedient even when you don't know where obedience may lead you"

9.6. "MOVE TOWARDS EMPOWERMENT"

Empowerment is a state of mind, a feeling of confidence, capability, and control over one's life. It is the power to make choices, set boundaries, and achieve goals. The journey to empowerment is a path of self-discovery, progress, and improvement.

In this chapter, we will explore the concept of empowerment, unlocking inner strength, and the ways to achieve it.

What is Empowerment?

Empowerment is not just about feeling powerful; it is about being in control of one's life. It is the ability to make decisions, take actions, and shape one's destiny.

Empowerment is a state of being that allows individuals to live a life that is authentic, values-driven, and meaningful.

Unlocking Inner Strength

Unlocking inner strength is the key to empowerment. It is the ability to cope with challenges, bounce back from failures, and stay true to oneself.

Inner strength is not just about being resilient but about being aware of one's thoughts, emotions, and values. It is the process of tapping into one's potential, overcoming uncertainties, and developing a stronger sense of self.

Ways to Unlock Inner Strength

So, how can you unlock your inner strength? Here are some ways:

- Build strong emotional intelligence and awareness: Understand your emotions, values, and thoughts. Recognize your strengths and weaknesses.

- Cultivate positive relationships: Surround yourself with people who support and encourage you.
- Nurture a sense of purpose and meaning: Discover your passions and values. Align your life with your purpose.

The Benefits of Unlocking Inner Strength

When you unlock your inner strength, you can:
- Develop a stronger sense of self and identity: You will be more confident, self-assured, and authentic.
- Build confidence: You will be able to leverage your strengths to achieve success and recognition.
- Strike a balance between humility and confidence: You will be able to navigate obstacles and capitalize on opportunities.
- Live a more authentic, values-driven life: You will be able to connect with your passions and long-term goals.

The Journey to Empowerment

The journey to empowerment is not easy. It requires you to:
- Accept your vulnerabilities: Recognize your weaknesses and limitations.
- Confront your fears: Face your fears and overcome them.
- Connect with your power: Discover your inner strength and resilience.

Conclusion

In conclusion, the path to empowerment is a journey of self-discovery, growth, and transformation. It requires you to accept your vulnerabilities, confront your fears, and connect with your power. By unlocking your inner strength, you can live a more authentic, values-driven life that truly reflects your soul's deepest desires and highest aspirations. You can create your unique story, forgive your past, and lead a life of profound fulfillment and impact.

Key Takeaways

- Empowerment is a state of mind, a feeling of confidence, capability, and control over one's life.
- Unlocking inner strength is the key to empowerment.
- Building strong emotional intelligence and awareness, cultivating positive relationships, and nurturing a sense of purpose and meaning are ways to unlock inner strength.

"Believe in yourself and take control now"

9.7. "BE A PLAYER, NOT A SPECTATOR!"

Life is a game that demands active participation, not just passive observation. To truly experience its thrill and fulfilment, you must be willing to step onto the field, take risks, and play with a purpose. As a player, you'll encounter challenges, learn from failures, and discover your strengths. You'll also develop the resilience, adaptability, and creativity needed to succeed in an ever-changing world.

The Power of Being a Player

Being a player is not just about achieving success; it's about living a life of purpose and impact. When you're a player, you're not just watching from the sidelines; you're actively participating in the game of life. You're taking risks, learning from your mistakes, and growing as a person.

Preparing for the Challenges Ahead

In the years to come, you could face many different and big challenges. You might not find a suitable job according to your passion or qualifications, and life might not be as easy as you think. But don't worry; you have the power to prepare yourself for these challenges. Today, you can focus on finding new opportunities, improving your skills, learning new technologies, and understanding the business or job markets.

Learning From Charles Darwin's Theory

Charles Darwin's theory of evolution teaches us that nature has always supported the idea of "survival of the fittest." But I'd like to modify the last term to "survival of the toughest" when it comes to facing challenges. You have to master yourself to stay sane and alive in this fast-paced erratic world. Being tough is not just about physical strength; it's more about your mental toughness, resilience, and adaptability to changing situations.

Difference Between a Player and a Spectator

Consider a team of football players – there are only 22 players on the field, but thousands of spectators watching from the sidelines. It's easy to watch players performing for their team, but it's a difficult task to be playing for that team. It requires lots of practice, stamina, and dedication. As a player in the team, you're not just watching the game; you're living it.

Being a Good Player

Being a good player is about more than just having the skills. If you want to improve the outcome of your game, you have to demonstrate perfection in the role your team demands of you, leading by example and being the best sportsman you can be. Teams need passionate and focused players. Firstly, you have to learn about your roles and responsibilities. What are the fundamental skills that are needed for your sport?

My Personal Experience

To keep myself organised and motivated in my life and business, and also to build my stamina, I remember joining a gym in my mid-twenties – At first, I struggled to keep up the pace and couldn't fixate on a particular activity for a long time, often making the workouts painful, but gradually I built up my endurance and eventually enjoyed taking up challenges and meeting my fitness targets. I consistently pushed myself to attain my set fitness goals and became a regular at the gym. I showed up regularly not only to be on routine, but also to sweat, grind, and improve with each rep and set.

Conclusion

Being a player, not a spectator, is a mindset that, if followed, can help you to achieve greater success and live a life of purpose. The true price isn't winning or losing: it's the evolution of your character, the expansion of your knowledge, and the emergence of your best self. So, don't be afraid to take risks, step onto the field, and play with a purpose. You have the power to shape your destiny and unlock your potential.

Key Takeaways

- Life is a game that demands active participation, not just passive observation.
- Being a player is about living a life of purpose and impact.
- Prepare yourself for the challenges ahead by improving your skills and learning new techniques.
- Being tough is not just about physical strength; it's about mental strength, resilience, and adaptability too.
- Be a good player not only by acquiring skills; but also through leading by example and being the best version you can be.
- Don't be afraid to take risks, take up challenges, and play with a purpose.

"Take action, make it happen, doesn't just be an observer in life"

9.8. "PRACTICE WORKING IN TEAMS"

Teamwork is the backbone of any successful organisation. When individuals with diverse skills and perspectives come together, they can achieve far more than they could be alone. However, effective teamwork doesn't happen overnight. It requires practice, patience, and dedication.

There are many benefits of teamwork:
- **Improved problem-solving:** Individuals with diverse skills and perspectives will lead to innovative solutions. Team members offer their different viewpoints, helping to identify potential pitfalls or opportunities that might have been overlooked by individuals working alone.
- **Enhanced creativity:** Collaborative environments can be beneficial to all by promoting the unique generation of ideas.
- **Increased productivity:** Members used to share workloads with more responsibilities.
- **Better decision-making:** Collective input leads to more informed choices with the best results.
- **Bonding with members:** This can create a good working environment and mutual bonding.
- **Support network:** Members rely on each other for proper guidance and encouragement.

Key Elements of Effective Teamwork:
- **Clear communication:** Open, honest, and respectful exchange of ideas among individuals.
- **Defined roles:** Clarity on individual responsibilities and meeting expectations of the team leader.
- **Trustworthiness:** Reliability, empathy, and mutual support among members.

- **Active Listening**: Engaged and attentive participation in the activities.
- **Adaptability**: Flexibility and willingness to adjust to the situations.

Practising Teamwork:
- **Start Small**: Begin with low-stakes projects or volunteer work.
- **Join a Good Team**: Practice and actively participate in group activities like sports and other group activities.
- **Seek Feedback**: Ask for useful suggestions, valuable insights and other support from team members.
- **Embrace Diversity**: Recognise diverse strengths.
- **Celebrate Successes**: Acknowledge and learn from achievements.

Overcoming Teamwork Challenges:
- **Conflict Resolution**: There may be many disagreements or disputes that can arise within a team. This can include differences in opinion, personality clashes, or varying work styles and philosophies. So, address your issues very promptly and respectfully.
- **Building Trust**: It refers to the process of forming and strengthening a sense of reliance, confidence, and mutual support among team members. When trust is built, team members feel secure in sharing their ideas.
- **Managing Different Work Styles**: Adapt to individual preferences, habits, and approaches to work. Reduce friction caused by differing work styles and promote a harmonious team environment. Refine work approaches to suit individual styles, driving excellence and efficiency.

Developing expertise in teamwork is a journey that requires dedication, persistence, and a willingness to learn. By recognizing the advantages of collaborative work, grasping the essential components, and honing your skills through active participation, you will evolve into a highly effective and sought-after team member.

Embrace obstacles as opportunities for growth, acknowledge and celebrate collective achievements, and continually refine your teamwork abilities to excel in today's dynamic and interconnected work environments.

"Unity ignites unstoppable momentum"

9.9. "BE AUTHENTIC"

In today's world, it's easy to get caught up in the idea of copying others. We see people we admire and want to be like them, whether it's a famous actor, musician, or businessperson. However, the truth is that originality is always better than copying someone else.

The Problem with Copying

When we copy others, we risk losing our own unique identity. We become a duplicate of someone else, rather than forging our path. This can lead to a sense of disconnection and dissatisfaction, as we're not being true to ourselves.

Moreover, copying others can also stifle our creativity and innovation. When we're too focused on emulating someone else, we're not pushing ourselves to think outside the box and come up with new ideas.

The Importance of Originality

Originality is what sets us apart from others. It's what makes us unique and valuable. When we're original, we're not bound by the limitations of others. We're free to create, innovate, and express ourselves in our way.

Originality is also what leaves a lasting impact. Think about it - the people who have made the biggest impact on the world are those who have been original and innovative. They're the ones who have dared to be different and have created something new and unique.

Finding Your Path

So, how do you find your path and cultivate originality? It starts with self-discovery. Take the time to reflect on your values, passions, and goals. What makes you unique? What sets you apart from others?

Don't be afraid to take risks and try new things. This is where the magic happens, and you'll discover new aspects of yourself. Remember, it's okay to make mistakes - it's all part of the learning process.

My Story

I'd like to share my own story of finding my path and cultivating originality. Growing up, I was inspired by my father's hard work and dedication to our family. I wanted to support and alleviate his workload, so I started assisting him in his contract work as soon as I graduated.

Then soon after, came the responsibility of being a husband too. With added responsibilities at such a young age and experiencing major accidents personally and with accidents involving my employees, I was shattered and in complete shock! I wasn't prepared to take further experiments that risked people's lives.

With each passing year, I realised that I wanted to make a difference in my way. I didn't want to copy someone else's path; I wanted to forge my own. So, I took calculated risks, tried new things, and stayed true to myself.

Conclusion

In conclusion, originality is always better than copying someone else. When we're original, we're unique, valuable, and free to create and innovate. Don't be afraid to take risks and try new things - it's where the magic happens.

As we celebrate the beauty of uniqueness and the freedom to create without bounds, let's remember that our originality is what will leave a lasting impact. So, dare to be different, think differently, and create boldly. The world needs more originality, and it starts with you.

Key Takeaways

- Originality is what sets us apart from others and makes us unique and valuable.

- Copying others can stifle our creativity and innovation.
- Self-discovery is key to finding our path and cultivating originality.
- Taking risks and trying new things is where the magic happens.
- Our originality is what will leave a lasting impact.

"Be original, reject copy, success is authentic"

9.10. "HOLD YOURSELF ACCOUNTABLE"

Accountability is the key to turning your intentions into achievements. It's the difference between setting goals and realising them. When you hold yourself accountable, you take ownership of your actions, decisions, and outcomes. In this chapter, we'll explore the importance of self-accountability and provide strategies for implementing it in your life.

Why Self-Accountability Matters

Self-accountability is essential for personal growth and development. By holding yourself accountable, you:

- **Boost self-awareness and introspection:** You can gain a deeper understanding of your thoughts, feelings, and actions.
- **Encourage personal growth and development:** You can identify areas for improvement and work on developing new skills.
- **Promote coping skills and adaptability:** You can learn to handle challenges and adapt to new situations.
- **Build trust and credibility with others:** You can demonstrate your reliability and commitment to your goals.
- **Drive results and achievements:** You stay focused and motivated, achieving your goals and realising your dreams.

Strategies for Self-Accountability

Here are some strategies to cultivate self-accountability in your life:

- **Set Clear Goals:** Establish specific, measurable, and attainable objectives. Break down large goals into smaller, manageable tasks.

- **Track Progress:** Regularly monitor your advancement. Note down, or find apps to log your successes and setbacks.
- **Create an Accountability System:** Share your goals and progress with a trusted friend or mentor. Schedule regular check-ins for support and guidance.
- **Embrace Failure:** View mistakes as opportunities for growth. Analyse what went wrong and adjust your approach accordingly.
- **Celebrate Successes:** Acknowledge and celebrate your achievements. This reinforces positive habits and motivates continued progress.

Putting Self-Accountability into Practice

Here are some practical tips to help you implement self-accountability in your life:

- **Develop a morning routine:** Set intentions and focus on your goals.
- **Implement a 'stop doing' list:** Eliminate non-essential tasks and activities.
- **Schedule time for self-reflection and journaling:** Regularly reflect on your progress and identify areas for improvement.
- **Seek constructive feedback:** Ask for feedback from others to gain new insights and perspectives.
- **Embrace challenges:** View challenges as opportunities for growth and development.

Conclusion

In conclusion, self-accountability is the key to achieving your goals and realising your dreams. By implementing the strategies outlined in this chapter, you'll cultivate a strong sense of self-accountability and stay focused on your objectives.

Remember, accountability is not about being perfect; it's about being consistent, resilient, and committed to your goals.

Key Takeaways

- Self-accountability is essential for personal growth and development.
- Setting clear goals, tracking progress, and creating an accountability system are key strategies for self-accountability.
- Embracing failure and celebrating successes are important aspects of self-accountability.
- Implementing self-accountability in your daily life can help you stay focused and motivated.
- Self-accountability is not about being perfect; it's about being consistent, resilient, and committed to your goals.

"Own Your Actions; Achieve Your Goals"

PART 10:

Legacy and Impact

10.1. "REALISE YOUR UNIQUENESS AND POWER"

As we navigate through the complexities of life, it's easy to get caught up in the idea that we need to conform to certain standards or expectations. But what if I told you that your greatest strength lies not in trying to fit in, but in embracing your uniqueness? I'd love to know – what does the phrase "realize your uniqueness and power mean to you? Have you ever had a moment where you felt truly empowered by staying true to your individuality? Try sharing your stories with your near and dear ones and explore this journey of self-discovery together.

Self-acceptance and self-love are the keys to unlocking your true potential. When you learn to love and accept yourself, you begin to see your strengths and weaknesses in a new light. This self-awareness gives you the confidence to tap into your inner power, overcome obstacles, and achieve your goals.

By embracing your unique qualities and imperfections, you can unleash a profound sense of purpose and fulfillment. By accepting and loving yourself, you realise the power and potential that lies within you. The more you clasp your uniqueness, the more you can connect with others who appreciate and value your distinctiveness. This paradoxical truth frees us from the need to conform, allowing us to forge deeper, more meaningful relationships that are built on authenticity and mutual appreciation, rather than mere familiarities.

Every being in this world is a wonderful creation of God; especially humans are considered unique. Everyone is different in their nature, appearance and demeanour. This universal truth can be realised only when you are capable of exploring your true self. Nothing in this universe can stop you from enhancing your personality.

You should know your uniqueness as you can't find a true replica of yours in appearance, experiences, thoughts, actions, emotions, genetics, beliefs, hobbies, sense of humour and all. You express your uniqueness in the way you appear in front of others. When you dress up and stand in front of a mirror you can see the virtual image of yourself which makes you believe that you are looking great.

You know the basics of what sets you apart from others. It can be a great idea to tune in or hone in on the qualities where you shine. Set aside some time to brainstorm and train yourself. Make a schedule with a date and time to complete any particular task.

Hold yourself to it and then write down your answers to the following questions:

- When should I wake up so that I can finish all my necessary tasks?
- Which is the best compliment that I have ever received in my life?
- What is that special quality or skill in me that I was always proud of?
- When in my life did I truly enjoy and appreciate my life?
- What was the best gift I ever received? And who gave that gift?

Just find the answers to the aforesaid questions. You will be surprised to find answers to those as you would have never thought of it before. There is one thing to remember during this process though – it's not always easy to be you! I would also suggest you use this self-realisation tool if you are considering a career change as this can help you to realize your uniqueness and interests.

Conclusion

Self-realisation at times is a must for establishing your mental peace and happiness. At Least once and at some point in your life, you might feel lost and wonder what exactly are you doing in your life. You might think about what brought you to a point where you don't feel motivated any longer! At this moment you can ask yourself these self-realisation questions to re-discover what you are, where your passion lies and what you want from life. Never lose the knowledge of right and wrong. Live life to the fullest and perform those tasks that will give you peace and happiness. The only quality you have to nurture is your approach and intentions so that people here will make it happen.

Everyone has gone through periods of darkness and periods of light. Try to understand that darkness is inevitable which is also called companion of light. When you find yourself in darkness, you get a chance to study yourself and discover yourself so that you adhere to shut up for hours closeted in a room in a meditative state learning some effective ways of state change. If you can't change your state of mind, you have to repeat this action until you bring back yourself into the realm of light. This act of pulling you into the light is one of the most important skills that you can achieve and cultivate for a better living.

"Your uniqueness will make you perfect; others will look up to you"

10.2. "TRANSFORM THOUGHTS INTO ACTIONS"

Your thoughts have the power to shape your life. They drive your actions, influence your self-esteem, and determine your destiny. The mind is a powerful tool, and once you learn how to harness its power, you can unlock your true potential.

The Power of Self-Talk

One of the most effective ways to transform your thoughts into actions is through uplifting self-talk. The way you talk to yourself matters, as it serves as a set of instructions for your mind. Positive self-talk can motivate and inspire you, while negative self-talk can hold you back.

The Thought-Feeling-Action Cycle

So, how do thoughts turn into actions? It's a simple yet powerful cycle:

- **Thought:** A thought generates a feeling.
- **Feeling:** The feeling motivates you to take action.
- **Action:** The action produces a result.

If you change your thoughts, you can change your feelings, and ultimately end up changing your results in life.

From Principles to Actions

Having principles and ideas is not enough. You need to put them into action. Many people lack the desire to work hard and make sacrifices to turn their ideas into reality. Remember, principles are useless if they remain just ideas. They need to touch your heart and motivate you to take action.

Starting Your Day on a Positive Note

The way you start your day sets the tone for the rest of it. Instead of beginning your day with negative news, it's better to focus your mind on positivity and inspiration. In a world filled with corruption and scandals, it's easy to feel overwhelmed. However, instead of cursing the darkness, drive it away by lighting a candle.

Overcoming Fear and Taking Action

When a new idea pops into your head, it's natural to feel excited, and then fearful once the novelty fades. Your brain may resist the idea, warning you of potential risks and dangers. However, if you don't take action, your idea may never see the light of day. Remember, hesitation kills. Its human nature to feel fear, but it's up to you to focus on your vision and push through.

Conclusion

In conclusion, transforming your thoughts into actions is a powerful way to unlock your potential. By harnessing the power of self-talk, understanding the thought-feeling-action cycle, and taking action, you can achieve your goals and make a positive impact. Remember, it's not about being brave; it's about being brave for five minutes longer.

Key Takeaways

- Your thoughts have the power to shape your life.
- Self-talk is a powerful tool for transforming your thoughts into actions.
- The thought-feeling-action cycle is a simple yet powerful process.

- Principles are useless if they remain just ideas; they need to be put into action.
- Starting your day on a positive note can set the tone for the rest of the day.
- Overcoming fear and taking action is crucial for achieving your goals.

"Think big, act bigger, and achieve the greatest success"

10.3. "CELEBRATE YOUR TRUE FREEDOM"

What is *true freedom*? Is it the freedom to do as we please, whenever we please? Or is it something more profound? True freedom is something no one can take away from us; it's the freedom to be ourselves and live life on our terms.

The Misconception of Freedom

Many of us believe that our circumstances or others' behaviour have a direct effect on how we feel. But this is a misconception. True freedom is not about external circumstances, but rather internal liberation. It's about being free from the constraints of our minds and emotions.

The Rules That Bind Us

We are all bound by rules and regulations, whether it's in our personal or professional lives. We have to follow traffic rules, obey our teachers, and adhere to occupational health and safety guidelines. But does this mean we are not free? Not necessarily. These rules are in place to maintain social order and ensure our safety.

The Abuse of Freedom

However, some of us abuse our freedom, using it as an excuse to be selfish, ignoble, weak, or irresponsible. We use our freedom to indulge in anti-social activities, such as crime, substance abuse, or other forms of destructive behaviour. But this is not true freedom. True freedom is about living a life of purpose, responsibility, and integrity.

The Power of Positive Thinking

So, how do we celebrate this true freedom granted to us? Well, for starters, we can do so by cultivating a positive mindset. We can choose to see the world in a positive light, to focus on the good, and to be grateful for what we have. We should also let go of our fears, anxieties, and doubts, and learn to trust ourselves and our abilities.

The Journey to True Freedom

True freedom is a journey, not a destination. It's a journey of self-discovery, growth, and transformation. It's a journey that requires us to confront our fears, to challenge our assumptions, and to push beyond our comfort zones.

But the reward is worth it. When we embark on this journey, we discover a sense of freedom that is uncontainable, a sense of joy that is unshakeable, and a sense of purpose that is unrelenting.

Conclusion

In conclusion, true freedom is not just about external circumstances; it's about internal liberation. It's about being free from the constraints of our minds and emotions. It's about living a life of purpose, responsibility, and integrity. So, let us celebrate our true freedom, and let us embark on the journey to discover it.

Key Takeaways

- True freedom is the freedom that no one can take away from us.
- It's about internal liberation, not external circumstances.
- We are all bound by rules and regulations, but this doesn't mean we are not free.

- True freedom is about living a life of purpose, responsibility, and integrity.
- It's a journey of self-discovery, growth, and transformation.
- The reward is worth it – a sense of freedom that is uncontainable, a sense of joy that is unshakeable, and a sense of purpose that is unrelenting.

"True freedom is not just a state, but a state of mind."

10.4. "LEAD A PRACTICAL YET MEANINGFUL LIFE"

Life is a journey, and it's up to us to make the most of it. Instead of dwelling on the past or worrying about the future, we should focus on living in the present moment. This is where true happiness and fulfillment can be found.

Let Go of the Past

The past is gone, and no amount of thinking or worrying can change it. Holding onto painful memories or regrets can weigh us down and prevent us from moving forward. It's time to let go of the past and start living in the present.

Live in the Present

The present moment is all we have. We can't predict the future, and we can't change the past. But we can control how we live in the present. By focusing on the here and now, we can make the most of every moment and create a life that is meaningful and fulfilling.

Be Practical

Being practical means being organized and focused. It means using tools like "to-do" lists and digital calendars to stay on top of tasks and responsibilities. It means being intentional about how we spend our time and energy.

Manage Your Emotions

Our emotions can be a powerful force in our lives. But if we're not careful, they can also control us. It's up to us to manage our emotions and choose how we respond to situations.

This means letting go of anger, bitterness, and resentment, and instead choosing love, compassion, and understanding.

Avoid Negative Patterns

Whining and complaining can be a slippery slope. It's easy to get caught up in negative patterns of thinking and behaviour, but it's not worth it. Instead, let's focus on finding solutions and taking action.

Surround Yourself with Positivity

The people we surround ourselves with can have a big impact on our lives. Let's choose to surround ourselves with positive, supportive people who encourage and uplift us.

Love Yourself First

Finally, let's remember that love starts with ourselves. When we love and accept ourselves, we're better able to love and accept others. This means taking care of our physical, emotional, and spiritual needs, and being kind and compassionate towards ourselves.

Conclusion

Leading a practical yet meaningful life is within our reach. By letting go of the past and living in the present, alongside being practical and managing our emotions, we can avoid negative patterns. When we combine this with surrounding ourselves with positivity, and loving ourselves first, we can create a truly fulfilling life.

Key Takeaways

- Let go of the past and focus on the present moment.
- Be practical and organized in your daily life.

- Manage your emotions and choose how you respond to situations.
- Avoid negative patterns of thinking and behaviour.
- Surround yourself with positive, supportive people.
- Love and accept yourself first.

"Yesterday was a dream and tomorrow is a vision. But today well lived makes every yesterday a dream of happiness and every tomorrow a vision of hope"

Dale Carnegie

10.5. "TURN YOUR VISIONS INTO REALITY"

Turn Your Visions Into Reality

Success is not just a destination; it's a journey that begins with a clear vision. A vivid dream that fuels your passion and drive is essential, but it's not enough to simply imagine a bright future.

You must take deliberate action to make it a tangible reality. In this chapter, we'll explore the strategies and mindset necessary to turn your vision into a triumphant success story.

The Power of Success

Success has a magnetic power that attracts everyone. However, many people fail to achieve it, not because they cannot perform better, but because they fail to develop their dreamful vision into reality. Teamwork plays a crucial role in achieving success. A successful team is one where everyone's unique skills and strengths come together to achieve a shared goal productively.

The Role of a Visionary Leader

A visionary leader is essential in turning a vision into reality. They ensure that their vision is clear, and they sketch a tactical plan to fulfil those goals. They also authorize each individual to initiate action on the plan at personal and organisational levels. A good leader must have excellent people skills, communication skills, and a good mental attitude to make their team special.

The Importance of Accuracy

Accuracy plays a vital role in achieving success. It can only be achieved through practice and a clear vision. A shooter, for example, must evaluate various factors like the height and speed of the target to hit it accurately. This kind of vision and perfection can transform your dreams into reality and make you a grand successful person.

The Characteristics of a True Visionary

A true visionary must have the capability to assess various factors like a great mind, ideas, decision-making skills, and thinking ahead of time. They must be able to conceptualise new ideas and think outside the box. Leonardo Da Vinci, for example, conceptualised numerous things like parachutes and mechanical robots ahead of their time.

Inspiration from Great Visionaries

Great visionaries like the late M.K. Gandhi, late Nelson Mandela, late Martin Luther King Junior, late Henry Ford, late Steve Jobs, Bill Gates, and Elon Musk have shaped the world we live in today. Their visionary leadership and relentless pursuit of innovation have inspired millions of people around the world.

Conclusion

In conclusion, turning your vision into reality requires a clear vision, a tactical plan, and a mindset that is willing to take deliberate action. It also requires teamwork, accuracy, and a true visionary leader. Remember, visionaries will always meet opposition from weak minds, but the seeds they plant will always save the world.

Key Takeaways

- Success begins with a clear vision and a vivid dream.
- Teamwork plays a crucial role in achieving success.
- A visionary leader must have excellent people skills, communication skills, and a good mental attitude.
- Accuracy can only be achieved through practice and a clear vision.
- A true visionary must have the capability to assess various factors like a great mind, ideas, decision-making skills, and thinking ahead of time.

- Great visionaries have shaped the world we live in today, and their legacy continues to inspire millions of people around the world.

"Believe in yourself, and always turn your dreams into reality"

10.6. "SET YOUR SOUL ABLAZE"

Inspiration is the little spark that takes place to ignite passions within, and reminds us of our purpose, thus setting our souls ablaze.

This reminds me of Elvis Presley and Ann Margret's song 'Viva Las Vegas' which goes like this:

"Bright light city set my soul, gonna set my soul on fire!"

Our soul serves as the engine in the body which ignites the spirit of feelings and gives us the sense of liveliness and inner strength. This spirit of feeling should be alive in you even when someone instigates anger, fear and insecurity, to reflect on your thoughts before any potentially dangerous action.

You should nurture your spirit without fear of negative outcomes and that could help you move forward to your dreams.

This move should be consistent and you can see how this will bring you closer to your goals. We humans always find ways to be happy even during our lowest phase of life, to avoid feeling sad and hopeless for a while. One who loses hope, and is mostly despondent will likely experience a fear of failure or miss happenings in his life. Deepa Malik, a Paralympics performer who won 17 international medals and is also a motivational speaker once told –

*"There is ability beyond disability.
My body is paralysed, my soul is not."*

Another motivational speaker Muniba Mazari, who was a survivor of domestic violence and a horrific accident too once said:

"Don't die before your death"

This was said during a speech in which she told the story of her car accident and her journey to recovery.

She also said that the words have the power to heal the souls. The one sentence from her mother:

"This too shall pass"

Helped her to keep going during the most difficult phase in her life.

Methods to set your soul on fire:
- **Discover your purpose**: Think about what's most important to you. What makes you happy and excited? What drives you to get up in the morning? Understanding your priorities and aspirations will help you find your purpose in life.
- **Chase your desires**: Do things that bring you joy! Engage in activities that make you feel alive. Whether it's playing music, painting, or cooking, make time for things that will make you happy.
- **Plot your path and pitfalls**: Don't be afraid to step out of your comfort zone. Set goals that challenge you and motivate you to grow. Think about what might probably hold you back and prepare yourself for those obstacles.
- **Enjoy your personality**: Love yourself just the way you are! Don't try to be a clone of someone else. Your unique qualities and quirks make you special and will help you find your life's purpose.
- **Revitalize your spirit**: Take utmost care of your body, mind, and soul. Engage in activities that will help nourish your soul, such as meditation, yoga, or just a small walk and spending some time alone in nature. Observe nature and its inhabitants. Take some time to play with your pets and children.

- **Validate your experiences:** Share your stories and experiences, both bad and good with others. Share the things that you did to overcome those experiences, and about what inspired you. Learn from your mistakes and don't be afraid of being vulnerable. While going through some quotes, I came across a quote which implied that great minds discuss ideas, mediocre minds talk about what they learnt through their experiences with people and small minds discuss people.

- **Connect with visionary minds:** Spend time with people who inspire and motivate you. Avoid people who constantly try to bring you down and drain your energy. Negative people can only offer you negative thoughts and outcomes. But if someone is genuinely pointing out your mistakes then take those criticisms positively and work on it. Surround yourself with positive, genuine and supportive people who help you grow and keep you sane.

Remember, setting your soul ablaze is a continuous journey. Keep igniting your passions, purpose, and inner fire.

"Ignite your passion and fuel your dreams with it"

10.7. "BE A BEACON OF LIGHT AND WISDOM"

As we navigate the complexities of life, we often search for guidance and inspiration to illuminate our path.

But what if we could be the light for others? What if our words, actions, and presence could bring hope, comfort, and direction to those around us?

In this chapter, we will explore the power of being a light to the world, and how we can share our wisdom, kindness, and compassion to make a positive impact on the lives of others.

The Power of Knowledge

Knowledge is a treasure that can never be stolen or broken. It is the invisible jewellery of our mind, and nobody can enact laws to steal it. One can acquire this treasure by educating oneself. However, knowledge is not just about accumulating information; it's about applying it in practical ways to transform our lives and the lives of others.

The Outcomes of Education

The two natural outcomes of education are information and formation. Formation leads to the transformation of one's life, and as a result, one who is properly educated can bring about positive change not only in their personal life or family life but also in society as a whole.

The Importance of Wisdom

Knowledge without wisdom can be highly dangerous and destructive. Wisdom is the ability to know how something can be done and delivered in the best way. It's the ability to discern what is right and wrong and to make informed decisions. Wisdom can protect us from problems and help us navigate life's challenges effectively.

The Value of Experience

Always obey what your teachers and parents say, as they want to give you sincere advice for your transformation. Their experience, whether good or bad, can teach you valuable lessons and help you avoid mistakes. Remember, everyone's life is filled with problems, and it's up to us to be wise enough to react to life and face the problems effectively.

The Power of Inspiration

Knowledge can empower anyone by enlightening them to do great things in their life. It can inspire many who are directly or indirectly connected to us. The power of knowledge itself shows our ability to make others understand what we know. By sharing our knowledge, we can shape the society and make it beneficial for all.

Conclusion

In conclusion, being a beacon of light and wisdom is not just about accumulating knowledge; it's about applying it in practical ways to transform our lives and the lives of others. By sharing our wisdom, kindness, and compassion, we can make a positive impact on the world and create a ripple effect of kindness that resonates far and wide.

Key Takeaways

- Knowledge is a treasure that can never be stolen or broken.
- Education is not just about accumulating information; it's about applying it in practical ways to transform our lives and the lives of others.
- Knowledge without wisdom can be highly dangerous and destructive.
- Wisdom is the ability to know how something can be done and delivered in the best way.
- Experience can teach us valuable lessons and help us avoid mistakes.

- Knowledge can empower anyone by enlightening them to do great things in their life.
- By sharing our knowledge, we can shape the society and make it beneficial for all.

"You can illuminate the world with a spark of wisdom"

10.8. "LEGACY IS BUILT THROUGH NOBLE ACTIONS"

Legacy is not just something that we leave behind. It's much more than wealth or possessions. It's the remembrance of the impact that your actions will bring into people's lives and to society. It can be the contributions or the sacrifices you made to uplift people and their lives. Legacy is something inspiring that you do for the community through several means like charity, providing support or mentorship, professional guidance and so on. It should bring positive changes in people's lives and make positive impacts which can outlive you. Just think about what you want to change and what difference you would like to see in your community.

Why is leaving a legacy so satisfying?

- It gives you a sense of purpose since it will have an impact on someone's life.
- It gives you a sense of achievement, motivating you to do more challenging tasks.
- It grows empathy in you and makes you more approachable.
- You'll feel a sense of satisfaction and be more fulfilled in life.
- With your legacy, you will be satisfied knowing that the things you do now will continue to contribute to the betterment of someone's life even after you're gone.
- Your legacy will inspire generations to come to contribute to society.

How to make the legacy more meaningful?

- Ask yourself what matters most to you in life. How would you want the world to remember you after you are gone?
- Do you have the skills to innovate something that can benefit people at large? What skills and resources will you need to achieve that?
- Just having good intentions and ideas won't help. You need to act on them too.
- Discuss your thoughts and ideas with others who share the same vision and thoughts as you.
- Don't lose focus and authenticity even if challenges arise.
- Help and mentor someone who you think will benefit from your expertise, experience and knowledge.
- Start small but make sure the impact will last long.
- Motivate someone to do better in life, give respect and talk respectfully.
- Always stand up for what's right and defend the vulnerable. Oppose what is wrong and damaging to society.
- Influence others to follow the cause that you stand for, and ask them to contribute too if needed.

Conclusion

Leaving a noble legacy needs acts of kindness and compassion. Discover the purpose or the idea that will drive you to make a positive impact on people's lives. Set small goals that will contribute to your legacy. Make small contributions to uplifting people every day, and make sure that your actions have a ripple impact on them and their connections too. Make small but purposeful and conscious steps each day. Share your thoughts and vision with others who share your values. Make choices wisely and look for improvements within you and others. Take time out to volunteer for good and noble causes.

> *"Set your noble vision, and work towards it to leave a lasting legacy"*

10.9. "BE A GAME CHANGER"

Through this chapter, let's explore the fantastic benefits of being a game changer through a progressive mindset and a clear vision! Since several objectives are bundled into this exercise; it has become a bit complex and possibly will be dragged on a bit. So bear with me, and be patient while I try to make it sound as simple as I can.

Why do we need to be a game-changer, and how do we do it?

There should be continuous and consistent efforts for your personal growth. First of all, you have to plan and craft a road map to your final goal. For this firstly, take a moment to envision your life's destination. Now think about the aspirations you have to set to secure your short-term and long-term goals. Creating a clear and effective vision will act as a guiding force, helping you to set milestones on your way towards your final goal.

Moreover, you will have to focus your attention on acquiring new knowledge and skills if needed to enhance your chances of achieving your goals faster. By doing so, you will stay competent without being stagnant and lacking confidence to move forward.

The process of continuous learning is very much needed in today's world which is constantly evolving. If you are unsure about what knowledge you need to acquire to achieve your desired dreams, then try exploring different areas of skills that might be useful to your goals. Cultivate a mindset that sees every experience as an opportunity to learn and grow. You might have to face challenges in your journey, but seeing them as opportunities for personal growth and development will help you in the long run.

Remember that you have to show resilience, acquire, adjust, and evolve through each encounter in your life. Building social networks or having influential people in your circle can be considered great assets in your life. Try to encircle yourself with people who will encourage, inspire and ignite passion for betterment in each step of your life.

You should also be brave enough to take some considerable risk in your life, after researching and learning about the potential dangers it might pose. When you consider taking risks after lots of research and study, you need to have a proper backup plan too.

Having a plan B will give you the confidence and boost needed to take risks and will motivate you to do things without worrying about the profit at first. This will help you to step out of your comfort zone and to constantly thrive for your venture's substantial growth. The great men in history were great risk-takers too who reaped the rewards immensely by stepping out of their comfort zones.

You should also need to practice self-care physically and psychologically which will further fuel your transformational journey towards success. Try reinforcing positive habits that can boost your confidence level and make you believe in yourself. When you have that go-getter attitude, you will see miracles happening in your life. You can see your well-wishers rejoicing in your success, and in some situations, you might also experience people's wrath as you move forward.

Stay away from the latter type of people as they are not happy with their own lives, and they can't stand to see others happy too. They will try to diminish every effort that you took towards your successful career and will drain away your energy, focus and happiness. That's why you are advised to surround yourself with successful people as they will be happy with your achievements. Celebrate every small victory that takes you one step closer to your dream. This will significantly contribute to you becoming a real game changer in your own life.

To be a game changer in your life, you need to value your time too. You should have effective time management and should cultivate the habit of prioritising your tasks according to your needs but without any unnecessary distractions. When you are well-armed with the above strategies and knowledge, you are now all set to be a game-changer in your life. Personal growth is a lifelong journey and every positive step you take will bring you closer to your goals.

Conclusion

The most important thing you as a game changer should first consider doing in this modern era is to clean up all the weaknesses and unnecessary negative thoughts from your mind. In today's world, no one considers working on their mental state like stress, anxiety, depression, anger, hatred, etc. We assume that these emotions are natural, and thus are unavoidable. As I mentioned before, try changing and moving away from the environment that drags you down and from the negative people you are surrounded with. Once you become successful, you can consider changing your social circle and migrating to where other successful people live.

This will reduce your association and interactions with people who can only offer you negativity. Value your time and focus on updating yourself with new skills. These efforts can further help you bring a big change in your life and perspectives, and you can continue your journey towards becoming a true game changer with more confidence.

Real game changers are not only self-aware but are also aware of other's needs and emotions. They will always be driven by determination, commitment, curiosity and focus. They will never be satisfied by normal results and will be persistently working towards their objectives. They will not try copying others' ideas but will create their own unique, innovative and efficient solutions, considering all practical issues that they may face. They break all norms and conventions to achieve their unique and distinctive goals. Let your life as a game changer be an inspiration to other youngsters who can take calculated risks in life and help them to become game changers in their lives.

"A true game-changer lives with purpose, impacting lives"

10.10. "EXECUTE LIKE A TRUE VISIONARY"

We all know that great ideas are not rare, but the visionaries that make those ideas happen are very rare. Visionaries are not just people who can do everything by themselves, but most of them are great minds who can inspire and support people to make great things happen. They might not have the right skill sets to do everything, but they will have the ability to gather the right people and resources to accomplish their vision. There are only a few visionaries who have both the skillset and executing power to make their dreams happen. To be a visionary you just need to have the right mindset and the knowledge of how to execute the dreams into reality.

Principles of Being a True Visionary

- **Have a clear vision:** Think about the societal issues that concern you and have a clear idea of your vision of how to address them.

- **Prepare yourself to act on your goals:** Decide on how to solve the problem and work consistently towards attaining it.

- **Find ways to empower people:** A true visionary will be empathetic and believe in improving the lives of the less fortunate. It can be through collaborations, mentoring or creating new jobs or business opportunities for the community.

- **Have innovative ideas and solutions:** Work towards attaining solutions for societal challenges, and advocate for bringing in new ideas that benefit generations to come.

- **Never pursue fame:** Your focus should be to improve the lives of others and to contribute to the progress of your community. Serve selflessly, and never focus on getting fame. Your legacy should be built upon selflessness and lasting impact.

- **Inspire others through your own experiences:** Great visionaries want their efforts to be carried forward even after they are gone. Inspire and influence like-minded individuals to work together towards the shared vision.
- **Never stop trying to create an impact:** Be persistent in your efforts, adapt to the changing environment and show resilience in executing your visionary ideas.
- **Calculate the success of your vision:** Analyse the positive impact that your ideas and efforts have brought into people's lives. Will the effort be enough to create a ripple effect on the generations to come? Look beyond your ambitions and achievements. That's what makes you a great visionary.

*"True visionaries are not just dreamers;
their actions leave lasting impact"*

CHAPTER 101

"UNLOCK YOUR FULL POTENTIAL, MANIFEST YOUR DREAMS"

This chapter ties my book together with a strong conclusion that may help you to understand the best practices and principles you need to follow to achieve your objectives. So stay motivated and apply the following strategies to achieve the goals you have always dreamed of:

- **Align yourself with your goals:** It's important to align your emotions, thoughts and actions with your goals, vision and values.
- Small actions towards big dreams: Set big goals, but break them into achievable small ones.
- **Visualise success and believe in achieving it:** Imagine your success and believe in your potential and strength to achieve it.
- **Follow certain routines to achieve excellence:** Certain routines and positive habits if followed consistently will lead you to achieve your goal soon.
- **Never underestimate yourself:** Identify your limiting force and ascertain your potential to eliminate the habit of holding yourself back.
- **Take bold actions where necessary:** Challenge yourself to come out of your fear and comfort zones if you want to experience success. Welcome new opportunities with enthusiasm.
- **Be in good company:** Always try to surround yourself with positive like-minded people who will support and

help you grow. Be in company with people who share similar aspirations, passion, values and visions as yours.
- **Reflect on your journey and achievements:** Just take a moment to reflect on where you started your journey from and where you've come to. Look back and see how far you've progressed since you started this journey of self-improvement. Check what all you need to reach your fullest potential. Pat yourself on your back for the effort you put into achieving this.
- **Continue and never stop:** Commit yourselves to keep moving forward without losing hope and with much dedication. To achieve something great, you have to keep going forward without losing faith in the process.
- **You are the creator of your destiny:** Always remember that you have the power and ability to transform your own life. No obstacle can stop you from achieving your goals until you stop trying. So trust your potential and abilities to make your dream life come true.

*"Dreams don't have deadlines,
but determination does"*

www.ingramcontent.com/pod-product-compliance
Lightning Source LLC
LaVergne TN
LVHW091702070526
838199LV00050B/2256